War and Memory in the
Twentieth Century

War and Memory in the Twentieth Century

Edited by
Martin Evans and Ken Lunn

Oxford • New York

First published in 1997 by
Berg
Editorial offices:
150 Cowley Road, Oxford, OX4 1JJ, UK
70 Washington Square South, New York, NY 10012, USA

Berg is an imprint of Oxford International Publishers Ltd.

Library of Congress Cataloging-in-Publication Data

A catalogue record for this book is available from the Library of Congress.

British Library Cataloguing-in-Publication Data

A catalogue record for this book is available from the British Library.

ISBN 1 85973 194 5 (Cloth)
1 85973 199 6 (Paper)

Typeset by JS Typesetting, Wellingborough, Northants.
Printed in the United Kingdom by WBC Book Manufacturers, Bridgend,
Mid Glamorgan.

Contents

Contents

Foreword

Geoff Eley

The 1990s have seen a boom in memory. It's hard to know how exactly to read this phenomenon – how to judge its social and cultural meanings, as well as its political valencies, and how to situate its explanation, or historicize its occurrence. But its presence is palpable. One way of making sense of it would be to use the languages of postmodernism, where the turning to memory is a 'nostalgia for the present' (in Fredric Jameson's phrase), an anxiety about the loss of bearings and the speed and extent of change, in which representations of the past, the narration and visualizing of history, personal and collective, private and public, spell the desire for holding onto the familiar, for fixing and retaining the lineaments of worlds in motion, of landmarks that are disappearing and securities that are unsettled. In this understanding, 'memory' becomes the crucial site of identity formation in the late twentieth century, of deciding who we are, and of positioning ourselves in time, given the hugeness of the structural changes currently occurring in the world – in the new era of globalization, the end of Communism, and the capitalist restructuring of the post-fordist transition, at the much-vaunted 'end of history', and in the 'postmodern condition'.[1] It is part of the 'cultural logic' of this contemporary transition, we might say. Mass media play a big part in this too. Processes of commodification and the commercialization of culture, in the consumer economies of entertainment and stylistic display, amidst the new electronic communications, produce a postmodern economy of signs in which the mobility of historical imagery and citation has become unavoidable. In all of these ways the contemporary sensibility has become a memorializing one. We are constantly being asked to place ourselves in relation to one kind of 'past' or another, and the public spheres of the contemporary world provide constant incitements to memory in this sense.

The endless procession of anniversaries is another part of this story. The national referents, of course, vary, but the great extravaganza of 1989 in France, which sought to declare the French Revolution finally over, was only the most dramatic and visible of these culturally particular events. The most familiar cross-national commemoration has involved the extended and ramified remembering of the Second World War, beginning of course with the fortieth anniversary of the European peace in 1985, and continuing through the sequence of fiftieth anniversaries from the outbreak of the war in 1939 to the D-Day celebrations and the liberation six years later. This public calender has generated an extraordinary amount of commemorative excess, saturating the spaces of public representation and the TV screens in particular, while simultaneously triggering a plethora of private reflections. But once again, the meaning of all this activity, of so much public and obsessional remembering, lies outside the formal framework and the substantive conditions of change. It is the sense of an ending – both internationally with the end of the Cold War, the strengthening of the EU and the transnationalized shrinkage of the globe, and domestically with the definitive dissolution of the post-war settlement, and the recomposition of the social landscape of class – that sends us to these earlier moments. In effect, we are returning home, revisiting the origins, reopening the history that produced our contemporary world, or at least the one that is now lost, going back to the foundations. It is this that sensitizes us so easily to the past as a field of meaning.

Of course, there are other reasons to do with history as a specialized activity – as a discipline, as a field of professional knowledge – that help explain the salience of memory as a kind of thematics. The very fact of the opening up of the post-war era for legitimate and accepted historical work has played its part, claiming the period since 1945 for both teaching and research, so that large numbers of historians are now writing about the years in which they were also themselves formed as adults. Until recently, 1945 acted as a boundary of the present in a limiting way, and it is only slowly, as the years since the Second World War stretch into more than half a century of historical time, that contemporary history has established its credentials, gradually supporting the necessary apparatus of discussion and publication (through the launching of journals, societies, institutes, the holding of conferences, and so on), so that courses on the post-war world are now being taught conventionally in history departments for the first time (rather than just in sociology and political science). We can then add a series of other influences. The growth of oral history as an accepted sub-disciplinary area since the mid-1970s is an obvious one of these, again with its own journals, professional associations, conferences, institutional bases, individual classics, methodologies, technologies and evolving traditions.[2] The power of interdisciplinarity, with its early institutional bridgehead in the 1960s with the foundation of the new universities, and then later in the former polytechnics (I'm writing here mainly about Britain), also created a home for sophisticated intellectual work on memory, because until historians' suspicions towards anthropology, psychology, psychoanalysis and other theoretical traditions became breached, discussion would stay within a set of narrow technical debates about the problems of using oral sources.

In this last respect, there can be no question that cultural studies has provided the main framing and impetus for the growth of memory as an intellectual priority and an academic preoccupation. The terms in which the editors of this volume frame their project – in which memory is presented as 'a complex *construct*', and the interdisciplinary bases for organizing a conference, or any collective discussion, are taken as axiomatic, with the 'public field of representations' as the shared ground of inquiry – owe everything to the analytical languages developed in cultural studies during the past two decades. Work in cultural studies has enhanced and expanded our perceptions of the past in the present, pointing us to all the ways in which history becomes evoked and addressed, and the wide range of sites and media through which remembering (and forgetting) occurs in a public sphere, consciously and unconsciously, through film and television, photographs and advertisements, radio and song, theatre, museums, exhibits, tourist spots, fictions, ceremonial, school curricula, political speeches and so on. In this way, the wider domain of ideas and assumptions about the past in a society has been claimed for historical study, so that the customary ground of the historian – the boundaries of accepted historical analysis, and the nature of the appropriate archive, the definition of what *counts* as a legitimate source and an acceptable subject – has been called radically into question.[3]

The possibilities have become either unsettling or exciting, depending on the conservatism of one's disciplinary orientation. They confuse many of the older ways of defining the historian's distinctive practices and identity, freeing the established disciplinary constraints, and opening the imagination to a far more mobile agenda, with a much richer repertoire of legitimate methods and approaches. This is an extremely fruitful indeterminacy. It destabilizes the customary approach to conceptualizing the boundary between 'memory' and 'history', where the one used to be straightforwardly the professional organizing and contextualizing of the other, as it called into action the superior languages of objectivity, and faced the partial and subjective accounts of individuals with the truth of the archive, the 'facts', and the 'reality' of the historical record. For the late Raphael Samuel, the most eloquent and creative chronicler and theorist of the current process of redefinition, this makes history 'an organic form of knowledge', 'one whose sources are promiscuous, drawing not only on real-life experience but also memory and myth, fantasy and desire; not only the chronological past of the documentary record but also the timeless one of "tradition"'.

> History has always been a hybrid form of knowledge, syncretizing past and present, memory and myth, the written record and the spoken word. Its subject matter is promiscuous. . . . In popular memory, if not in high scholarship, the

great flood or the freak storm may eclipse wars, battles and the rise and fall of governments. As a form of communication, history finds expression not only in chronicle and commentary but also ballad and song, legends and proverbs, riddles and puzzles. Church liturgies have carried one version of it – sacred history; civic ritual another. A present-day inventory would need to be equally alert to the memory work performed (albeit unintentionally) by the advertisers, and to the influence of tourism. . . . As a self-conscious art, history begins with the monuments and inscriptions, and as the record of the built environment suggests, not the least of the influences changing historical consciousness today is the writing on the walls. The influence of video-games and science-fiction would be no less pertinent in trying to explain why the idea of chronological reversal, or time travelling, has become a normal way of engaging with the idea of the past.[4]

Some of cultural studies' favourite subject matters – museums and exhibitions, cinema and photography, magazines and popular fictions – have provided the best ground for historical work to begin reconceptualizing the relationship of history and memory, and the new journal *History and Memory*, the main flagbearer of this development in the profession, displays exactly this range of influences.[5] Film, both as a visual record of the past and as the production of history in its own right (subject to all the constructionist caveats we now bring to the integrity and authenticity of the 'archive', we must never forget), as well as the medium of fantasy and desire in a continuing and active fashion, is attracting increasing attention. The critical and eclectic appropriation of psychoanalytic theory of various kinds has played a key part here, whose possibilities historians have only gradually begun to explore, while photography also provides rich opportunities, particularly for the social and cultural history of the family and of personal life.[6] Finally, in all of these areas the impact of feminist theory and politics has been enormous, clearing the path for new initiatives, and directly inspiring many of the most creative departures. The dynamics and effects of women's history inside the profession have been extraordinarily important in their own right, but more fundamentally the challenge of feminism has legitimized the study of subjectivity, and over the longer term has forced historians to address such questions too. The analytical uses of autobiography, and various combinations of cultural theory, psychoanalysis and history, have been especially exciting. Caroline Steedman's work deserves a special mention, for instance. Moreover, while the editors of this volume rightly refer to the work of Ronald Fraser in outlining the salient influences in their thinking, his later volume, *In Search of a Past*, is arguably as important from our point of view as the classic *Blood of Spain*, which is the book they mention.[7]

So far, as I have suggested, the main impetus has come from people working in cultural studies, film and literary studies, particularly with a feminist orientation. Even when such work is historical, as it so often is, the authors are invariable non-historians in the strict professional and disciplinary sense, and even if they *are* historians by training and self-identification, they frequently speak from the margins, either because they have travelled the cultural studies route, or because history departments have ignored them.[8] One recent volume of essays on the cultural history of the Second World War, for example, which touches on the history–memory complex in all sorts of ways, assembles exactly the hybrid team of contributors I've been describing, coming from History certainly, but also from Media Studies, Film Studies, English, Art History, Design History, Communications, Women's Studies, and of course Cultural Studies itself.[9] Consequently, it is extremely important, and very refreshing, to find a volume on *War and Memory* consisting so impressively of historians. A willingness to engage with the unstable and indeterminate interrelationship of 'history' (in the professional and disciplinary senses of the term) and 'memory' (as a general name for the construction of the past's cultural meanings and the associated representational archive) has become a pressing necessity for historians of the contemporary world, and this excellent collection provides an admirable start.

Notes

1. See the emblematic texts by Fredrick Jameson, *Postmodernism, or The Cultural Logic of Late Capitalism* (Durham: Duke University Press, 1991), and David Harvey, *The Condition of Postmodernity. An Enquiry into the Origins of Cultural Change* (Oxford: Basil Blackwell, 1989). 'Nostalgia for the present' is the title of one of Jameson's chapters focused around film (see *Postmodernism*, pp. 279–96). The 'postmodern condition' originates with Jean-François Lyotard, *The Postmodern Condition* (Manchester: Manchester University Press, 1984). The phrase 'the end of history' was launched into public discourse by Francis Fukuyama *The End of History and the Last Man* (London, Hamish Hamilton, 1992).
2. For examples of recent oral history classics, which engage explicitly and creatively with the history and memory problematic, see the three volumes of *Lebensgeschichte und Sozialkultur im Ruhrgebiet 1930 bis 1960*, Lutz Niethammer, '*Die Jahre weiß man nicht, wo man die heute hinsetzen soll*': *Faschismuserfahrungen im Ruhrgehiet* (Bonn: Dietz, 1983), and '*Hinterher merkt man, daß es richtig war, daß es*

schiefgegangen ist': *Nachkriegserfahrungen im Ruhrgebiet* (Bonn: Dietz, 1983); and Lutz Niethammer and Alexander von Plato (eds), *'Wir kriegen jetzt andere Zeiten': auf der Suche nach der Erfahrungen des Volkes in nachfaschistischen Ländern* (Bonn: Dietz, 1985). Also Luisa Passerini, *Fascism in Popular Memory: The Cultural Experience of the Turin Working Class* (Cambridge: Cambridge University Press, 1987); Allessandro Portelli, 'Oral Testimony, the Law and the Making of History: The "April 7" Murder Trial', *History Workshop Journal*, 20 (Autumn 1985), pp. 5–35. For a landmark collection, originating in a conference on 'Myth and History' (Oxford, September 11–13, 1987), see Raphael Samuel and Paul Thompson (eds), *The Myths We Live By* (London: Routledge, 1990).

3. If I had to choose three examples of this crucial effect – the rethinking of the history–memory relation, and the consequent opening up of history's disciplinary boundaries and inhibitions – I would propose the following: Patrick Wright, *On Living in an Old Country: The National Past in Contemporary Britain* (London: Verso, 1985), and *A Journey Through Ruins. The Last Days of London* (London: Radius, 1991); Carolyn Kay Steedman, *Landscape for a Good Woman: A Story of Two* Lives (London: Virago, 1986); and Raphael Samuel, *Theatres of Memory*. Vol. 1: *Past and Present in Contemporary Culture* (London: Verso, 1994).

4. See Raphael Samuel, *Theatres of Memory*, pp. x, 443f.

5. The home of this journal in Tel Aviv University is also significant, for the presence of especially powerful collective memories in a political culture and its national pedagogies, embracing both the academic and the popular, does much to complicate the history–memory relationship and to bring the latter to the surface of intellectual debate. Addressing and representing the legacies of the Holocaust has been an especially difficult and challenging task for historians, and Saul Friedländer, one of the key voices in this continuing discussion, is also a moving spirit behind the journal *History and Memory*. See for instance the relationship between his own memoir, *When Memory Comes* (New York: Farrar Straus Giroux, 1979), and the landmark collection of essays he edited, *Probing the Limits of Representation. Nazism and the 'Final Solution'* (Cambridge, Mass.: Harvard University Press, 1992). For a general history of the place of the Holocaust in Israeli political culture, see Tom Segev, *The Seventh Million. The Israelis and the Holocaust* (New York: Hill and Wang, 1993). The film *Schindler's List* (Stephen Spielberg, 1993) provides an excellent opportunity for exploring the history–memory relationship in relation to the Holocaust. For my own thoughts, see Geoff Eley and Atina Grossmann, 'Watching *Schindler's List*: Not the Last Word', forthcoming in *New German Critique*, origin-

ally published as *'Schindler's List* hat nicht das letzte Wort', *Historische Anthropologie, Kultur–Gesellschaft–Alltag*, 3, 2 (1995), pp. 293–308.

6. For historians and film, see the volume edited by Robert Rosenstone, *Revisioning History. Film and the Construction of the Past* (Princeton: Princeton University Press, 1994). The recent exhibit *Assembling the Family* at the National Portrait Gallery (London, Summer 1996), on the use of photographs and albums to compose the histories of families between the mid-Victorian years and the present, is an excellent indication of what can be done. See Liz Jobey, 'Keeping Aunty out of the Picture: Ruthless Cut and Paste in the English Family Album', *New Statesman*, June 28, 1996, pp. 38–9. See also Judith Williamson, 'Family, Education, Photography', in Nicholas B. Dirks, Geoff Eley and Sherry B. Ortner (eds), *Culture/Power/History: A Reader in Contemporary Social Theory* (Princeton: Princeton University Press, 1994), pp. 236–44; and Annette Kuhn, *Family Secrets: Acts of Memory and Imagination* (London: Verso, 1995).

7. See Steedman, *Landscape for a Good Woman*; Ronald Fraser, *In Search of a Past. The Manor House, Amnersfield, 1933–1945* (London: Verso, 1984), and *Blood of Spain: The Experience of Civil War 1936–1939* (London: Allen Lane, 1979). See also the discussion in *'In Search of a Past*: A Dialogue with Ronald Fraser', *History Workshop Journal*, 20 (Autumn 1985), pp. 175–88.

8. To illustrate the seriousness of this syndrome, four of the most widely respected nineteenth- and twentieth-century British historians in international terms, Carolyn Steedman, Sally Alexander, Denise Riley and Catherine Hall, have not held appointments in history departments until very recently, if at all.

9. Pat Kirkham and David Thoms (eds), *War Culture: Social Change and Changing Experience in World War Two* (London: Lawrence & Wishart, 1995). By contrast, see several other key volumes dealing with the immediate post-war era, where these cultural questions of memory and the constructedness of the past are absent: Jim Fyrth (ed.), *Labour's Promised Land? Culture and Society in Labour Britain 1945–51* (London: Lawrence & Wishart, 1993); Jim Fyrth (ed.), *Labour's High Noon. The Government and the Economy 1945–51* (London: Lawrence & Wishart, 1993); James Obelkovich and Peter Catterall (eds), *Understanding Post-War British Society* (London: Routledge, 1994). In some ways the most striking example, which deals intentionally with the 'mythology' of 1945, but brackets the conceptual issues of popular memory *per se* completely, is Steven Fielding, Peter Thompson and Nick Tiratsoo, *"England Arise!" The Labour Party and Popular Politics in 1940s Britain* (Manchester: Manchester University Press, 1995).

Preface

Martin Evans and *Ken Lunn*

In June 1994 Portsmouth was the focus of an international event marking the fiftieth anniversary of the D-Day landings. Recognizing the pivotal role played by the city during the Normandy invasion, the event was one in a cycle of fiftieth anniversaries remembering the Second World War, a commemorative process which began in September 1989 and ended in August 1995 with the anniversary of Victory over Japan. Such a sustained and popular expression of remembrance has no precedent within British history. During the nineteenth century, whether it be Trafalgar, Waterloo or the Crimean campaign, the men who fell for their country were quickly forgotten. Now, in contrast, hundreds of thousands attended the Victory over Japan celebrations; whilst 1.5 million were present in Hyde Park in May 1995 for the Victory in Europe Day. In this way the place of the Second World War within the British national memory was emphatically reaffirmed.

Although the tone and content was very different, all the other combatant nations staged similar commemorations. The Russians with Stalingrad; the Germans with the bombing of Dresden; the Polish with the Warsaw uprising: these three examples are indicative of a generalized will to remember. Significantly too, they underline how, fifty years on, the Second World War is still recognized as one of the defining experiences of the twentieth century. If one feature of these commemorations was the sheer scale of public remembering, another was mounting acrimony. The further the commemorative cycle went the more memory became fraught with tension, and nowhere was this more obvious than with the anniversary of the dropping of the atomic bomb on Hiroshima. Calls from within Japan, demanding that the Allies should apologize, led to fury amongst Far East veterans in America, Britain and several other former dominions. For many of the latter, the atomic bomb was justified because it shortened the war and thus saved lives. And anyway, they went on, does not undue focus upon Hiroshima risk forgetting the terrible atrocities carried out by Japanese militarism?[1] What about the large numbers of women from conquered countries who were herded into camps and used as prostitutes by the Japanese army? What about the thousands of Allied prisoners who died building the Burma railway? Or, even before the Second World War, what about the Nanking Massacre of December 1937, when the Japanese invaders slaughtered hundreds of thousands of defenceless soldiers and civilians, in an event sometimes termed as the Japanese 'Auschwitz'? Surely the Japanese government should be willing to acknowledge these aspects of the war as well. The Hiroshima controversy was symptomatic of a general problem facing each anniversary, namely *what* was the purpose of remembering? Was it to be celebratory or commemorative; triumphalist or reflective; based upon international reconciliation or narrowly national-istic? Furthermore, the Hiroshima anniversary underlined the significance of the national perspective, namely how any one person's memory of the Pacific conflict is heavily dependent on whether you are American, British, Australian or Japanese.

To explore the complexities of war and memory in the twentieth century an interdisciplinary conference was held at the University of Portsmouth in March 1994. This book grew out of that conference and it is structured by the same intellectual concerns, namely how war in the twentieth century has been commemorated. What are the function and place of historical memories of war? How do they relate to concepts of national identity? How have the memories of war been constructed? What have been the contours of these memories and how have they altered over time? How do memories of war circulate and how are they transmitted from one generation to the next? How are memories of war constructed in terms of race, class and gender? In asking these questions the present volume cannot claim to be exhaustive; it does not cover all the conflicts that have taken place in the twentieth century. Instead the book is designed to raise fundamental questions about different processes of memorialization. In particular it investigates the various 'sites' of memory, exploring 'public' ways of remembering, expressed in films, television, public monuments, museums, war crimes trials, as well as more 'private' ways of remem-bering, such as personal testimonies, letters and diaries. Part 1 focuses on the specific example of the Holocaust and war crimes trials; whilst Parts 2 to 5 examine different types of memory, oral testimony, museums, monuments and film. Part 6 then draws together what is a central theme throughout the book, that is how memory within popular culture is a focus of continual conflict and contestation.

In approaching war and memory in this manner the editors and con-tributors have been influenced by a growth of recent research in this area. One starting point has been the pioneering work of Paul Fussell, *The Great War and Modern Memory*.[2] Published in 1975, and focusing on the literary representations of the conflict, Fussell opened up the complexities of remembering by analysing the ways in which the imagery of the Great War became inscribed within British culture and society. In doing so Fussell convincingly argued that the Great War generated new images and, as such, has become part of the fibre of our own lives. A further starting point was Ronald Fraser's oral history of the Spanish Civil war, *The Blood of Spain*.[3] This book broke new ground because of the way in which testimony was used. In presenting the interviews he deliberately shifted the emphasis away from a narrow historical empiricism; it was not how it was which interested Fraser, but how people remembered it as having been. Thus Fraser made the omissions, prejudices and reworkings of memory into a legitimate object of historical enquiry. The work of Fussell and Fraser is testament to the gathering interest in remembering, an interest which is also exemplified in, amongst others, the brilliant scholarship of Adrian Gregory, Luisa Passerini, Henry Rousso, Jay Winter and James E. Young, all of whom have subjected war and memory to new and ever more detailed modes of scrutiny.[4] However, of all recent research we would like to underline the significance of two people in particular: Pierre Nora and Alistair Thomson.[5] Nora's notion of 'sites of memory' has been hugely influential, not only in expanding our notion of what constitutes remembering, but also in opening up the field to comparative analysis by making us reflect upon the nature and form of different types of memory. For Nora the purpose of each site of memory is to express the will to remember, whether it be on the part of a local community or at the level of the nation-state, by blocking forgetting, stopping time and materializing the immaterial. In this sense, Nora argues, the place of memory is created by a complex interplay between a sense of the past and a sense of the present. Thomson's work on Australian veterans from the First World War is equally suggestive, this time in respect to the relationship between public and private memory. In looking at the memories of Australian veterans he highlights how private memories cannot be separated from the effects of dominant public discourses. Indeed he shows how the latter often furnish the very images by which private history is thought through. When conducting his initial interviews in Melbourne he was struck by the extent to which individual memories had become entangled with more public representations; for instance, some veterans related scenes from the film *Gallipoli* as if they were their own.

What Nora and Thomson do is remind us how memory is a complex *construct*. At the same time they underline how memory is a process used by both individuals and more institutional forces to connect the past with the present and the future. One illustration of this is the research of Graham Dawson and Bob West on popular memory and national identity in Britain.[6] They argue that the 'public field' of Second World War representations, through innumerable cultural images, constitutes a very powerful reworked national identity, one which was effectively invoked by Margaret Thatcher during the Falklands crisis in 1982. This is not to suggest any crude conspiratorial construction of such imagery, nor to deny the existence of contrasting and challenging memories of war, but to note the complex workings whereby this particular national myth becomes the dominant discourse. In recognizing such processes this book is concerned with how memory is a battlefield, an arena of contestation where conflicting social groups assert conflicting memories. What are the dominant memories associated with war? What images and symbols do these dominant images draw upon? Why do certain memories remain central within the arena of public representations whilst those of others, such as women or working-class people, are often marginalized? Moreover what are the differing political, cultural and historical determinants which go together to compose what James E. Young has imaginatively termed the 'texture of memory'?

As a collective venture the initial conference could not have been achieved without the financial backing of the School of Social and Historical Studies at the University of Portsmouth, as well as the support of the Oral History Society and the Parkes Library at the University of Southampton. In terms of the final volume the editors would like to thank the British Academy, which financed the research leave necessary to complete the project. We would also like to acknowledge the patience and tact of Kathryn Earle at Berg Publishers. Importantly, too, we would like to thank friends and colleagues at the University of Portsmouth. Portsmouth benefits from a lively research culture and we are particularly grateful for the energy invested in this project by Tacey Hurd, as well as the intellectual and financial support provided by the Nation and Identity and the Francophone research groups, collaborative projects which work on contemporary nationalism and French colonial and post-colonial relations respectively. Donna Loftus, who provided the index, also deserves our grateful acknowledgement. Finally, and most importantly, we wish to acknowledge the efforts made by all the contributors to both the conference and the book. We thank you for your time, your expertise and, above all, the shared sense of intellectual discovery which you all brought to this collective venture.

Notes

1. Ian Buruma, *Wages of Guilt: Memories of War in Germany and Japan* (London: Cape, 1994).
2. Paul Fussell, *The Great War and Modern Memory* (Oxford: Oxford University Press, 1975).

3. Ronald Fraser, *The Blood of Spain* (London: Allen Lane, 1979).
4. Adrian Gregory, *The Silence of Memory* (Oxford: Berg, 1994); Luisa Passerini, 'Work, ideology and consensus under Italian fascism', *History Workshop Journal*, vol. 8 (1979), pp. 82–108; Henry Rousso, *Le Syndrome de Vichy* (Paris: Seuil, 1987); Jay Winter, *Sites of Mourning, Sites of Memory* (Cambridge: Cambridge University Press, 1995); James E. Young, *Holocaust Memorials and Meaning* (New Haven and London: Yale University Press, 1993).
5. Pierre Nora, 'Between memory and history: *Les Lieux de Memoire*', *Representations*, vol. 26 (1989), University of California, pp. 7–25; Alistair Thomson, *Anzac Memories: Living with the Legend* (Melbourne: Oxford University Press, 1994).
6. Graham Dawson and Bob West, '"Our Finest Hours": the popular memory of the Second World War and the struggles over national identity' in Geoff Hurd (ed.), *National Fictions: World War Two in British Films and Television* (London: BFI, 1984).

Notes on Contributors

Bernice Archer is a Ph.D. student at the University of Essex. Her thesis is a comparative study of civilian internment in the Far East during the Second World War in which she focuses on a small group of camps in China, Hong Kong, Singapore, the Philippines, Java and Sumatra. She is a keen oral historian.

David Cesarani is Professor of Modern Jewish Studies at the University of Southampton. His publications on the Holocaust and Nazi war criminals include, as editor, *The Final Solution: Origins and Implementation* and *Justice Delayed*, a study of how Nazi collaborators entered Britain after 1945.

Barry M. Doyle teaches modern British social and political history at the University of Teesside. His research has concentrated on the social, political and cultural world of the Norwich middle class in the early twentieth century. He is currently working on a social history of twentieth-century Britain.

Geoff Eley is Professor of History at the University of Michigan, Ann Arbor. His publications include *Reshaping the German Right* and *From Unification to Nazism: Reinterpreting the German Past*.

Martin Evans is Lecturer in French and European Studies at the University of Portsmouth. His research has concentrated on colonialism and post-colonialism. He is the author of *The Memory of Resistance: French Opposition to the Algerian War*.

Sue Harper teaches cultural history and film at the University of Portsmouth. She has published widely on British cinema, including *Picturing the Past: The Rise and Fall of the British Costume Film*.

John Hellmann is Professor of English at the Ohio State University, where he teaches at the Lima Campus. He is the author of *Fables of Fact: The New Journalism as New Fiction*, and *American Myth and the Legacy of Vietnam*.

Margaretta Jolly is researching for a doctoral thesis at the University of Sussex on women's letters and letter-writing during the Second World War. She has worked with older women in reminiscence projects and is a member of the Brighton Workers' Educational Association.

William Kidd is Senior Lecturer in French at the University of Stirling. He has published extensively on twentieth-century French literature and sociology, war and memory, and psychocriticism. His forthcoming work (co-authored) will be *La Moselle monumentale*.

Gerd Knischewski is Senior Lecturer in German Politics and Society at the University of Portsmouth. His current research project is the changing historic identities of Berlin.

Tony Kushner is Marcus Sieff Lecturer in Jewish/Non-Jewish Relations at the University of Southampton. His most recent book is *The Holocaust and the Liberal Imagination: A Social and Cultural History.*

Jane Leonard is Senior Research Fellow in the Institute of Irish Studies, the Queen's University of Belfast. She is currently working on the cultural and political history of twentieth-century conflict commemoration in Northern Ireland.

Ken Lunn is Reader in Social History at the University of Portsmouth. He has published extensively on the history of 'race' and immigration in modern British history and on radical Right politics.

Phil Melling is Senior Lecturer and Head of Department in American Studies at the University of Swansea. Among his books are *Vietnam in American Literature, Hotel Vietnam* and *Man of Amman.* He has also written on American popular culture in the 1920s and 1930s.

Catherine Moriarty is the Curator of the Design Council Archive at the University of Brighton. Formerly she was the Co-ordinator of the National Inventory of War Memorials at the Imperial War Museum, London. Her research into commemorative sculpture and the First World War was based at the University of Sussex.

Lucy Noakes is Lecturer in Media Studies at the University of Brighton. Her research has focused on the relationship between gender, memory and national identity. Her forthcoming book is *Just for the Duration: Gender and National Identity in Wartime Britain.*

Notes on Contributors

Martin Shaw is Professor of International Relations and Politics and co-director (with Mary Kaldor) of the graduate programme in Contemporary War and Peace Studies at the University of Sussex. His books include *Post-Military Society*, *Global Society and International Relations* and *Civil Society and Media in Global Crisis.*

Ulla Spittler is Senior Lecturer in German at the Language Centre, University of Brighton. She is currently working on public commemoration in post-war Germany.

Jeffrey Walsh is Principal Lecturer in English at the Manchester Metropolitan University. He is the author of *American War Literature: 1914 to Vietnam* and *The Gulf War Did Not Happen: Politics, Culture and Warfare Post Vietnam.* His forthcoming book is *Analyzing Television.*

Part I

Holocaust and War Crimes Trials

'I Want to go on Living after my Death': The Memory of Anne Frank

Tony Kushner

For Gentiles Only!, one in a series of Holocaust-denial pornographic publications that have circulated in Britain since the 1980s, refers to 'The "Holocaust" Myth and one of its central pillars, the Anne Frank *"Diary"'*. A study could be devoted to the particular obsession of the 'revisionists' (in reality, antisemitic followers of anti-history) in their insistence that the diary is a forgery. On one level, this is peculiar as the diary of Anne Frank finishes, of course, before her arrest and deportation eastward. It ends without the horrors of Auschwitz, where most of the inhabitants of the secret annexe were killed, the death marches and the final days of Anne and her sister in Belsen. Her last entry, dated 1 August 1944, was written just three days before members of the Dutch SS raided the hiding place and sent the occupants to the concentration camps. Yet it is still necessary, if their message is to carry any weight, for the collection of misfits, eccentrics and neo-Nazis who refuse to accept the reality of the gas chambers also to question the authenticity of a document written hundreds of miles away from the major killing centres.[1] *The Diary of Anne Frank* has become the most important source of knowledge in the world today concerning the Holocaust and as Alvin Rosenfeld points out, 'the most widely read book of World War II'. It is now seen as one of the key writings of the twentieth century, a landmark in the educational experiences of those in liberal society and more generally 'stands today, almost unrivalled, as a contemporary cultural icon'.[2]

In Britain and Ireland alone well over 1 million people have visited the 'Anne Frank in the World' exhibition since it started touring in 1986. Indeed, interest in the story of Anne Frank is, if anything, growing. In 1993 it was the most popular non-fiction work in terms of library borrowing. Today her work has gained in relevance with the Bosnian disaster; thousands of British youngsters needed no prompting to see the connection when they sent parcels and letters of support to their contemporaries in former Yugoslavia after reading *The Diary*. The parallel for those in Bosnia is more than apparent:

> Our youth is very similar. After fifty years, history repeats itself in Bosnia – war, hate, killing, hiding, displacements. We are 12 years old and we can't influence politics or war, but we want to say to all the world that we want to continue our lives in freedom and peace. We wait for peace, like Anne Frank fifty years before. She didn't live to see peace, but we . . .?

wrote the pupils of Class V13, Ivan Goran School, Zenika, Bosnia-Herzogovina in March 1993. It is clear that *The Diary of Anne Frank* loses none of its freshness to new generations in many different circumstances. This chapter, however, will concentrate on the 1950s when *The Diary*, in what was an uneven pattern, moved from obscurity to its status at the end of the decade when, as *The Times* stated, it had become 'known to millions of people all over the world'. But what did *The Diary* mean to contemporaries? How was Anne Frank interpreted just a few years after her death? Why is it that Anne Frank became such an enduring image of the Second World War to the liberal world?[3]

It is now hard to envisage a situation where *The Diary* would not be taken seriously. Yet in the years immediately after the end of the war this was essentially the case. It was a result more of the work having no context in which to operate than because its authenticity was under question. The first barrier was in Holland itself. Otto Frank, the only member of the annexe to survive, returned to Amsterdam in 1945 and was presented with the diary by Miep Gies, one of the family's close circle of helpers. After initial hesitation, he then devoted all his energy to getting *The Diary* published and circulated. It was not an easy task – after some initial refusals a small publisher was found to print the first edition in 1947. The print run was just 1,500 and although there was enthusiasm from those whose who came into contact with *The Diary*, the overall impact in the Netherlands and certainly beyond was limited. Rosenfeld comments that these difficulties 'no doubt reflect[ed] the sense that people were tired of the war and probably did not want to be reminded all over again of the suffering that had marked the years of occupation'.[4] Here he presents a rather generous interpretation of Dutch popular memory in the immediate post-war years. This memory was in fact selective – the misery inflicted by the German occupiers was recognized but the role played by Dutch collaborators was largely forgotten. The plight of the Jews in occupied Holland was subject to particular amnesia. Returning Jewish survivors were often treated with antipathy and sometimes open resentment. They were an unpleasant reminder of the recent past to a Dutch society experiencing an extension and perhaps an intensification of earlier anti-semitic tendencies. It was especially unpleasant that this hostility was focused on the Holocaust survivors. Elie Cohen in his classic analysis *Human Behaviour in the Concentration Camps* wrote in the early 1950s that interest in the subject was 'very much on the wane'. He added that 'particularly in the Netherlands there is a notable paucity of scientific works' on the camps. There was thus little space for consideration of the difficult issues raised by *The Diary of Anne Frank*.[5]

Holland, however, was far from isolated in its absence of Holocaust commemoration – even if its specific construction of war memory was, like that of every country involved in the conflict, unique. But Otto Frank was now on a mission to market *The Diary* in book form on a worldwide basis. His next 'success' was in France and Germany – again leading to minor publishers producing limited editions of *The Diary*. In France, however, the book did achieve critical acclaim which led to it being noticed more internationally – most importantly through the American Jewish author, Meyer Levin, whose obsession with *The Diary* started after reading its French translation (published by Calmann-Levy in 1950). Even with intellectual backing, however, it was far from being a best-seller in France, although early sales were more impressive than in Germany.[6] Moreover, in Germany, some anti-German sections were subtly but fundamentally altered, such as her comment on 9 October 1942 that 'Germans and Jews are the greatest enemies in the world', so as not to embarrass the book's readers. The hesitant early history of *The Diary* was yet more pronounced in the United States and Britain. In the former, ten leading publishers turned *The Diary* down before it was accepted by Doubleday in New York and published in 1952. There was also a similar lack of enthusiasm from the major publishing houses in Britain – *The Diary* was published by a subsidiary of Vallentine Mitchell also in 1952.[7]

The situation at the point of the British and American editions reflected a general pattern. The mission of Otto Frank was rewarded, but only in the form of small print runs from relatively obscure publishers. In the British and American cases it should be added that Doubleday and Vallentine Mitchell were both small publishing outfits with strong Jewish connections. The reluctance of Germany and German-occupied countries to confront their role in the murder of their own Jewish citizens in the years immediately following the end of the war is perhaps not surprising. Selective amnesia, along with myth-making, has been essential in constructing successful national memories in the modern era. Yet the apparent equal unwillingness of the major allies in the war against Nazism to recognize the fate of the Jews is less straightforward.[8]

Anne Frank has now become a symbol for all the Jews killed in the Holocaust. Until the late 1950s or early 1960s, however, the very concept of the Holocaust as a distinct historical event was not part of general popular or historical consciousness. Not even the terminology was in place.

Thus if the *Wiener Library Bulletin* (which was first published in 1949 and was perhaps the first journal specifically devoted to Nazism and the Jewish tragedy) is examined, the subject is referred to under the heading 'Terror and Resistance'. The word 'Holocaust' was used in Jewish publications, along with the Hebrew words 'Churban' and 'Shoah', as early as the 1940s, yet even Yad Vashem, which until the early 1990s was firmly established as the most important Holocaust commemoration centre in the world, struggled to establish itself throughout the 1950s in Israeli society. Although some were anxious to preserve the memory of those who had perished, for many Jews, including those in the new Jewish state, there was no desire to remind themselves of their total vulnerability in the very recent past. It was memory that was problematic in the extreme for a country forced to defend itself militarily from its creation. The Israeli nation remained, at best, ambivalent to Holocaust survivors in its midst.[9]

The situation in Britain and the United States was less complex. The Second World War, as a specific Jewish tragedy, was simply not recognized. The liberations of the western camps – Belsen by the British and, amongst others, Buchenwald and Dachau by the Americans – were presented in ways that would minimize their Jewish aspect. On the one hand, they were universalized, thereby showing the triumph of good over evil or democracy over totalitarianism. They were proof that this had been a 'just war', and a fitting if somewhat disturbing end to the conflict. On the other hand, they were particularized, but only to strengthen British and American nationalistic myths. The bad 'Hun' had been overcome by the forces of decency represented by the British soldier or the American GI. The victims were faceless; they were presented in the liberation films as a people without a past and with no foreseeable future. For the British in particular, any attention given to the Jewishness of the survivors was additionally dangerous because it gave credence to Zionist arguments with regard to the promotion of Jewish nationalism in the last days of the British mandate in Palestine. But beyond issues of international diplomacy and *realpolitik*, both the British and American governments were wary of straying from liberal universalism by in any way stressing Jewish particularity – even in suffering and mass murder.[10]

By the early 1950s there was ample material to shape an understanding of the Jewish fate in the war provided by war crimes trials, survivor testimony and underfunded research bodies in Europe and beyond. It was not the shortage of information, but an unwillingness to accept the uniqueness of the Jewish plight during the war which acted as a barrier to comprehension. If anything, the knowledge of what we now call the Holocaust actually declined in British and American societies in the first half of the 1950s. The Second World War was being reconstructed, especially in film and literature, as a more 'traditional' military conflict fought along gentlemanly lines. Nowhere can this be seen more clearly than in the Anglo-American production, *The Desert Fox*, released in 1951. In contrast, detailed work by Leon Poliakov and Gerald Reitlinger on the destruction process published in the early 1950s received limited attention on both sides of the Atlantic. There was simply little or no understanding of the immensity of the Jewish fate, and thus *The Diary of Anne Frank* in the 1950s (and beyond) lacked a Holocaust context in which to illustrate its full complexity. Meyer Levin wrote in 1950 about the hesitation of American publishers with regard to *The Diary*: 'In the main, the[y] sprung from the same nominal sources. The book was "too special"'.[11]

The process by which *The Diary* became estranged from its Holocaust/ Jewish connections can be viewed at its most extreme and, at times, at an almost farcical level in the British marketing of *The Diary* in 1952 and 1953. When Vallentine Mitchell, the publishing wing of the *Jewish Chronicle*, agreed to produce the English edition, there is no doubt that they did so for more than commercial reasons. Indeed, they were probably the most important publishers of Holocaust-related material in Britain during the 1950s and 1960s. As David Kessler, the managing director of Vallentine Mitchell, told Otto Frank: 'We took the book in the first instance because we believed that it was one which ought to be read in England.' He added that 'at the same time, we had sufficient confidence in it to estimate that it would cover its expenses'.[12] These comments were not simply made to keep quiet the irrepressible Otto Frank, who was complaining about the failure of the British marketing operation. In an editorial meeting in September 1952, the book was seen to be coming to the end of its natural sales life. After just four months the marketing manager reported that 'though ANNE FRANK might not be a best-seller, we had never anticipated that it would be and that to dispose of a 5,000 edition in about six months was very creditable'. In spite of Otto's complaints, a second print run was rejected – in 1953, remarkably, the book was unavailable for sale in the United Kingdom.[13] The refusal to republish *The Diary* may with hindsight be deemed one of the great marketing failures of the twentieth century. This, however, would be unfair on Kessler and his colleagues, who wrote firmly to Frank in June 1953 that 'we are not in the least ashamed of what we achieved. Publishing conditions in different countries vary and it is no use to think that a success in one country necessarily portends a success elsewhere.' Kessler reminded Frank that many other British publishers had rejected *The Diary* and that no other publishers in the country could be found who would take it. Kessler concluded that 'It is quite certain that publishers in this country have come to the conclusion that there is no large pent-up demand for the book.' As the twentieth century draws to a close, at least 25 million copies of *The Diary* have been sold globally. Why then were British sales so slow in the first few years in a country where subsequently over 2 million copies have been bought?[14]

One simple and tempting explanation was that taken by Otto Frank – the shortcomings of Vallentine Mitchell. In 1956, the limitations of the publishing house at that time were recognized in an internal memorandum which stated bluntly that 'it is common ground that we have no future in the general publishing business'. Two reasons were given: firstly, that good titles 'were not available to us' and secondly that 'we have no adequate sales organisation for a profitable general list'. Yet in the case of *The Diary* neither factor, certainly not the first and not even the second, were at work. For once and briefly, Vallentine Mitchell, under the part-sponsorship of a certain Captain Ian Maxwell (later more famously known as Robert Maxwell), employed a reasonably large sales team. His representatives reported as early as September 1952 that 'the book was not selling very well in the provinces. In two weeks, they had only sold three copies. The *Cookery Book*, on the other hand, was selling quite well.'[15]

It was not only the representatives who were struggling to get the book noticed in Britain. Although the reviews received by *The Diary* were very positive, they were patchy and very slow in appearing. Although it is clear that a more professional approach to *The Diary* from its publishers in the United States resulted in greater sales, it is far too simplistic to blame Vallentine Mitchell for its relative failure in Britain. Indeed, when Doubleday were eventually persuaded to take the book in the United States, there were some within the company who regarded the 5,000 print run as 'something as a gamble and assuredly large enough to meet what was expected to be the demand for such a chronicle'. Ultimately, however well marketed, *The Diary* needed to appeal to a particular audience, and in 1952–3 it was far from clear who this was in Britain. Britain's war memory was essential to its post-1945 national identity. It was too precious, it must be argued, to have been brought into question by the experiences of another people whose suffering and losses made British sacrifices pale into insignificance. Moreover, the history of the Jews in the war was particularly problematic: it was a story with no redemptive ending, which contrasted markedly with the British case. VE Day, in a European Jewish context, fitted very uneasily with the reality of the war. Furthermore, Britain, in reconstructing its own war memory, had a particular place for Belsen, which was liberated by the British in April 1945. It had become 'our camp'. Even though the vast majority of its victims were Jewish, the anglicizing of its memory meant that it no longer 'belonged' to the Jews. Yet the British fixation with Belsen of all the camps in the Nazi system meant that consideration of other specifically murderous sites such as Birkenau and Treblinka was extremely rare in British society and culture during the 1950s. In 1958 a survivor came to Britain lecturing on the history of Auschwitz. A former British cabinet minister was incredulous and 'exclaimed that before this talk he had thought that most of the deaths were caused by epidemics due to overcrowding and lack of sanitation'. Not surprisingly, after his British tour the survivor concluded that 'The real facts are not well known.'[16]

British Jewry internalized many of these tendencies, keeping the Holocaust at a distance – a terror that was ever-present but could not or would not be confronted. Peace and quiet, and especially the suburban lifestyle, was the goal and realized ambition of many. The Jews of Britain engaged in what the writer Bernard Kops has called the post-war pursuit of 'the semi and the three-piece suite'. It was perhaps for this reason that Vallentine Mitchell had discovered that sales of Florence Greenberg's classic Jewish cookery book far outreached those of *The Diary of Anne Frank*. Indeed, Bernard Kops was almost alone of all the new British Jewish writers of the post-war era until at least the 1970s in even touching upon the history of the Jews of Europe during the war.[17]

It is against this background that the marketing and understanding of *The Diary* has to be understood for Britain in the 1950s. The book was, in Kessler's mind, 'unique', but he added in 1953 that 'The fact that it records war-time experiences is, to my mind, far less important than its qualities as a remarkable document of a girl's adolescence.' In Britain the book was therefore universalized not in the form of a symbol for all of the horrors of the Second World War, but for the age-old problems of growing up. It was thus to a child psychiatrist rather than a historian of the war (or an expert on Jewish literature) that Vallentine Mitchell turned to obtain material for advanced publicity:

> We are anxious for the book to reach not only the widest but the most suitable public, and we are looking for the right note to strike in our publicity. Although it was written by a young girl it is unlikely it will be read by adolescents. We believe it will be of interest to parents and for all those interested in the inner problems of growing children. The book is exceptionally honest and intelligent and seems to reveal authentically all the pains and joys of adolescence.

Here then was the possible market – a book made for those parents in 1950s Britain failing to understand the younger generation. It is easy to be dismissive of Vallentine Mitchell's failure to see the possible teenage market available with *The Diary*. Yet on another level, they were not mistaken – the book's appeal in the latter part of the decade and subsequently has been through children identifying with Anne in terms of her adolescent struggle with her parents. Unfortunately for Vallentine Mitchell, it was from Dr Spock rather than Anne Frank that parents would seek reassurance in child-rearing in the 1950s.[18]

By the end of the 1950s, *The Diary* was a best-seller everywhere, including Britain. In 1955 a Broadway play of *The Diary* was transported to Europe and a Hollywood film was released in 1959 – both with immense success. As early as 1953 *The Diary* had headed sales lists in the United States and Japan. Demand for the book in Germany expanded massively in 1955 after the enormous acclaim and national trauma caused by the theatre version. Sales took off in Britain at the same time. What had changed, and why did the British and American markets follow different paths for several years?[19]

Britain, of all the major countries involved in the Second World War, was most at ease with its memory of the conflict. The myth of 'Britain alone' was firmly established, and with ultimate victory, the military and civilian losses and suffering it had incurred were not in vain. In short, there was no suppressed memory to confront, no need for a symbol that both represented the horrors of war and provided a redemptive ending. The British liberation of Belsen provided the proper finishing point: the forces of good triumphed over the monsters that had created a 'living hell'. Britain did not require the specific recognition of victims such as Anne Frank and her sister Margot who had died in abject misery in the weeks preceding British entry into Belsen. Dunkirk, the Blitz, D-Day, the flying-bomb raids and, to a lesser extent, the prisoners of war in Japan were the British reference points for war suffering.

In contrast, the Japanese desperately required Anne Frank. The country's war memory was problematic in the extreme. Humiliation in defeat for what had been a martial society; the fighting of an unjust war which could not be recognized as such; and the trauma of Hiroshima and Nagasaki left a nation in need of healing and of bolstering its own self-image. Sales in Japan after its publication in 1952 were spectacular. Over 100,000 copies were sold by early 1953 as *The Diary* reached its thirteenth printing. The Japanese publisher had been gloomy about its commercial prospects and, like his British counterpart, did not think 'it would be a profit making affair'. His marketing strategy was to 'protest against the great misfortunes brought by war. Japanese of all ages and classes have sent in [favourable] comments.' Yet in contrast to the situation in Britain, book stores across Japan instantly displayed portraits of Anne Frank in their window displays. To the Japanese, Anne Frank, although European, had become an acceptable and accessible cultural figure of the war – a young victim, but one who inspired hope for the future rather than a sense of guilt for the past. Her sex further emphasized the stress on innocence, reflecting a broader trend of war representation in Japanese society. Memorials to the atomic bomb victims emphasized women and children (whilst simultaneously excluding mention of marginal groups such as the Korean immigrants who suffered massive losses). Since the 1950s *The*

Diary has sold 5 million copies in Japan. The possibly problematic nature of this national interest was revealed in a Japanese cartoon version of the book released in 1995. The internationally acclaimed producer, Seiya Araki, was criticized by the Anne Frank Foundation in Amsterdam. The Foundation did not want to be associated with the 1½-hour film, because it felt that 'it paint[ed] a too idealised and romantic picture of the reality'.[20] The reasons for the success of the book in Japan found echoes in many European countries during the 1950s. Anne Frank became universalized, she was a way of connecting to a troubled history in a non-threatening way: everyone was now a victim of the war. Whereas in Britain the book could only be marketed as one about adolescence, continental Europe (and particularly Germany) and Japan relished the book, or rather sanitized and warped versions of it, as *the* text of the Second World War. But why should it be taken to heart so quickly in the United States and why was it that by the end of the decade the dominant image of Anne Frank was American?

Sales in the United States were remarkably similar in the first year of publication to those in Japan – 100,000 with the book heading the best-seller list for many weeks. Judith Doneson has written of 'the Americanization, and ultimate universalization, of the Holocaust through the *Diary*'. There is no doubt that the universal was the objective of both the award-winning Broadway play of 1955 and the film of 1959. The latter was made clear in the film company's statement that 'this isn't a Jewish picture, this is a picture for the world'. Although it was essentially Jewish writers and others who were responsible for the transformation of the diary to stage and film, there was anything but a desire to stress Jewish particularity.[21]

It was this issue, above all others, that prompted the heated and long-standing argument between Meyer Levin, who had in many ways 'discovered' *The Diary* for an American audience, and Otto Frank. Levin, a complex figure, had been haunted by the images he had witnessed as a reporter in the American liberation of the western concentration camps in the spring of 1945. The shock encountered in confronting the indescribable was common among the many thousands of Allied troops involved in such camp liberations. Levin, however, was unusual in becoming deeply involved on a personal level with the survivors in the months following on from the first days of their 'freedom'. As Lawrence Graver has illustrated, Levin became obsessed with the need to communicate the Jewish tragedy to a wider audience. After reading *The Diary* in 1950, Levin believed this was the text that, through the words of one individual, could be used to represent the horrors of the Holocaust: 'Anne Frank's voice becomes the voice of six million vanished Jewish souls.' At first Otto Frank and Meyer Levin had a common mission –

both wanted Anne Frank's words to reach the largest possible audience. Indeed, Meyer Levin was of immense importance in gaining an American publisher for *The Diary* and also in launching its successful critical acclaim in a key piece in *The New York Times Book Review*.[22]

The falling-out of the two men occurred with the transformation of *The Diary* into a playscript. Levin wrote a version that used extensive quotations from *The Diary* and put great stress on the Jewishness of the inhabitants of the secret annexe. He framed his script with constant and clear references to the fate of European Jewry during the war. Although amended versions of Levin's play of *The Diary* have been successfully produced in small auditoriums, it is almost inconceivable that it would have gained the popular success of the more famous version of the play scripted by Frances Goodrich and Albert Hackett which avoided key passages, such as that of 9 October 1942, which highlight the broader Holocaust context and also the moments of despair felt by Anne Frank:

> Dear Kitty,
> I've got dismal and depressing news for you today. Our many Jewish friends are being taken away by the dozen. These people are treated by the Gestapo without a shred of decency, being loaded into cattle trucks and sent to Westerbork, the big Jewish camp in Drente. Westerbork sounds terrible . . . It is impossible to escape . . . . If it is as bad as this in Holland whatever will it be like in the distant and barbarous regions they are sent to? We assume that most of them are murdered. The British radio speaks of their being gassed.
> Perhaps that is the quickest way to die. I feel terribly upset, I couldn't tear myself away while Miep [Gies] told these dreadful stories . . .

Reaching the widest popular audience was certainly the goal of Otto Frank. How much Frank, as Levin was to argue for decades to come, wanted a less particularistic *Diary* is still unclear. What is not debatable, however, is that the Goodrich–Hackett version of the play (which remained little changed in the film of *The Diary* four years later) minimized both the Jewish content and the Holocaust context.[23] The accessibility of both Broadway play and Hollywood film was further strengthened by ending with the very partial quote from Anne's diary, 15 July 1944: 'in spite of everything, I still believe that people are really good at heart'. Whereas Levin's version was highly sombre, Goodrich and Hackett's was uplifting with a classic Hollywood 'happy ending'. Levin by no means avoided the much-quoted words from 15 July 1944 but he was also anxious not to avoid those that immediately followed in which Anne Frank provided far more complex reflections on the present and future: 'I simply can't build up my hopes on a foundation consisting of confusion, misery and death. I see the world gradually being turned into a wilderness, I hear the ever-approaching thunder, which will destroy us too, I can feel the sufferings of millions.' Although she concluded the entry with the comment that 'I think it will all come right, that this cruelty too will end, and that peace and tranquillity will return again', the mixing of hope and despair is typical of many of *The Diary*'s entries, especially in its later stages.[24]

The American 1950s version of Anne Frank was thus used to buttress the liberal ideal. Firstly, she was an individual determined to pursue her right to happiness. Secondly, Anne Frank became a universal figure whose Jewishness could be almost ignored – Anne Frank had become every person, she was accessible to all regardless of ethnicity, religion or nationality. Thirdly, and most importantly, she was portrayed as a figure of hope, one who never abandoned the crucial liberal ideal of progress even in the direst of circumstances. Indeed, if there had been any natural justice, the Frank family should have been an American family, and the figure of Anne that emerged from both Broadway and Hollywood was impeccably American. The middle-class credentials of the Frank family further enhanced their rights to occupy an American suburban status in the 1950s. Algene Ballif, reviewing the Broadway version in *Commentary*, astutely observed her 'metamorphosis into an American adolescent'. Ballif commented further that 'Anne Frank was not an "American" adolescent, as Mr. Hackett and Miss Goodrich would have us believe. She was an unaffected young girl, exceedingly alive, deep, and honest – experiencing more, and in a better way perhaps, than many of us do in the course of a whole lifetime.' It was, however, a far more comfortable, unchallenging and accessible image of Anne Frank with a happy ending to her diary that was transported to the world by American culture in the second half of the decade.[25]

The ease with which Anne Frank was Americanized still does not explain her appeal to a massive domestic market. It must be suggested that the United States revealed tendencies different from both the British example (where the untarnished war memory limited the adult market) and those of countries such as Japan and Germany (where the reverse was true). The Second World War was simply less important in the formation of national identity in the United States. Post-war international and domestic traumas played a far more significant role – Judith Doneson refers in particular to the internal wounds caused by McCarthyism, and suggests that the universal figure of Anne Frank was crucial in re-establishing commonality. Ballif argued in 1955 that 'if we in America cannot present her with the respect and integrity and seriousness she deserves, then I think we should not try to present her at all'. But, Alvin Rosenfeld has suggested, Anne Frank has meant 'different things to different people' and the need for an all-loving, all-forgiving figure far removed from the horrors of the Second World War proved to be irresistible for American culture and society during the 1950s.[26]

It was thus a bizarre image of the Holocaust which was exported by American liberal culture through the play and film of Anne Frank – a Holocaust with only muted references to Jewishness and a Holocaust with, in essence, a happy and even a romantic ending. The Broadway play reached Britain in 1956 and its liberal Americanization was hardly challenged. The producer announced that he would 'emphasize the universality of the theme as he had learnt from experience . . . that any attempt [in Britain] to stress the Jewishness of a character always end[ed] in unreality'. Not surprisingly, the play, with its non-Jewish Jews and ultimate redemption, struck a chord on the Continent and further boosted the already enormous sales that were occurring. In Britain, the play lacked relevance. A refugee critic sensed that the audience 'around me [did not feel] quite that profound disturbance of the soul which I had expected and which performances of the play in Germany seem to have accomplished'. He added 'But then, this story has a very special significance for all decent Germans.' In the Britain of the 1950s, the play had little to say to most adults about either contemporary society or memory of the war.[27]

Whereas it was the play that really stimulated demand for the book in Germany, a very different development took place in Britain. In the latter country, large-scale sales of the book occurred earlier, from 1954. In that year it was published in a cheap pocket, paperback edition by Pan Books. Pan took some persuading to take *The Diary* – and following its earlier hesitant publication history, many similar companies rejected the opportunity in 1953. Pan, again with Jewish connections, were still not utterly convinced of its commercial possibilities but were proved to be pessimistic. By 1959 they were producing the tenth printing of *The Diary*.[28]

It was undoubtedly the cheap version that enabled its increased sales in Britain, yet this was not a factor in the United States. Rather than reflecting the relative prosperity of the latter, it was in fact the greater accessibility to children and adolescents made possible by the paperback that changed its success. For the younger generation, who were ambivalent to the precious and untouchable memory of the war presented by their parents, *The Diary* offered a new perspective and one which they could identify with through the adolescent struggles of a young girl – in spite of her being imprisoned in an Amsterdam attic. A problem still remained – how to deal with the ending. The late Jill Tweedie, perhaps the leading female liberal journalist in post-war Britain, related the trauma of reading the diary in the mid-1950s. She found that after just three pages 'I was Ann[e].' She could assimilate the contents of *The Diary* and identify with its author, but not with its epilogue, which related in stark terms the fate of the inhabitants of the annexe: 'No-one and nothing prepared me for the shock of the end, I couldn't take it in, it broke all the rules.' Her surprise seems all the more remarkable in that Tweedie also related how her 'most vivid childhood memory, apart from the bomb that blew in our house, is of being taken to see [aged nine] the filmed horrors of Belsen. Every detail is with me still, the half-dead with their somnambulist eyes, the dead looking more ancient than the corpses of ancient Egyptians.'[29]

But these dead were not connected by the British to real people, Jews with such pasts as Anne Frank. There was no place for them to operate in other than the context of sheer horror. As such they were put to the back of the mind, a secret nightmare of growing up in post-war Britain, never explained or contextualized. As the critic Milton Shulman put it, reviewing the Anne Frank play in London during 1956: 'It takes such an effort of memory to recall the horrors of Belsen and Buchenwald. Time has inured us to the statistics of mass murder.' *The Diary of Anne Frank,* however, especially in its dramatic and filmic versions, could still avoid those horrors. Even for those wishing to forgive and forget, *The Diary* was still an acceptable text.[30]

The publication of Lord Russell of Liverpool's immensely successful *Scourge of the Swastika* in 1954 – it sold 400,000 copies in 1956 alone – raised questions of whether it was, in the words of the journal of the Council of Christians and Jews, 'desirable that interest in the concentration camps should be kept alive'. The Council (ironically in this context, brought into existence in 1942 out of British Christian outrage at the destruction of European Jews) believed generally that it was not. They felt that there was a 'certain danger in prolonging the emotional climate which [interest in Nazi atrocities] inevitably produce', especially hatred of the Germans. The Christian duty to forgive was more important than the Jewish duty to remember. Such strategies continued well beyond the 1950s and led to an almost total British Christian refusal to confront the Holocaust.[31] Nevertheless, *The Diary* was immune from such criticism, because Anne's writings stood on their own merits and had 'something important to say about life and its problems quite apart from the special conditions which caused them to be written'. Yet again the interpretation of a universalism within *The Diary* acted as a justification for its publication. Likewise in 1959 the film was welcomed by *The Times* by its major critic, even though the dilemma of to remember or not to remember the horrors of the Second World War was extremely difficult to solve. 'On balance', he concluded, 'it would seem that such a document as *The Diary of Anne Frank* should receive the widest publicity.' It should do so because 'the film is by [no] means a catalogue of horrors. Belsen remains throughout only a name.'[32]

The reviewer for the *Jewish Chronicle*, the MP Maurice Edelman, suggested that in the film 'Anne and her story are together a metaphor of the experiences endured by all of Hitler's victims'. From a Jewish perspective, this may have been true, though there were some such as Bruno Bettelheim who thought her image of passivity was dangerous and others who struggled to get an alternative model, that of the militant Jew, whether as ghetto fighter or forest partisan, better known. Although *The Diary of Anne Frank* had some success in Israel, it was the resisting Jew above all others who was commemorated there. Yet outside the Jewish minority in Europe, the United States and Israel, it is doubtful whether Anne Frank stood as any metaphor whatsoever for the Jewish experience, so watered down and sanitized had her writings become. The Holocaust, in both name and concept, still had not reached popular consciousness in liberal culture by the end of the 1950s. It is significant that an East German film, *A Diary for Anne*, which told the story of her deportation to Belsen, was rejected by the British Board of Film Censors in the same year as the Hollywood film was on general release. The British, Americans and others wanted their Anne with a happy ending. Thus an abridged school version of the diary published by Hutchinson in 1960 even omitted the epilogue.[33]

In conclusion, it is revealing that *The Diary of Anne Frank* is mainly referred to today in the context of Holocaust studies or the Second World War as a whole. Although general cultural histories of the post-war period give the impact of her writings no attention – in the British case writers as diverse as Alan Sinfield and Arthur Marwick have failed to mark the importance of Anne Frank – *The Diary* remains the most popular non-fiction work published since 1945. This is a serious absence in the literature because reading *The Diary of Anne Frank* was a crucial part of childhood and adolescence after the popularization of the book in the 1950s.[34]

A commentator remarked at the time of the first showing of the film in 1959 that it was a 'faithful presentation of a story so well known that it already seems like one of the great myths of a folksong to millions of people throughout Europe'. George Stevens, the producer, was known as 'a stickler for accuracy'. In fact this consisted in persuading Shelley Winters, who played Anne Frank's mother, to gain twenty pounds so that she could lose it gradually during filming. Steven's reticence to show more is even more curious in the context of his presence, with film crew, at the liberation of Dachau. Even *The Times* critic, who was worried about the dangers of representing Nazi atrocities, was forced to admit that it seemed that the attic inhabitants in the end seemed to have been subject only 'to an orthodox imprisonment of a few months'. Likewise Maurice Edelman pondered that 'The celebration of Chanukah [in the film] might almost have been translated from a peace-time London suburb.' But here was the appeal of the film, particularly to an American market. It was a Holocaust without tears, without bloodshed, without Belsen, let alone Auschwitz and the mass production of death.[35]

The Diary of Anne Frank is a complex text, far more so than its popularizers have realized. Anne Frank herself has often been represented as an attractive but far less interesting character than was the case. As a result there has been an absence of references to her moments of anger and despair and Anne Frank's increasing ambivalence towards the outside world. When *The Diary of Anne Frank* was popularized in the 1950s, attempts were made to universalize her writings. In the case of Hollywood–Broadway productions, she was every person. With Meyer Levin, she was every Jewish victim. In the process, the complexity, richness and development of her personality was lost. Anne Frank's very last entry in her diary (1 August 1944) reflected on what she described as her 'dual personality', but this more challenging, less clichéd figure has been far harder to assimilate than one who possessed a seemingly never-ending optimism and hope for mankind.[36]

The image of Anne Frank as perpetually cheerful was utterly unrealistic, but it has become almost totally accepted in many varied post-war societies. Few, therefore, could face up to the miserable reality of the last six months of her life. On the surface, the British novelist Storm Jameson, who wrote the preface for the first English version of *The Diary*, appears to have fallen into the trap of Anne as the eternal messenger of good news: Jameson prayed that Anne had gone to her death with 'a profound smile . . . of happiness and faith'. This was certainly the message that readers wanted to take away with them in the 1950s – if they wanted to face her death at all. But Jameson, who had immersed herself in the fate of the exiled and displaced as British chair of PEN in the late 1930s and during the Second World War, and who toured the ruins of Europe, including its death camps, immediately afterwards, was unwilling to let off so easily the concept of reason, the cornerstone of liberalism. Jameson confronted her readers with the horrifying reality of the twentieth century:

> Let us press just for a moment on the feeling – of stupefaction – that must start in us when we think that, in our lifetime, side by side with the amazing achievements of scientists and inventors, there existed these vast slaughter-houses for human beings, and that, to a number of her fellow beings, to send Anne Frank to one of them seemed a natural thing to do . . .. Human beings made Belsen.

This was not the message that the world wanted to hear in the 1950s; it was not one that could be accommodated within the liberal imagination.[37]

And how much progress have we made since the creation of this cultural legend? With the ending of Stalinism in Eastern Europe and the growth of pluralism in the West (in conjunction with the efforts of survivors and others, most recently Steven Spielberg), we can no longer have a Holocaust without the Jews. It is thus important that one of the latest British editions of *The Diary of Anne Frank* contains a preface by Auschwitz survivor Hugo Gryn. The very idea of using Holocaust survivors in such a way when *The Diary* first appeared would have been unthinkable, but now the world has come, belatedly, to respect the words and thoughts of individuals such as Primo Levi, Elie Wiesel, Hugo Gryn and others. But can we accept that the Holocaust is, as Claude Lanzmann suggests in his critique of Spielberg's *Schindler's List*, a story ultimately with 'no happy ending': that is, one about the destruction and not the saving of the Jews?[38] Some progress has been made – in the specific case of Anne Frank there is, for example, the remarkable documentary produced by Jon Blair made for the fiftieth anniversary of her death, which devoted half of its two hours to the story beyond the secret annexe.[39] The success of Spielberg's film suggests, however, that we are not yet, or may never be, ready for the message of a Storm Jameson or a Claude Lanzmann which represents the Holocaust focusing ultimately on murder and not survival and on mankind's capacity for evil, and not on the actions of a righteous minority. Too much of the liberal ideology is at stake. It will thus be appropriate to end with the comments of a schoolteacher in Dorset on the south coast of England and her fourteen-year-old students after reading *The Diary* in the 1990s:

'So you had a feeling of "let down" at the end did you?'

Teenager 1: 'Yes'.

Teenager 2: 'I reckon they should change the ending!' [laughter].

But, of course, to suit the post-war needs of the liberal imagination, in Broadway and Hollywood, as well as the classrooms of Britain, the theatres of Germany and many other places beyond, they already had.[40]

Notes

1. Society for the Dissemination of Survival Information Among Truth-Starved Gentiles [sic], *For Gentiles Only!*, 1993; for the campaign against *The Diary* in general see Barnouw (1989).
2. Rosenfeld (1991), pp. 243, 245. Rosenfeld's important article remains the fullest account of the impact of *The Diary* in the post-war world, although he concentrates his coverage on the United States and Germany.

3. Information from *Diary: The Journal of the Anne Frank Educational Trust*, 1994; *The Guardian*, 7 January 1993 on library borrowing; *The Times*, 3 June 1959. For *The Diary*'s continuing appeal see *Dear Anne Frank: A Selection of Letters to Anne Frank Written by Children Today*, 1995, Harmondsworth: Penguin. The full letter collection is deposited at the University of Southampton archive (SUA).

4. For its Dutch history see Van Der Stroom (1989); Rosenfeld (1991), p. 246.

5. Hondius (1994); Cohen (1988), p. 1 and more generally Boas (1989), pp. 309–21.

6. For its early impact in France see Janet Flanner, 'Letter from Paris', *New Yorker*, 11 November 1950; and for Germany see Rosenfeld (1991), p. 239; Levin (1950a) and more generally Graver (1995), pp. 1–2, 14–15.

7. On the German changes see Van Der Stroom (1989), pp. 64, 71–3 and Rosenfeld (1991), pp. 267–8; *The Diary of Anne Frank* (1995), Basingstoke: Macmillan Children's Books, p. 35; Van Der Stroom (1989), pp. 73–4 comments that in contrast to the Dutch, French and German editions 'The English edition . . . had a more complicated history.' See also Levin, 'The restricted market', pp. 8–9 and Graver, (1995), pp. 17–19.

8. On Doubleday, see Graver (1995), pp. 21–4; Cesarani (1994), pp. 198–9 on the origins of Vallentine Mitchell; Fentress and Wickham (1992), pp. 127–37.

9. See more generally, Kushner (1994), ch. 7; *Wiener Library Bulletin*, 1949 onwards; Dafni (1990), p. 3. On Israel, the Holocaust and the survivors see Segev (1993) and Zerubavel (1994).

10. Kushner (1994), pp. 207–25. See, for example, *Daily Mail* (1945), *Lest We Forget*, London: Daily Mail.

11. Hurd (1984); Poliakov (1951); Reitlinger (1953); Levin (1950a), pp. 8–9.

12. Vallentine Mitchell published important works relating to the Holocaust in the 1950s and 1960s by Gerald Reitlinger, Leslie Hardman, Leni Yahil and others; Kessler to Frank, 17 June 1953 in *Jewish Chronicle* papers, 5/25, SUA.

13. Minutes of Vallentine Mitchell, 3 September 1952, in *Jewish Chronicle* papers, 5/11, SUA. Otto Frank wrote to Vallentine Mitchell on 9 May 1953 that he was 'not the only one who regards it as a disgrace that this book is not available on the English market', in *Jewish Chronicle* papers, 5/25, SUA.

14. Kessler to Frank, 17 June 1953, in *Jewish Chronicle* papers, 5/25, SUA. Sales figures from 1995 Macmillan Children's Books edition.

15. William Frankel to David Kessler, 16 August 1956, in *Jewish Chronicle* papers, 5/21, SUA; Vallentine Mitchell minutes, 21 May 1952 for Maxwell's role and 10 September 1952 for general sales, in *Jewish Chronicle* papers, 5/11, SUA. Maxwell's involvement queries his alleged indifference to the Holocaust in the post-war years suggested by Boyer (1991), p. 401.

16. See, for example, *The Spectator*, 30 May 1952. Kessler wrote to George Kamm within Vallentine Mitchell, 17 September 1953 that 'It was a rather strange feature of this book that although the reviews were excellent the demand was not particularly strong and, in fact, we sold far fewer copies than were sold in other countries', in *Jewish Chronicle* papers, 5/25, SUA; Graver (1995), p. 24 for Doubleday; Kushner (1995); survivor quoted in *AJR Information*, June 1958.

17. Bernard Kops in Paul Morrison's *A Sense of Belonging*, Channel 4, 1991; for an alternative analysis of post-war British Jewish writers see Sicher (1985), chs 3–6.

18. Kessler to Dr Emmanuel Miller, 25 February 1952 and Kessler to George Kamm, 17 September 1953, in *Jewish Chronicle* papers, 5/25, SUA.

19. Doneson (1987a); Rosenfeld (1991), pp. 266–78. For British sales figures see the minutes through the 1950s of Vallentine Mitchell in *Jewish Chronicle* papers, 5/11, SUA. The British Pan paperback edition went into its eleventh printing by 1960.

20. Gordon (1992); Buruma (1994); for Japanese sales and approaches to *The Diary* see letter of Otto Frank to Vallentine Mitchell, 9 May 1953 which includes publicity, reactions and sales details in Japan, in *Jewish Chronicle* papers, 5/25, SUA. All the victims portrayed at the 'Peace Museum' are children or women; Weiner (1995). See *Jewish Chronicle,* 2 June 1995, for Japanese sales up to 1955, and *The Independent*, 25 May 1995, for Araki's film.

21. Sales figures quoted in letter from Otto Frank to Vallentine Mitchell, in *Jewish Chronicle* papers, 5/25, SUA; Doneson (1987b), pp. 61, 66, 73. See also Graver (1995), ch. 2 for its American universalization.

22. Levin (1950b), for the impact of the liberations on his subsequent life; Levin (1952); Graver (1995), *passim* on the relationship between Levin and Otto Frank.

23. For the impact of Levin's play see Graver (1995), ch. 4; *The Diary of Anne Frank* (Macmillan Children's Books 1995), p. 34. See Levin (1973), for his version of the conflict; Goodrich and Hackett (1958).

24. Goodrich and Hackett (1958), p. 92; *The Diary of Anne Frank* (Macmillan Children's Books 1995), p. 229.

25. Algene Ballif (1955), p. 467. Her review also commented (p. 464)

that Miep in the play spoke 'in the pedestrian tones of a sensible young American housewife'.

26. Doneson (1987b), ch. 2 and see also Graver (1995), pp. 233–5 on the Cold War context; Ballif (1995), pp. 466–7; Rosenfeld (1991), p. 277.

27. *AJR Information,* November 1956 and January 1957. For British reviews of the play see Charles Landstone papers, A311 (2), Central Zionist Archives, Jerusalem.

28. For Pan's involvement see Kessler to George Kamm, 17 September 1953 in Jewish Chronicle papers, 5/25, SUA; *The Diary of Anne Frank* (1954 Pan edition), London: Pan. Pan used a drawing of Anne Frank on their cover with the text 'Astonishing, intimate, yet gay record of her two years' life in a secret hiding-place in Amsterdam before betrayal to the Gestapo – a human document of extraordinary quality'. Its tenth edition in 1960 used the film version to give it an added stimulus and had a slightly more restrained if still inaccurate text: 'The intimate record of a young girl's thoughts written during two years in hiding from the Gestapo – to whom she was at last betrayed.'

29. On youth rebellion in British society at this time see Hamblett and Deverson (1964); Osbergy (1992); Tweedie (1990).

30. Shulman in the *Evening Standard*, 30 November 1956.

31. Lord Russell of Liverpool (1954); *Common Ground* (September– October 1954), 8 (5), pp. 27–8; Braybrooke (1991), chs 3 and 10.

32. *Common Ground* (November–December 1954), 8 (5), n.p.; *The Times*, 3 June 1959.

33. *Jewish Chronicle*, 5 June 1959. See also Alexander Baron's review of the book in *Jewish Chronicle*, 2 May 1952; Bettelheim (1962); see Zerubavel (1994), pp. 74–7 and Graver (1995), pp. 132 and ch. 4 for Israel; *The Times*, 19 September 1959 for 'A Diary for Anne'. Rosenfeld (1991), p. 259 refers to Ernst Schnabel's *Anne Frank: Spur eines Kindes* (1958), 'a book that traced the story of Anne Frank beyond the point of her last diary entry to her death in Bergen-Belsen'; *The Diary of Anne Frank* (slightly abridged edition, London: Hutchinson, 1960).

34. Sinfield (1989) and Marwick (1991). This is also the case with Rousso (1991), which ignores the impact of *The Diary*, reflecting a broader trend amongst cultural studies scholars, who perhaps reject the importance of what is perceived to be a text of minor literary importance.

35. *Jewish Chronicle,* 5 June 1959; *The Times*, 3 June 1958 for Stevens and Winters; for the images taken by Stevens see Hastings (1985), ch. 7. Stevens's colour film of the Dachau liberation was rediscovered and shown in 1994; *The Times*, 3 June 1959.

36. *The Diary of Anne Frank* (Macmillan Children's Books), pp. 230–1.
37. Storm Jameson, preface in *The Diary of Anne Frank* (1952 Vallentine Mitchell edition), pp. 9–11; Jameson (1969), pp. 323, 328, 344; Jameson (1970), p. 96 and part 2, and esp. p. 257 on Anne Frank.
38. *The Diary of Anne Frank* (Macmillan Children's Books), pp. vii–xi and Kushner (1995), pp. 3–11 on the role of survivors in the commemoration of Auschwitz in January 1995; Lanzmann (1994), and more generally Cheyette (1994) and Manchel (1995).
39. Blair's award-winning documentary was shown on BBC2, 6 June 1995 and repeated, 26 December 1995. See also van der Rol and Verhoeven (1993).
40. Cory (1993).

Bibliography

Archive Sources

Jewish Chronicle papers, 5/11, 5/21, 5/25, Southampton University Archive
Charles Landstone papers, A311 (2), Central Zionist Archives, Jerusalem.

Printed Sources

Newspapers and Journals
AJR Information, November 1956; January 1957; June 1958.
Common Ground (September–October 1954), 8 (5), pp. 27–8; (November–December 1954), 8 (5), n.p.
Diary: The Journal of the Anne Frank Educational Trust, 1994.
Evening Standard, 30 November 1956.
The Guardian, 17 December 1990; 7 January 1993.
The Independent, 25 May 1995.
Jewish Chronicle, 2 May 1952; 5 June 1959; 2 June 1995
New Yorker, 11 November 1950.
The New York Times Book Review, 15 June 1952.
The Spectator, 30 May 1952.
The Times, 3 June 1958; 3 June 1959.
Wiener Library Bulletin, 1949 onwards.

Books and Articles
Ballif, Algene (1955), 'Anne Frank on Broadway', *Commentary*, November, vol. 20, no. 5.
Barnouw, David (1989), 'Attacks on the authenticity of the Diary', in Netherlands State Institute for War Documentation, *The Diary of Anne*

Frank: The Critical Edition, New York and London: Viking, pp. 84–101.

Bettelheim, Bruno (1962), 'Freedom from ghetto thinking', *Midstream*, 8 (2), Spring, pp. 16, 24–5.

Boas, Henriette (1989), 'Commemorating the Holocaust in Holland: positive and negative aspects', in Netherlands State Institute, *The Diary of Anne Frank.*

Boyer, Tom (1991), *Maxwell: The Outsider*, 2nd edn, London: Mandarin.

Braybrooke, Marcus (1991), *Children of One God: A History of the Council of Christians and Jews*, London: Vallentine Mitchell.

Buruma, Ian (1994), *Wages of Guilt: Memories of War in Germany and Japan,* London: Jonathan Cape.

Cesarani, David (1994), *The Jewish Chronicle and Anglo-Jewry, 1841–1991*, Cambridge: Cambridge University Press.

Cheyette, Bryan (1994), 'The Holocaust in the picture-house: *Schindler's List'*, *Times Literary Supplement*, 18 February.

Cohen, Elie (1988), *Human Behaviour in the Concentration Camps*, New York: Greenwood Press.

Cory, Doreen (1993), '"Real World or "Secondary World"? A study of students' responses to "The Diary of Anne Frank"', University of Southampton unpublished MA dissertation, section C7.

Dafni, Reuven (1990), *Yad Vashem: The Holocaust Martyrs' and Heroes' Remembrance Authority, Jerusalem,* Jerusalem: Yad Vashem.

Dear Anne Frank: A Selection of Letters to Anne Frank Written by Children Today (1995), Harmondsworth: Penguin.

The Diary of Anne Frank (1954), London: Pan.

Doneson, Judith (1987a), 'The American history of Anne Frank's *Diary*', *Holocaust and Genocide Studies*, 2 (1), pp. 149–60.

Doneson, Judith (1987b), *The Holocaust in American Film*, Philadelphia: Jewish Publication Society.

Fentress, James and Wickham, Chris (1992), *Social Memory,* Oxford: Blackwell.

Goodrich, Frances and Hackett, Albert (1958), *The Diary of Anne Frank*, London: French.

Gordon, Andrew (ed.) (1992), *Postwar Japan as History*, Berkeley and Los Angeles: University of California Press.

Graver, Lawrence (1995), *An Obsession with Anne Frank: Meyer Levin and the Diary*, Berkeley, Los Angeles and London: California University Press.

Hamblett, Charles and Deverson, Jane (1964), *Generation X*, London: Heinemann.

Hastings, Max (1985), *Victory in Europe: From D-Day to V-E Day,* London: Artus.

Hondius, Dienke (1994), 'A cold reception: Holocaust survivors in the Netherlands and their return', *Patterns of Prejudice*, 28 (1), pp. 47–65.

Hurd, Geoff (ed.) (1984), *National Fictions: World War Two in British Films and Television*, London: British Film Institute.

Jameson, Storm (1952), Preface in *The Diary of Anne Frank*, London: Vallentine Mitchell, pp. 9–11.

Jameson, Storm (1969), *Journey from the North*, vol. 1, London: Collins.

Jameson Storm (1970), *Journey from the North*, vol. 2, London: Collins.

Kushner, Tony (1994), *The Holocaust and the Liberal Imagination: A Social and Cultural History*, Oxford: Blackwell.

Kushner, Tony (1995), '"Wrong War Mate": fifty years after the Holocaust and the Second World War', *Patterns of Prejudice*, vol. 29, nos 2–3, pp. 3–13.

Lanzmann, Claude (1994), 'Twisted truth of *Schindler's List*', *Evening Standard*, 10 February.

Levin, Meyer (1950a), 'The Restricted Market', *Congress Weekly*, vol. 17, no. 29, pp. 8–9.

Levin, Meyer (1950b), *In Search: An Autobiography*, New York: Simon & Schuster.

Levin, Meyer (1952), 'The child behind the secret door', *The New York Times Book Review*, 15 June.

Levin, Meyer (1973), *The Obsession,* New York: Simon & Schuster.

Daily Mail (1945), *Lest We Forget*, London: Daily Mail.

Manchel, Frank (1995), 'A reel witness: Steven Spielberg's representation of the Holocaust in *Schindler's List*', *Journal of Modern History*, vol. 67, no. 1, pp. 83–100.

Marwick, Arthur (1991), *Culture in Britain since 1945*, Oxford: Blackwell.

Michman, Jozeph (ed.) (1989), *Dutch Jewish History vol. II,* Assen and Maastricht: Van Gorum.

Osbergy, Bill (1992), '"Well, it's Saturday night an' I just got paid": youth, consumerism and hegomony in post-war Britain', *Contemporary Record*, vol. 6, no. 2, pp. 287–305.

Poliakov, Leon (1951), *Breviare de la haine,* Paris: Calmann-Levy.

Reitlinger, Gerald (1953), *The Final Solution: The Attempt to Exterminate the Jews of Europe 1939–1945,* London: Vallentine Mitchell.

Rosenfeld, Alvin (1991), 'Popularization and memory: the case of Anne Frank', in Peter Hayes (ed.), *Lessons and Legacies: The Meaning of the Holocaust in a Changing World,* Evanston, Illinois: Northwestern University Press.

Rousso, Henry (1991), *The Vichy Syndrome: History and Memory in France since 1944*, Cambridge, Mass. and London: Harvard University Press.

Lord Russell of Liverpool (1954), *The Scourge of the Swastika,* London: Jonathan Cape.

Segev, Tom (1993), *The Seventh Million: The Israelis & the Holocaust,* New York: Hill and Wang.

Sicher, Ephraim (1985), *Beyond Marginality: Anglo-Jewish Literature after the Holocaust,* Albany: University of New York Press.

Sinfield, Alan (1989), *Literature, Politics and Culture in Postwar Britain,* Oxford: Blackwell.

Society for the Dissemination of Survival Information Among Truth-Starved Gentiles [*sic*], *For Gentiles Only!,* 1993, London: no publisher.

Tweedie, Jill (1990), 'The silent byways of the righteous gentiles', *Guardian,* 17 December.

Van der Rol, Ruud and Verhoeven, Rian (1993), *Anne Frank: Beyond the Diary,* New York: Viking.

Van Der Stroom, Gerald (1989), 'The diaries, *Het Achterhuis,* and the translations', in *The Diary of Anne Frank: The Critical Edition,* pp. 62–72.

Weiner, Michael (1995), 'Out of the very stone: Korean Hibakusha', *Immigrant & Minorities,* vol. 14, no. 1, pp. 1–25.

Zerubavel, Yael (1994), 'The death of memory and the memory of death: Masada and the Holocaust as historical metaphors', *Representations,* vol. 45, pp. 72–100.

2

Lacking in Convictions: British War Crimes Policy and National Memory of the Second World War
David Cesarani

'Official Memory' and 'Popular Memory' of the Second World War

The newspaper furore in March 1994 over the prospect of German military participation in the proposed VE-Day celebrations to take place in London the following year illustrated that the Second World War remains a touchstone of British national identity. After the organizers of the event declared that no serving German soldiers would take part, Britain's largest circulation tabloid boasted on its front page that 'The *Sun* Bans the Hun'. Inside, a montage showed 1940s Wehrmacht troops marching through Whitehall. The paper declared that only its courageous defiance of Mr Major prevented a parade by German troops such as their Nazi forebears had failed to achieve. *The Times* and the *Guardian* devoted editorials to the controversy. Both thought it was time to 'bury the hatchet' and the *Guardian* remarked that 'After fifty years, the Second World War's grip on British society is too strong.' A perceptive article by Martin Woollacott succinctly expressed the reasons for this bizarre eruption: 'Second World War celebrations have a meaning in Britain that they do not have in any other former allied country. The war, for some Britons at least, is a kind of icon of our inner superiority.'[1]

If the images and myths of the war are still central elements in British popular culture, what values do they embody? Kenneth Morgan has proposed that in the post-war era the years 1939–45 offered 'a last fleeting vision of greatness' from which both the left and right in British politics could take inspiration. The war 'supplied images that were satisfying and self-confirming'. It was 'crucial to Britain's usable past'.[2] In both 'official memory' and 'popular memory' the Second World War stands out as 'The People's War' and 'The Good War', untainted and uncomplicated by the lost illusions, ironies and traumas of the Great War.[3] Apart from a few blunders and blemishes, the war is understood almost universally as honourable and noble, fought with right and justice exclusively on the Allied side.[4] Hence the incomprehension, and indignation, in the face of German protests over the erection of a statue in London to honour the memory of Sir Arthur 'Bomber' Harris in the summer of 1993.

As the 'Bomber' Harris incident showed, to this day it is almost unthinkable to hold that the Allies committed unjust acts in the pursuit of victory, or that the eventual success of the Allied armies signified anything other than the supremacy of right over might. In the popular view, post-war Europe, and Britain within it, was then reconstructed by the 'good guys' working with the highest of motives. At home it was the era of 'The People's Peace', the content of which was embodied in the slogan 'Never Again'.[5]

Certainly, by the 1980s some historians had begun to question the romanticized view of the war and triumphalist versions of the Attlee governments of 1945–51.[6] Yet this revisionism took place quite separately from the equally close and critical examination of Britain's role in the denazification and regeneration of post-war Germany.[7] The Australian historian R. J. B. Bosworth has recently claimed that in Britain the consensual interpretation of the war, and the peace, began to collapse as early as 1961, with the publication of A. J. P. Taylor's *Origins of the Second World War*. However, although Bosworth entitles his comparative study of the historiography of the war *Explaining Auschwitz and Hiroshima*, like other critics and iconoclasts he ignores the presence or absence of the Holocaust and Nazi war crimes in British history writing, or parallel debates in politics and the press since 1945.[8]

The peripheral treatment of Jewish concerns can be seen most clearly in the place assigned to the Holocaust and Nazi war crimes in 'national memory' and British historiography after 1945. While the liberation of Bergen-Belsen and the Nuremberg Tribunal bulk large in the nation's memory, they exist mainly as legitimating symbols, the 'fitting capstone', of the Just War.[9] Lucy Dawidowicz famously excoriated British historians from the 1950s to 1970s for their neglect of the 'Final Solution'.[10] Until quite recently, detailed teaching about Nazi crimes against the Jews was rare in British schools and universities. The United Kingdom has no large-scale Holocaust memorial, or a museum of the Holocaust.[11]

The failure to exclude Nazi collaborators and war criminals from this country after 1945, or to prosecute them once their presence was detected, can only be understood completely when it is located in this cultural milieu and the context of national memory. Equally, the recent opposition to demands for legislation to facilitate war crimes trials in the United Kingdom cannot be comprehended only on legal, constitutional or political grounds.

The allegations against persons in Britain and the demands that they be investigated and, possibly, put on trial involved a serious challenge to consensual notions of the 'Good War' and the 'People's Peace'. To assert the presence of unpunished Nazi collaborators in this country made a mockery of British war aims. It contradicted the widespread belief that in 1945–6 right was victorious and the guilty were subjected to retribution. It undermined the cosy vision of the welfare state by injecting into the body politic a foreign and toxic presence. The question of how these men arrived also opened up almost forgotten aspects of post-war immigration.[12]

The war crimes issue is one of a series that has provoked an interrogation of recent British history. Through its lens attention has been drawn to the impact of the Cold War on British administered denazification in Germany and the treatment of Nazi collaborators; the ethics and practice of the 1945–51 Labour governments; post-war immigration and population policy; the Jewish experience in Britain after the war; and the very meaning of the war itself.

The Occlusion of Memory

The occlusion of memory began with the way the war ended. British troops liberated concentration camps in western Germany, but not the killing sites in Eastern Europe. Consequently, from the beginning of the peace these troops and the British public obtained only a partial understanding of the 'Final Solution'. It was common for the press to telescope the concentration camps of the early 1930s into those overrun in April–May 1945, with little awareness of the radical difference between their functions or the gulf between them and the extermination centres in Poland. In some camps, such as Buchenwald, Jews were a small minority of the inmates. In others, where they predominated, Jews were not identified explicitly in radio or press reports, in line with the Ministry of Information's policy of not specifying atrocities against the Jews.[13]

This partiality was reinforced by British war crimes policy and the post-war trials of war criminals. When the British government adopted a policy of seeking retribution for Nazi war criminals, it was ill-informed about the killing operations in the east, or the role of East European collaborators. The Soviet Union declined to join the United Nations War Crimes Commission in 1942 and did not supply information on East European collaborators to the Central Registry of War Criminals and Security Suspects. Consequently, in the aftermath of hostilities, the British occupation authorities in Germany and Austria deployed their resources for detection and prosecution on a narrow and unrepresentative front. Moreover, they actively avoided any responsibility for apprehending and dealing with former citizens of the Soviet Union.[14]

The Belsen Trial and the International Military Tribunal (IMT) at Nuremberg made a considerable impression on British public opinion, but the depth and duration of this impact have been exaggerated. The trials subsumed the attempted genocide against the Jews under the category of war crimes and crimes against humanity. Only Germans were on trial, and little attention was paid to their East European collaborators. Even before the IMT had finished its work, boredom with war crimes trials had set in. By the time of the trial of senior German generals, including von Manstein, in 1948–9, there was actually a popular reaction against 'dragging out' the process of retribution. Winston Churchill caught this mood by subscribing to Manstein's defence fund. A stream of books and pamphlets appeared attacking the Nuremberg Tribunal as a case of 'victors' justice'. Public figures as authoritative as Lord Hankey, a former member of Churchill's war cabinet, argued that the Tribunal's value was nullified by the participation of the Soviet Union.[15]

During the course of 1948 the British government succumbed to pressure to discontinue war crimes trials in the British Zone of Germany. In June 1948, 4,251 suspected war criminals were still in detention in the British Zone. However, only 753 were tried there and 1,001 surrendered for trial in other countries. Over 2,500 were released in the months before the 1 October 1948 deadline, or immediately after it had passed. Since the focus of these proceedings had been on Germans and the aim had been to deal with them in Germany, or to surrender them to the governments of the countries in which they were alleged to have committed war crimes, it was thought that the war crimes issue had now been resolved. As Anthony Glees has noted in an important study of British war crimes policy, 'by 1948 it was genuinely believed that most war criminals had been tried and that none had been able to enter the UK'.[16]

However, a conjunction of war crimes policy and post-war immigration and labour policy had inadvertently achieved exactly the opposite. 'Official' and 'popular' memory would recall the celebrated post-war trials of war criminals, but in fact at the same time a gross injustice was being facilitated. Partly due to the blinkered view of Nazi atrocities and the blurred identity of their perpetrators this blunder was hardly noticed at the time. Since it concerned groups and issues that were marginalized in the course of the 'People's Peace' it was almost wholly ignored subsequently.

In 1946–7, the British government was faced with acute labour shortages and a balance of payments crisis. In order to boost the production of vital fuels, raw materials and manufactured goods it resolved to recruit foreign labour from amongst Displaced Persons (DPs) in the British Zone of Germany. Eligibility for these labour schemes was supposedly restricted to those who were designated as DPs according to the criteria of the United

Nations Relief and Rehabilitation Administration. However, in the British Zone thousands of East Europeans who had fought for the Germans, or served them in various capacities, and were therefore ineligible for DP status, had been classed as Displaced Persons by the British authorities. When they applied for work schemes they were obliged to undergo interviews by Ministry of Labour recruiting teams and a security screening process, but this was woefully inadequate. As a result, men who had served in the Baltic Waffen SS, as well as police and militia units were allowed to enter Britain.[17]

In addition, the Foreign Office used the cover of the European Voluntary Worker scheme to bring to Britain an entire Ukrainian Waffen SS division in 1947. These men had been held in a POW camp in Rimini, where a selective screening had revealed that many had long served the SS, and some were likely to have committed war crimes. Despite this, they were transported to Britain to forestall Russian demands for their forced repatriation. After being held as surrendered enemy personnel for two years they were civilianized, against the wishes of the Home Office, and allowed either to emigrate or to settle in the United Kingdom.[18]

Finally, Nazi collaborators entered Britain in the ranks of the Polish army. During the last two years of the war the Polish Armed Forces (PAF) fighting under British command in North Africa and Italy regularly accepted Poles and other East Europeans captured in German uniform as replacements for their own losses. At the end of the war, the British government accepted a moral and political responsibility for the vast majority of Poles who had fought in British uniform and who declined to return to Soviet-dominated Poland. A Polish Resettlement Corps (PRC) was formed in May 1946 'to facilitate their repatriation to Poland, emigration to other countries, or resettlement in civilian life here'. Just over 114,000 Poles opted to join the scheme. There was little effort at political screening or any attempt to find out whether these men had chequered war histories. Yet events were soon to show that there were chronic weaknesses in the PRC settlement process.[19]

In 1946, the Polish government sought the extradition of Dr Wladyslaw Dering who was accused of conducting medical experiments on prisoners in Auschwitz. Dering had left Poland in 1945, made his way to Italy and become a medical officer in the PAF. It was by this route that he arrived in England in August 1946. Although he was on a UN list of war crimes suspects, he was not detected at any stage of his admission into the army or on his entry into Britain. Once he was located by the Polish authorities, however, his case proved a headache for the British government. In the climate of souring relations between Britain and the USSR it became British policy not to permit extradition to an Eastern Bloc country. After using some 'squalid' stalling tactics to frustrate the Polish government, the British allowed Dering to emigrate overseas. He could have been tried in the United Kingdom, but according to Anthony Glees British war crimes policy 'did not work because there was no will to make it work'.[20]

This lack of will was partly a function of occluded memory. War crimes in the east did not figure largely in official or popular consciousness. The Jews, who were their main victims, were deeply unpopular due to the struggle in Palestine, where the Jewish Zionist military underground was waging a war against the British forces upholding the Mandate.[21] With little knowledge about the perpetrators, or sympathy for the victims, there was no impetus or desire to screen East Europeans more carefully or, if they were suspected of war crimes, to investigate and prosecute them. Although there was some awareness in government and Parliament that Waffen SS men, Nazi collaborators and suspected war criminals had entered the United Kingdom, this information was not acted upon. Indeed, a major screening exercise in the early 1950s appears to have been more concerned with detecting Communists. Over the following years men who would later be exposed as alleged war criminals and Nazi collaborators routinely obtained British naturalization.[22]

The Selectivity of Memory

The insouciance showed towards East Europeans with dubious histories was the reverse side of a blithe absence of interest in the 'Final Solution'. During the 1950s, few books on the Nazi genocide were published in Britain. Those which had the greatest impact, *The Diary of Anne Frank* (1952) and Lord Russell's *Scourge of the Swastika* (1954), gave an incomplete, unrepresentative version of the Holocaust.[23]

The small number of survivors who came to Britain after the war were preoccupied with building new lives for themselves, and found little appetite for recollections of the horrors they had endured. The Eichmann trial momentarily directed public attention to the Nazi attempted genocide, but this was not reflected in any sustained public debate, educational initiatives or cultural projects.[24]

By contrast, nostalgia for the war years found embodiment in a stream of books and films that appeared throughout the 1950s.[25] Paul Brickhill single-handedly generated *The Dambusters* (1951), *The Great Escape* (1951) and *Reach for the Sky* (1954). P. R. Reid published *The Colditz Story* in 1952, E. S. Montagu, *The Man Who Never Was* in 1953. *I was Monty's Double* by M. E. C. James appeared in 1954, and *Carve her Name with Pride* by R. J. Minney in 1956. Desmond Young's sympathetic account of Rommel came out as early as 1950, creating the enduring dyad of Desert Fox and Desert Rat. All of these books were turned into films within a short space of time, most by British studios. Through the cinema they reached an even wider audience and supplied the powerful visual tropes that inform the filming of war to this day.[26]

The years after 1945 also saw a boom in novels of the war such as Eric Williams's *The Wooden Horse* (1949), Nicholas Monsarrat's *The Cruel Sea* (1951), J. Harris's *The Sea Shall not Have Them* (1953). These stories, too, were filmed between 1950 and 1955. Evelyn Waugh's *Men at Arms* (1952) and *Officers and Gentlemen* (1955) were hugely influential without reaching the screen. According to the literary historian Ken Worpole, 'It is likely that in the 1950s the most widely read books in Britain were books that dealt with the experience of male combatants in the Second World War.'[27] The journalist and writer Frank Barrett speaks for more than one generation of post-war children when he remembers that 'The Second World War obsessed us all. We avidly read about war in comics with characters such as Rockfist Rogan and Captain Hurricane. There were endless war programmes on television.'[28]

Over the same period only two novels explicitly and solely about the Jews in Nazi-occupied Europe were published in the United Kingdom, both by foreign writers: John Hersey's *The Wall* (1950) and Ka-Tzetnik's *House of Dolls* (1956). Neither was filmed, although *The Diary of Anne Frank* reached the screen in 1959.[29] As Bernard Bergonzi notes in his survey of British letters in the aftermath of war, 'the English were capable only of an aestheticized or evasive response' to the catastrophic events of the 1940s.[30]

Running parallel to the construction of an insular interpretation of the war in British culture was the institutionalization of a narrowly defined national memory in the form of commemorations and monuments.[31] Armistice Day, Battle of Britain Day, VE-Day were established as foci of national memory. 'Official' and 'popular' memory in the 1950s justly commemorated the sacrifice of British service personnel and civilians, and celebrated the victory of democracy over totalitarianism; but the discrete experience of the Jews went unrecognized. For example, in 1960 the *Wiener Library Bulletin* pointedly noted the contrast between the scale of attention being paid to the twentieth anniversary of the Battle of Britain and the silence over the twenty-fifth anniversary of the Nuremberg Laws, with which it coincided.[32]

Even though consensual notions about the meaning of the war began to break down from the 1960s, this did not entail any greater inquiry into the experiences of previously marginalized groups or the issues that concerned them. Notwithstanding the challenge of 'youth culture' and irreverence towards the generations that had lived through wartime, national memory of the war in the 1960s and 1970s remained highly selective. For this reason, the information that suspected Nazi war criminals might be domiciled in the United Kingdom was met at first with incredulity, while demands that something should be done about their presence even aroused resentment.

National Memory and the War Crimes Debate, 1986–93

Selective memory was to underpin selective justice, making the campaign for British war crimes legislation long and hard. The campaign opened in the summer of 1986 when Greville Janner, a Labour MP, raised with the Home Office the case of Krylo Zvarich, a Ukrainian accused by the Soviet Union of war crimes. Soon afterwards, the Los Angeles Simon Wiesenthal Center gave the British consul general in Los Angeles a list of seventeen suspected war criminals living in Britain. An All-party Parliamentary War Crimes Group was set up in November 1986 to lobby for an inquiry, and then for a change in the law that would make it possible to try persons domiciled in the United Kingdom who were suspected of committing war crimes in areas not under British jurisdiction at a time when they were not British citizens.[33]

Such was the scepticism of the Home Office that an official government inquiry into the alleged presence of war criminals in Britain was not announced until February 1988. The inquiry, conducted by two senior retired law officers, was widely regarded as a device to pigeonhole the matter. However, its report in July 1989 went further than expected in verifying the presence of war criminals, identifying how they had gained access to Britain, and then recommending action against them.[34]

In December 1989, the government gave both Houses of Parliament an opportunity to register their feelings on whether legislation should be introduced to enable the trial of alleged war criminals. The House of Commons voted by a large majority in favour of the principle, but the House of Lords was clearly hostile. A War Crimes Bill was introduced into Parliament in March 1990 and had passed through the Commons by substantial majorities a year later. However, the Lords defeated the bill in June 1990 and again in May 1991, obliging the government to resort to a rarely used constitutional device to force it into law against their Lordships' wishes.[35]

The debates in Parliament, amplified in the press and media, revolved around a set of interconnected constitutional, legal and moral issues.[36] The latter, involving questions of war and memory, will be dealt with here. Opponents of war crimes legislation repeatedly called on the advocates of war crimes trials to forgive and forget. For example, the *Daily Telegraph* described 'Nazi-hunting' as 'a new and frankly distasteful bloodsport . . . There is a futility, a sterility, about continuing a search for vengeance beyond certain limits of time and space.'[37]

Yet in the 1948 parliamentary debate on the suspension of war crimes trials in the British Zone of Germany, Winston Churchill had specifically excepted certain crimes from 'the limits of time and space'. He said, 'There may be some exceptional cases such as the slaughter of the men of the Norfolk Regiment . . . Our policy ought to be, subject to exceptional cases I have mentioned, henceforward to draw a sponge across the crimes and horrors of the past.'[38] What was to be applied to the men of Norfolk was to be denied to the Jews of Nowogrodek.

This selectivity of memory and justice recurred in another form in the debates over the war crimes bill in the House of Lords in 1986–91. A majority of peers was convinced that no one could safely act as an eye-witness to crimes committed in Eastern Europe fifty years previously. But they seemed well able to recall atrocities perpetrated by Jews against British soldiers in Palestine at around the same time.[39]

The memory that was being invoked by the War Crimes Group, which included Jewish and non-Jewish MPs, was implicitly extruded from British national memory. Proponents of war crimes trials were routinely stigmatized as the mouthpiece of a powerful Jewish-American lobby. War crimes legislation, allegedly based on a desire for revenge, was held to be foreign to British legal traditions. In a typical exchange in the House of Commons in February 1987, Ivor Stanbrook, a Conservative MP and leading opponent of war crimes trials in the United Kingdom, denounced the advocates of legislation as 'misguided, blinkered and not sufficiently imbued with a sense of the real spirit and purpose of British justice'.[40] *The Times* declared that 'Britain is a Christian country. Its laws enshrine principles of justice tempered with mercy, not vengeance.'[41] Hence the desire for war crimes legislation was ascribed to a desire for vengeance in accord with a bowdlerized version of Judaism. This was contrasted to the doctrine of mercy propounded by Christianity, a traditionally British preserve.

The memory of the 'Final Solution' and Nazi war crimes was deemed apart from and inferior to British national memory. Ivor Stanbrook maintained that British courts had no business to interfere in 'alleged crimes committed long ago by foreigners in foreign countries'. He accused the Home Secretary of surrendering 'to a lobby whose main motivations are hatred and revenge'.[42] Lady Saltoun of Abernathy asked 'Is it decent and fitting that we should take such a step in order to enable aliens to be revenged on other aliens for something done in a foreign country nearly half a century ago?'[43]

Antagonists also argued that it was wrong to rake over the ashes of history, to open old wounds. Edward Heath, Conservative MP and former prime minister, objected that it was particularly foolish to delve into the past when a new Europe was being born. The ideals of the European Community and Eastern European nations after the revolutionary year 1989 spoke to the future.[44]

Yet events since 1989 have provided ample warning that the 'Rebirth of History' gives good cause for watching over memory. Throughout Eastern Europe pro-Nazi collaborationist regimes of the 1940s are being rehabilitated.[45] Political and military leaders who co-operated in the Final Solution are being elevated to the pantheon of national heroes: Father Tiszo in Slovakia, Admiral Horthy in Hungary and General Ion Antonescu in Romania. In Latvia, former members of the Latvian SS are helping to instruct young men in the new Latvian army, while the veterans of the Ukrainian Waffen SS Division are fêted in Lvov.[46]

Whose War, Whose Memory?

Unlike these countries, Britain was spared occupation during the Second World War and the consequent rupture of memory or phenomena such as the 'Vichy syndrome'.[47] Yet Britain was not wholly immune to the experience which has scarred European societies. In a series of articles in the *Guardian* on the occupation of the Channel Islands, Madeleine Bunting showed that collaboration, betrayal and the deportation of Jews had, in fact, all occurred on British soil.[48] British national memory needs to be recalibrated to reflect our greater knowledge about the history of the war and its aftermath. Equally, it should pay heed to the diversity of memory of its multi-stranded population, for whom these neglected tributaries of British history are important channels of ethnic consciousness.

Ironically, the opponents of war crimes trials seized on revisionist interpretations of British actions in the war in order to frustrate passage of the War Crimes Bill. Several hostile MPs argued that to be consistent the bill ought to cover the 'crimes' allegedly committed through the bombing of Dresden in February 1945 and the British repatriation of Cossacks during the summer of 1945. On 19 March 1990, for example, in the course of the bill's second reading, Ivor Stanbrook asserted that 'The criminals were not restricted to the so-called Nazis but existed on all sides, including the Allied side.'[49] This attempt to relativize the Holocaust and blur the specificity of Nazi war crimes is not confined to the hurly-burly of politics.

Certain university-based historians have demonstrated an equal predilection to render dissonant or minority memory peripheral to 'national memory'. In his attack on Churchill's wartime leadership in *Churchill. The End of Glory* (1993), John Charmley maintains that the fate of the Jews was irrelevant to the British government's decision to go to war in 1939 or to stay in it in 1940–1. Charmley berates Churchill for demonizing Hitler and being obsessed with achieving his downfall. If anything, Stalin was worse and Britain's participation in the war was a disaster for the nation. Charmley said in an interview in *The Times* on 8 January 1993:

People like Martin Gilbert say 'what about the Jews?' Well, why just the Jews? What about the liberals and trades unionists who were in the concentration camps? When critics say I'm using hindsight, nobody in 1939 was saying we should go to war for the Jews. The real Holocaust only really got under way in 1943–44 when the Germans were losing. And while we're on the moral high ground, what about the people in Stalin's concentration camps. Were they not worth dying for?[50]

Charmley thus imports into British historiography the relativization of the Holocaust which was such a feature of the *Historikerstreit* in Germany in 1986–8. More particularly, his inability to understand why Britain went to war, and why Churchill was prepared to work with the Soviet Union to destroy Nazism, may not be unconnected with his inability to sympathize with Churchill's acute understanding of, and horror towards, the Nazi assault on the Jews.[51]

Memory of the 'Good War' may have been increasingly qualified by what we have learned in recent years about wartime disasters, errors of judgement, unsavoury alliances and the pettiness of life on the Home Front. But the heroism and the achievement of British service personnel and those who supported them is not diminished by greater public knowledge about the loss of Singapore, Britain's desertion of the Polish government-in-exile, the forced repatriation of Cossacks and White Russians, the imposition of racial segregation on Britain by the British government to interdict liaisons with Black GIs or the deportation of West Indians who had served the war effort.

Nor is the stature of the people who fought and endured the 'People's War' adversely affected by proof that at its end Nazi collaborators and war criminals escaped justice and found refuge in this country. It is, however, a stain on their courage and sacrifice that suspected war criminals who have been detected in the United Kingdom are to all appearances being allowed to evade prosecution once again. Although the War Crimes Act was passed in May 1991, not one suspect has yet been brought to trial despite several well-publicized cases, such as that of Antanas Gecas, in which strong *prima facie* evidence exists of war criminality.[52]

It is sad and ironic that, while Britain celebrates its part in the freeing of Europe from Nazi tyranny, Nazi collaborators live freely in British cities. Perhaps this festering sore explains why so little attention has been accorded to the dramatic contribution which D-Day made to the saving of Jewish lives. Although over 437,000 Hungarian Jews had been deported to Auschwitz between May and June 1944, around 120,000 still remained in Budapest and its environs. The Hungarian ruler, Admiral Horthy, ever sensitive to the tide of the war, was increasingly uneasy about his country's role in this phase of the genocide. He watched the progress of the Normandy landings with care, and by late June had decided that the Allied bridgehead would never be dislodged and that Germany's military fate was sealed. Hence, it was time to put some distance between Hungary and Nazi policy towards the Jews. The deportations were halted.[53] Yet not one of the mass of articles, radio or TV programmes on D-Day made this connection.

This omission further illustrates the narrowness of national memory. The fate of the Jews and the Allied war effort continues to run on separate lines, never intersecting until the liberation. The persistent failure to meld Auschwitz, and Nazi crimes in the East, into the history of the 'People's War' is reflected in and reinforced by popular accounts of the war.[54] The result is an inability to comprehend the presence of alleged Nazi war criminals in Britain today. Token action on this score, in turn, helps to preserve the selectivity of national memory.[55]

Notes

1. See *Sun, Daily Star*, 24 March 1994; editorials in *Daily Mail, The Times, Guardian*, 24 March 1994; Martin Woollacott in *Guardian* Section 2, 24 March 1994, p. 2.
2. Morgan (1994), p. 4.
3. For the concepts of 'official memory' and 'popular memory' see the introduction to Bodnar (1992).
4. Calder (1969), for long the definitive account of the war on the Home Front and the triumph of social justice in Britain and Europe.
5. Both epigrams, it is significant to note, are the titles of two of the best-selling histories of post-war Britain: Morgan (1994) and Hennesy (1992). The divergence of memory is illustrated nowhere better than in the mutually exclusive meanings of 'Never Again'. To the British it connotes the avoidance of mass unemployment and the social injustice of the 1930s. To Jews, it means simply no repetition of the Nazi Holocaust.
6. Morgan (1994), pp. 4–7.
7. Bower (1981).
8. Bosworth (1993), pp. 26–9, 51–2.
9. Bridgman (1990), pp. 110–12; Pronay (1988), pp. 41–5.
10. Dawidowicz (1981), pp. 31–4.
11. Fox (1989). Since this paper was given, the Imperial War Museum has announced the construction of a major new exhibition devoted to the Holocaust and has won a grant of £12.6 million from the Heritage Lottery Fund to support the project.

12. It is remarkable that in contrast to the huge amount written by sociologists, and, to a lesser extent, by historians, on immigration to the United Kingdom from the Commonwealth and Pakistan, an authoritative and fully sourced study of East European immigration to Britain did not appear until 1992: Kay and Miles (1992).
13. Bridgman (1990), pp. 34, 81–3, 103–4; Cesarani (1996), pp. 131–51; Kushner (1994), pp. 250–1; Kushner (1991). See also McLaine (1979), pp. 166–8, 169–70.
14. Glees (1992); Taylor (1993).
15. Cesarani (1992), pp. 169–74; Kushner (1991), p. 358.
16. Glees (1992), pp. 182–7.
17. Cesarani (1992), chs 3–5; Kay and Miles (1992), pp. 52–9.
18. Cesarani (1992), ch. 6.
19. Cesarani (1994).
20. Glees (1992), pp. 189–97.
21. Kushner (1993), pp. 149–68.
22. Cesarani (1992), pp. 91–101, 119–21. One leading example is the case of Antanas Gecas. Once a platoon commander in the 3rd Company, 12th Lithuanian Police Battalion, Gecas came to Britain in the PAF and settled in Scotland in 1946. Around 1982 he was exposed by the Soviet authorities and the American Office of Special Investigations. In 1986 his name was leaked to the British press and he was the focus of a Scottish Television documentary on war criminals in Britain. Gecas fought back by launching a series of libel actions. In the most important he protested that Scottish Television had defamed him by calling him a war criminal. However, on 17 July 1992, Lord Milligan gave his ruling in the case of Anthony Gecas v. Scottish Television. Milligan was 'clearly satisfied' that Gecas had 'participated in many operations involving the killing of innocent Soviet citizens including Jews in particular' in Belarus during the autumn of 1941. Milligan concluded that as a platoon commander in the 12th Lithuanian Police Battalion it 'inevitably follows' that Gecas was guilty of war crimes. No less than twelve other members who served the Nazis in this unit are alive and living in England. See Zuroff (1988); Opinion of Lord Milligan *in causa* Anthony Gecas *Pursuer* against Scottish Television PLC *Defenders*, 17 July 1992; *Independent*, 6 July 1992.
23. Cesarani (1992), pp. 178–9. On *The Diary of Anne Frank* see chapter 1 in this volume.
24. Cesarani (1996); Kushner (1991), p. 359.
25. On the post-war boom in books about the war, see Hewison (1981), pp. 11–12.
26. See Enser (1990), pp. 85–7. This useful bibliography provides a

valuable barometer of publishing about the war after 1945. See also
the valuable discussion in Worpole (1983), pp. 49–73.

27. Worpole (1983), p. 50.
28. *Independent*, 29 March 1994.
29. Paris (1990).
30. Bergonzi (1993), pp. 94–6 and 206.
31. Mosse (1990).
32. Editorial, *Wiener Library Bulletin*, 1960, 14 (3), p. 41.
33. For a detailed version of the following account see Cesarani (1992), chs 9 and 10.
34. Hetherington and Chalmers (1989).
35. Cesarani (1992), ch. 9.
36. For a detailed review of the issues see ibid., pp. 247–67.
37. Ibid., p. 204.
38. Glees (1992), p. 187.
39. Cesarani (1992), p. 237.
40. Ibid., pp. 201, 210.
41. Ibid., p. 204.
42. Ibid., p. 212.
43. Ibid., p. 262.
44. Ibid., p. 255.
45. Glenny (1990); Hockenos (1993).
46. Evidence on this is available for many different countries. On Croatia, see *Guardian*, 18 October 1993, 18 November 1993; on Hungary, see *Guardian*, 18 September 1993; on Romania, see *Guardian*, 25 February 1994; in general, Ian Traynor, *Guardian*, 16 September 1993. On Latvia, see *Jerusalem Post*, 24 November 1992 and *Guardian*, 12 February 1993; on Estonia, see *Sunday Times*, 19 July 1992. On the Baltic States in general, see Michael Ignatieff, 'In the New Republics', *New York Review of Books*, 21 November 1991. On Ukraine, see *Guardian*, 16 August 1993.
47. Rousso (1991).
48. Articles by Madeleine Bunting on collaboration in the Channel Islands: see *Guardian*, 4 May 1992, and editorial comment; 6 January 1993, 7 January 1993 and editorial comment; 11 January 1993; see also *Daily Mirror*, 5 May 1992 and editorial comment; *Independent*, 10 May 1992; *Independent*, *The Times*, *Daily Telegraph*, 7 January 1993.
49. Cesarani (1992), pp. 230, 232, 257–8.
50. *The Times*, 8 January 1993.
51. Cesarani, 'The law's delay' (1994).
52. For Gecas see *Glasgow Evening News*, 17 January 1994; *Independent*, 3 February 1994; *The Times*, 4 February 1994; *Guardian*, 4 February 1994; *Daily Telegraph*, 4 February 1994. In September 1995, Siemion

Serafimovicz was charged under the 1991 War Crimes Act. See *Sunday Express,* 30 May 1993, 6 June 1993, 24 October 1993.
53. See Braham (1981), vol. 2, p. 754.
54. Almost the only popular history of the Second World War to achieve this is Gilbert (1989).
55. The prosecution of Serafimovicz and the media coverage of the anniversary of the liberation of Auschwitz, which all followed the Portsmouth conference on war and memory for which this chapter was originally a contribution, have to some extent qualified this situation. But not entirely: see for instance Kushner (1995).

Bibliography

Bergonzi, Bernard (1993), *Wartime and Aftermath*, Oxford: Oxford University Press.

Bodnar, John (1992), *Remaking America*, Princeton: Princeton University Press.

Bosworth, R.J.B. (1993), *Explaining Auschwitz and Hiroshima*, London: Routledge.

Bower, Tom (1981), *Blind Eye to Murder*, London: Macmillan.

Braham, Randolph (1981), *The Politics of Genocide: the Holocaust in Hungary*, New York: Columbia University Press.

Bridgman, Jon (1990), *The End of the Holocaust and the Liberation of the Camps*, London: Batsford.

Calder, Angus (1969), *The People's War*, London: Cape.

Cesarani, David (1992), *Justice Delayed,* London: Heinemann.

Cesarani, David (1993), 'The law's delay', *Journal of the '45 Aid Society,* pp. 20–46.

Cesarani, David (1996), 'How England reacted to the Holocaust, 1945–90', in David Wyman (ed.), *The World Reacts to the Holocaust*, Baltimore: Johns Hopkins University.

Dawidowicz, Lucy (1981), *The Holocaust and the Historians,* Cambridge, Mass. and London: Harvard University Press.

Enser, A. G. S. (1990), *A Subject Bibliography of the Second World War and the Aftermath*, 2nd edn, Gower: Aldershot.

Fox, John P. (1989), *Teaching the Holocaust: The Report of a Survey in the United Kingdom*, Leicester: National Yad Vashem Charitable Trust and Centre for Holocaust Studies.

Gilbert, Martin (1989), *The Second World War*, London: Weidenfeld & Nicholson.

Glees, Antony (1992), 'The making of British policy on war crimes: history as politics in the United Kingdom', *Contemporary European History,* vol. 1, no. 1, pp. 174–81.

Glenny, Misha (1990), *The Rebirth of History*, London: Penguin.

Hennesy, Peter (1992), *Never Again,* London: Vintage.

Hetherington, Sir Thomas and Chalmers, William (1989), *War Crimes: The Report of an Inquiry,* London: HMSO.

Hewison, Robert (1981), *In Anger: Culture in the Cold War 1945–60,* London: Methuen.

Hockenos, Paul (1993), *Free to Hate,* London: Routledge.

Ignatieff, Michael (1991), 'In the New Republics', *New York Review of Books*, 21 November.

Kay, Diana and Miles, Robert (1992), *Refugees or Migrant Workers? European Voluntary Workers in Britain, 1946–51,* London: Routledge.

Kushner, Tony (1991), 'The impact of the Holocaust on British society and culture', *Contemporary Record*, vol. 5, no. 2, pp. 357–61.

Kushner, Tony (1993), 'Anti-semitism and austerity: the August 1947 riots in Britain', in Panikos Panayi (ed.), *Racial Violence in Britain 1840–1950,* Leicester: Leicester University Press.

Kushner, Tony (1994), 'Different Worlds: British perceptions of the Final Solution during the Second World War', in D. Cesarani (ed.), *The Final Solution,* London: Routledge.

Kushner, Tony (1995), 'Wrong war mate', editor's introduction to special issue on 'Fifty years after the Holocaust and Second World War', *Patterns of Prejudice*, vol. 29, nos 2–3, pp. 3–13.

McLaine, Ian (1979), *Ministry of Morale,* London: Allen & Unwin.

Morgan, K. O. (1994), *The People's Peace*, Oxford: Oxford University Press.

Mosse, George (1990), *Fallen Soldiers: Reshaping the Memory of the World Wars,* New York: Oxford University Press.

Paris, Michael (1990), *The Novels of World War Two*, London: Library Association.

Pronay, Nicholas (1988), 'Defeated Germany in British newsreels, 1944–5', in K. R. M. Short and Stephen Dolezel (eds), *Hitler's Fall: The Newsreel Witness*, London: Croom Helm.

Rousso, Henry (1991), *The Vichy Syndrome: History and Memory in France since 1944,* Cambridge, Mass.: Harvard University Press.

Taylor, Telford (1993), *The Anatomy of the Nuremberg Trials*, London: Bloomsbury.

Editorial, *Wiener Library Bulletin*, 1960, vol. 14, no. 3, p. 41.

Worpole, Ken (1983), *Dockers and Detectives*, London: Verso.

Zuroff, Efraim (1988), *Occupation: Nazi-Hunter*, Hoboken, NJ: Ktav.

Part II

Oral Testimonies

3

'A Low-Key Affair': Memories of Civilian Internment in the Far East, 1942–1945

Bernice Archer

'The Second World War may be defined as a war against civilian populations',[1] and this chapter focuses on one specific group of Second World War civilians. Hong Kong was the first British colony to be attacked by the Japanese during the Second World War, and Stanley Internment Camp was the first of many such camps set up for civilians. Part of my research on Stanley involved tracing survivors willing to be interviewed. The decision to concentrate on women was influenced by two factors: firstly, although women made up a large portion of the internees, they were underrepresented in the secondary and primary sources; secondly, my network of contacts directed me along that path. The fifteen women finally interviewed were all between sixteen and thirty years of age on entering the camp. They were white, middle-class, the daughters, wives or employees of British colonial officers and businessmen, and consequently they could not be called a typical sample. Seven of the women were married before internment, three of whom had a child in camp with them. One had her husband with her, two other husbands had died in the fighting and others were prisoners of war elsewhere. The remaining eight were single during internment.[2]

A theory, developed by the Popular Memory Group at the Centre for Contemporary Cultural Studies in Birmingham, claims that 'Our memories are risky and painful if they do not conform with the public norms or versions of the past. We compose our memories so that they will fit with what is publicly acceptable.'[3] This theory informs Alistair Thomson's analysis of First World War Australian veterans and their struggle to equate personal memories and identity with the public 'Jack the Lad' image of the typical Australian soldier. In his study, Thomson argues that the public expectations and perceived images of the Australian soldier were ones with which some veterans did not identify. Their 'risky and painful' memories, at odds with the public norm, therefore added to their post-war distress and sense of inadequacy. Thomson also highlights the need of other veterans to participate in public remembrance services to affirm the legend and to help 'filter out the memories that contradicted it'.[4] The same theory also informs this chapter, albeit in a different way. My research on the British civilian internees in Hong Kong from December 1941 to August 1945 revealed a similar yet different conflict to that faced by Thomson's Anzac soldiers. Rather than try to fit into a 'heroic legend' and needing to 'filter out' memories that contradicted it, the civilian internees interviewed devalued their experiences to conform with public expectations, and their memories were constructed and reconstructed accordingly. This chapter explores the contrast between the pragmatic, bearable and unheroic picture expressed by the interviewees and the image that appeared in diaries, intelligence and medical reports.

All memories are socially constructed and reconstructed, but, as Margaret Higgonet claims, the discourse of war and militarism stresses military qualities which permeate the whole of society and this, it will be argued, is an additional influence on civilian, and particularly female, war memories.[5] Images of military personnel, front-line dramas and heroics with their predominantly male actors dominate public perceptions of the war. Moreover, prisoners of war and wartime internees are still a masculine concept in the minds not only of the general populace but also of museum curators, the keepers and exhibitors of the public memory. Western civilians, which in general means women, children, the old and sick are considered the 'home front', the safe feminized area, which has to be protected and for whom men are fighting. To admit the capture and imprisonment of women by an enemy is politically and socially embarrassing as it denotes defeat and undermines masculine ideals. In this social atmosphere, civilians, and particularly women, have measured their war experiences against an inappropriate yardstick which has resulted in the public and private devaluation of both the experiences and related memories. The possible exceptions to this are the victims of the Holocaust. The sheer size, unmitigated horror and proximity of this genocide not only made it impossible for politicians and the public to ignore, but also overshadowed the smaller, less violent and distant civilian internment during the same period. Survivors of relatively less dramatic and more distant theatres of war have therefore been inclined either to play down or to dismiss their war memories as boring or inconsequential by comparison. Indifference by historians has further compounded this invisibility, and these stories have remained largely undisturbed in the Public Records Office files and the pages of private diaries and papers. All this has contributed in no small part to the repression of the public expression of Far East war memories but has not totally erased them. Hidden 'behind the innumerable war monuments in the city squares',[6] these individual memories are commemorated and communicated to the next generation in subtle, private and personal ways.

The commemoration services marking the fiftieth anniversary of the fall of Hong Kong serve to highlight this argument. At 9.45 a.m. on Saturday 7 December 1991, cars and coaches brought a large crowd of men, women and children to Sai Wan Military Cemetery, Hong Kong, where a remembrance service was to be held for those who died in battle. Chaplains from three religious denominations led a service attended by the Duke of Kent, the Governor and many other official wreath-layers. A military band accompanied the hymns and after Bible readings, prayers and an address, the haunting notes of the Last Post brought this well-organized, high-profile service to a close. The crowd dispersed among the lines of uniformly pristine white gravestones which covered the hillside like a miniature regiment of the soldiers whose bodies they represented.

At 2 p.m. on the afternoon of the same day, a few cars and the odd taxi brought a much smaller group to attend another remembrance service at Stanley Cemetery on the southernmost tip of the island. This cemetery is adjacent to Hong Kong prison where, in the severely war-damaged warders' quarters, approximately 2,500 civilian men, women and children were interned for three and a half years. The Governor and the Duke of Kent were conspicuous by their absence. A lone bugler replaced the military band and one priest conducted a short service during which a member of the Royal British Legion laid a wreath. It was a simple but moving ceremony for the small group present who, holding single poppies or small posies, stood among the uneven granite headstones which marked the final resting places of the ninety-four men, twenty-eight women and five children who had died during internment. It was to be, according to the programme, 'a low-key affair'.

The irony of these two contrasting services was highly significant. Surrender and humiliation are unpleasant memories, but they are regularly commemorated. The military personnel who fought and died bravely during those three weeks attempting to defend an indefensible Hong Kong were honoured and remembered with due ceremony. However, the dead amongst those civilians who lost their 3½-year battle against the distressing conditions of internment, when survival was a victory for human adaptability, innovation, resilience and determination, were clearly considered by those in authority to have made a modest sacrifice by comparison with the soldiery, and were commemorated accordingly. These services not only highlight the prioritizing of military personnel but also symbolized the post-war British public attitude to civilian internees returning from the Pacific War at the end of 1945. This attitude reflected official policy but also stemmed from war weariness and the post-war eagerness to forget the past and build for the future. The internalization of these two dominant discourses by the survivors of Stanley Internment Camp helped affirm their sense of insignificance and they have continued to undervalue their experience of Japanese imprisonment.

This devaluation is strengthened by the fact that 8 December 1941 is remembered for the Japanese attack on Pearl Harbor the previous day, whilst the simultaneous, and not totally unexpected, attack on Hong Kong is either forgotten or considered by many as a relative sideshow. As the threat of a Japanese attack loomed ever nearer, various defensive measures were taken by the Hong Kong Government Office, including the formation of evacuation plans for British and European women and children.[7] However, many were still in the colony, and were interned along with other Western nationals when the colony fell just three weeks later. Why was this? Although some British service people rated Japan's military capabilities very highly, Roger Perras argues that others were influenced by racist and ethnocentric views. Thus the historian John Ferris argues that when in December 1941 Field Marshall Wavell claimed that 'The Japs are just bogeymen', he was speaking for the general run of British military officers in Asia, leading men and officers to underestimate the enemy. Comments such as '[the Japanese] would not dream of fighting at night . . . they are subhuman specimens . . . I cannot believe they would form an intelligent fighting force . . . we have nothing to fear from the Japanese', fatally misled the armed forces and contributed to the colony's downfall.[8] As similar comments were made by the interviewees this suggests that such beliefs, however erroneous, also filtered through to the Western civilian population and contributed to their false sense of security.

In June 1940 the evacuation of approximately 5,750 European women and children was planned. By August all service families had been withdrawn, along with some civilian women and children, making a total of 3,474 evacuees. However, the evacuation order had been received unenthusiastically in some quarters. Many thought it unnecessary, and an anti-evacuation pressure group called the Evacuation Representative Committee vigorously challenged the legality of the compulsory order. Consequently, in November 1940 the Governor replaced compulsory evacuation by a voluntary scheme. This upset many women who had already been forced to leave. Their return was banned but a few are reputed to have returned illegally. Exemption was allowed for essential services such as nursing, and some women did not register because they were awaiting notification of their nursing applications, a few of which were deliberately lodged to avoid evacuation. Some secretaries were encouraged to stay when it was realized that businesses would grind to a halt if deprived of European female staff. Two women missionaries also refused to leave until their appeals against evacuation had been heard. Other women deliberately avoided evacuation while some families were caught in transit.

Consequently, at the time of the evacuation 900 women had been neither registered nor evacuated.

The naiveté which prompted the anti-evacuation group was based on a belief in imperial superiority, fuelled by the attitude of political and military personnel. Later this was to be the cause of guilt and embarrassment to politicians, military personnel and civilians alike. It was also the cause of much anti-government feeling which was further exacerbated by the fall of Singapore, the so-called bastion of defence of the Far East, just weeks later. The rounding-up of Western nationals who were subsequently interned by an enemy considered as 'bogeymen' and 'unintelligent fighters', but who had swept through the Far East with an unexpected speed and ferocity that could be neither repulsed or contained, was an unforgettable humiliation.

If the colony was ill-equipped for battle it was even less prepared for surrender. Nor were the Japanese prepared for large numbers of prisoners. The stunned confusion during the first few weeks after the Japanese invasion is strongly reflected in memories of the period. The battle, pre-internment and early internment periods were universally described in one word – chaos. The disorientated civilians who were rounded up by the Japanese immediately after the surrender were crammed, under guard, in emptied brothels along the waterfront on the mainland. This appeared to be the only place in which such a large group of civilians could be herded together in a restricted area by an enemy himself surprised by the numbers he had to cope with. The three weeks spent in these brothels were hazily remembered as 'five to six men and women to a cubicle sharing one bed, little food and limited sanitation'.[9] The other civilians, scattered in pockets around the colony, waited in shock for whatever should befall them amidst the rapidly deteriorating conditions of a colony whose infrastructure was severely war-damaged, where the water was cut off, electricity erratic and drains and sewers blocked. Meanwhile, some disorderly Japanese soldiers were still rampaging around the countryside.

Many civilians were relieved by their move to Stanley, pleased that the state of disorder was apparently over, and not expecting to be incarcerated for very long. Indeed, for many it was the first time they were able to gain information about friends and loved ones from whom they had parted a few weeks earlier. Having been told to take only what they could carry, personal decisions about appropriate clothing and equipment reflected the confusion and misconceptions of what internment would entail. For example, one trained secretary claimed to have prepared herself to march by 'wrapping a blanket around my shoulders; hung as much as possible, cup, water bottle, shoes etc. from string around my waist and put as much as I could carry in a Chinese basket'.[10] In contrast, a much older woman arrived in camp carrying only an armful of flowers from her garden. Nurses who had been on duty since the start of the invasion had no choice and arrived with only what they stood in. One remembers returning covertly to her house to collect some belongings, only to find that looters had removed everything except her wedding dress and the dog's collar, both of which were obviously considered useless. A young mother prioritized her baby's pram and baby food, while another woman, reflecting the sentiments of those who clung to their belief in the strength of the British Empire, refused to pack anything because 'Churchill will not let us stay more than a few days'.[11] She and others were unaware that Winston Churchill had told General Ismay in January 1941 'if Japan goes to war with us there is not the slightest chance of holding or relieving Hong Kong'.[12]

Surrounded by the prison walls on one side, the Japanese guards' quarters on another and the open sea on a third side, the looted, battle-scarred prison-warders' quarters and adjacent school became Stanley Internment Camp. Enclosed by barbed wire, this was the 'home' for 2,500 internees, of whom approximately 900 were women and 300 were children under sixteen. In spite of the efforts of an advanced clearing-up party there were still unburied bodies lying around and little had been done, or could be done, to prepare the camp for the internees' arrival. There were no cooking facilities, furniture, cutlery or crockery, and toilet arrangements were shamefully inadequate. These distressing early days were recorded by the British businessman who was eventually to become the camp billeting officer: 'All the rooms were overcrowded and in many cases one room contained a collection of men, women and children whether related or not . . . all possible odd spaces, holes under staircases, corners in passages, kitchens and servants' quarters came to be occupied with no thought given to hygiene or public health.'[13] Other official reports document the desperate food shortages with the resulting weight loss and illness. Meat was almost non-existent and the internees were told to eat grass when there were no vegetables. The medical reports record the acute shortages of drugs and medical equipment to treat recurring malaria and dysentery, and the many other malnutrition- and vitamin deficiency-related illnesses. Diaries reveal the loneliness: 'Mary was sitting in the front row and the shadows showed the lines on her face, I felt like weeping all evening . . . Mrs Grant's face full of worries past and present . . . Sheila looking wistful about her mother who died the week before the Japanese attack . . . all these people missing their men and humming softly.'[14] The 128 granite headstones in Stanley cemetery are evidence that the conditions were more than some internees could bear.[15]

Yet surprisingly, interviewees were inclined to stress the positive sides of internment, the comradeship, survival techniques, development of skills and independence – even the fun. Official reports were not disputed, but omissions, such as the innovative ways in which they tried to make food more interesting and edible, were recalled. One woman remembers using a yeastvite tablet and a hot-water bottle as raising agents for 'hot-cross buns'. Another described her daughter's birthday cake: 'made from hand ground rice from the precious rice ration . . . banana skin for fruit, the icing was boiled sugar beaten until creamy and coloured with Recketts' blue bag and mercurochrome. Very patriotic but vile to the taste.'[16]

Other stories revealed the underlying discomfort of the unpleasant overcrowding. One woman showed me a drawing of her room. To gain at least an element of privacy she had created living space on a balcony, moving inside only during typhoons. Another recalled a move to 'better' quarters: the fact that she now slept under a shattered window exposing her to the elements was mentioned only casually. Difficult room-mates were alluded to, their names avoided or forgotten. However, the names of those responsible for kindnesses such as those who had given them food, clothes, support and friendship were remembered easily.

The distressing shortage of clothes was recalled in detail. Accounts of tea towels being adapted for shorts, flour sacks or men's underpants used for knickers, and old car tyres made into clogs are just a few examples. Recollections of the entertainments organized by the internees were also readily recounted; costumes for plays and musicals were created from anything and everything, mosquito nets were used for ballet costumes with bits of tin for sequins. 'We were just a herd of elephants,' one woman recalls, 'but we did enjoy ourselves.'[17] However, the more sinister reason for the enthusiastic participation in the entertainments is revealed by another woman, 'as we might have been machine-gunned down at any time we had the nerve to do things we'd never attempt normally'.[18] References to the Japanese were also relatively lighthearted, even though their erratic behaviour, unpredictable tempers and at times extreme cruelty, as well as the burden imposed by curfews, roll calls, and room searches had kept the internees in a state of suppressed fear. Lessons in bowing to their conquerors, and the numerous ways they were able to demonstrate at least symbolic resistance, such as hanging out washing or planting a vegetable patch in the shape of a 'V', or even a group demonstration of defiance (a whole concert party made a 'V' sign when the Japanese tried to film them) were recounted easily and with humour. All this could mislead the interviewer into thinking that three and a half years of internment was indeed 'a low-key affair'.

Could these modest collective memories purely be the result of old age or poor recall or are there other explanations? Undoubtedly there was trauma. The constant fear and uncertainty affected all the internees, but trauma is relative, individual levels depending on many things. Whether one had lost a relative, was alone or with family and friends in the camp all made a considerable difference. For those severely traumatized the construction of positive memories was possibly, as Thomson claims, 'an unconscious way of dealing with deeply repressed experiences and feelings . . . humour [is] used to overcome embarrassment and pain'.[19] An alternative explanation is offered by psychologists at the recently established Centre for Crises Psychology in Yorkshire: 'people tend to think that good things happen to good people and bad things happen to bad people. Therefore, as something bad has happened to them some survivors believe they must be bad.'[20] Was there a sense of shame and of 'being bad'? Avoidance of the evacuation order was racially determined. 'We thought the Japanese were poor soldiers and when they came up against a real army they would never win.'[21] Consequently, although many of the women had enrolled for voluntary nurse training prior to the invasion, and their work was indeed invaluable during internment, their motives for doing so were not altogether altruistic. Some women illegally returned from evacuation and some had deliberately avoided it. Others in genuine war employment, who became pregnant after the evacuation order, were guilt-ridden for subjecting babies to the rigours of internment. But these plausible theories are only contributory factors. The overriding reason for the unheroic picture painted by the interviewees was the influence of dominant social discourses which not only existed during internment, but awaited them after liberation and have remained up to recent times.

Once in camp, survival was the prime motivator, and unpleasant feelings were repressed. An excerpt from a First World War poem captures the internees' philosophy:

> Fear is a wave
> beating through the air
> and on taut nerves impinging
> till there it wins
> vibrating cords.
>
> All goes well
> so long as you tune the instrument
> to simulate composure.[22]

Inherent in all aspects of survival was the simulation of composure, both individually and as a group. 'Making the best of a bad job' was the unspoken social agreement and those 'out of tune', the pessimists and complainers, were avoided. This was an indication that this behaviour was socially unacceptable. Keeping busy with an outward display of optimism was the order of the day. Cooking, entertainments, dressmaking and gardening were all part of this. When 'vibrating cords of fear impinged on taut nerves', as it often did, especially when six male internees were executed for using a radio in the camp, the optimistic rumours of liberation and repatriation helped the prisoners to 'retune and compose'. However, this outward optimism concealed an inner disquiet, as one diary note explains: 'had we known that we would be prisoners for over three years there would have undoubtedly been many suicides. As it was, the followers of the Ouija board and the readers of the tea cups were unable to find other than cause for optimism . . . good news was never more than a month ahead.'[23] Another woman recorded inner feelings which were at odds with her outward behaviour: 'I can't imagine being out of here by Christmas despite my bold assertions in public.'[24] These bold assertions were a cloak of confidence which the internees donned in Stanley, and proved impossible for them to discard after liberation because of the expectations of the social discourse which greeted them in Britain and Hong Kong at the end of the Pacific War.

After liberation, those internees remaining in Hong Kong found a desperately depleted and starving Chinese population who had suffered even more acutely under the Japanese occupation than they had. As they had not only to restore the colony to its former glory but also to repair the severely damaged reputation of the British, it would have been neither politic nor appropriate to dwell on the unpleasant experience of internment. Those internees who returned to Britain found an unreceptive, unsympathetic society with its own war experiences, scars and memories. The priority both publicly and privately was to look forward, to reconstruct lives, homes and relationships, as well as repairing the physical and economic damage inflicted on the country. The internees, with few obvious scars, and little sign of the privations they had suffered, since most had regained their lost weight by the time they reached Britain, found their internment-constructed behaviour had to be continued. 'Many adjustments had to be made . . . we especially needed to be mindful of the suffering and deprivations of people in England.'[25] They had to bite back responses to complaints about rationing: to them an egg a week was luxury. As one interviewee said ironically, 'when they knew we had not been raped by the Japanese they lost interest'.[26] A flippant remark, but a summary of the attitude of the public at large. Memories of internment were reconstructed within an acceptable framework, anecdotal, humorous and modest. Thus survivor memories of Far Eastern internment have been constructed and reconstructed with the building blocks provided by the pressures of dominant social discourses which demanded 'low key' responses regardless of the reality. Eventually, these memories became subordinated to marriages, children, new homes, new jobs: new lives. They appear to have remained hidden, for, as Gabrielle Rosenthall claims, 'where narrating is met with little or no interest ... then further attempts at narration will become even more difficult'.[27]

Why, then, were these interviewees prepared to retrieve their hidden memories now? The answer is that it is now more socially acceptable for civilians and especially women to have personal war experiences and to articulate them. Recently we have seen that returning civilian hostages from the Middle East and traumatized civilian men, women and children in Eastern Europe have been encouraged to relate their ordeals. Also, the greater credence given to oral history, and the relatively recent recovery of women from the historical margins by the increasing number of women historians, have raised social awareness of the relevance of women's experiences. The sound of the female voice is becoming not only more acceptable but more audible within social and historical discourses.

For those women who attended the memorial services in December 1991, the striking contrast between the two ceremonies highlighted the tension between the public and private memories; their awareness of this was clear from the disappointment they showed at the modest public recognition. Age is also an influence. All interviewees are in the evening of their lives and wanted some record made to validate and confirm their place in history. Breaking the silence had an additional purpose. As 'narrative is the first memorial',[28] by adding their voices and stories to the official and unofficial records of Stanley Internment Camp these women have created a memorial for the next generation – all the interviewees asked for a copy of the project, mainly to 'give to my children'.

War memories are bequeathed in other ways, through the planting of commemorative trees, by exhibitions, by the display or publication of photographs, by the wearing of red poppies and, of course, by the erection of public war memorials, which 'like other representations of events . . . juxtapose, narrate and remember events according to taste . . . [and] political needs, interests of the community, the temper of their time'.[29] As such they can 'threaten to deny the specificity of our own experiences'.[30] However, it should also be noted that 'the sites of memory are many and diverse, deliberate and accidental . . . where medical men and administrators recorded day-to-day illnesses, events, food qualities etc., others without access to the equipment to write, recorded in their own ways'.[31]

It is in this way that specific experiences can still be acknowledged. One such individual site is within the private locality of personal identity which, as Elizabeth Tonkin claims, is 'bound up with objects . . . which reassure their owners by reminding them of what they have been'.[32] The following extract from a letter demonstrates the significance of one such object: 'This is the famous camp spoon originally from the Cathay Hotel in Shanghai and which scraped heaven knows what awful food out of what makeshift mess tins in Stanley Camp. As children it was better known as a "disher out" of custard, chocolate mousse and jelly. Mum always wielded it with pride.'[33] This 'disher out' of sweet treats was a private memento, a memorial and commemoration which 'transformed an unpleasant experience into a pleasant and safe regular reminder'[34] of internment, and of the survival both of its owner and of her family.

Other objects served the same purpose: a sewing kit made from scraps of jerkin given as a birthday present in camp; a wooden cross carved from an old piece of wood sent from a man to his wife in another camp; a set of Chinese chequers cut from wood-block flooring; battered tin mugs; a child's faded dress made from odd scraps of material; a document file adapted from a beaten petrol can; and a pencil drawing of a child. Some are in daily use, but all are carefully treasured. These are not objects constructed or reconstructed after the event 'like the innumerable war memorials that block our view of the realities of war'.[35] These tangible, specific, objects *are* the realities of war. They capture the experience of the moment better than any photograph. These personal objects are not just recordings or reminders of internment, but are private commemorations and subtle forms of communication between the generations. They are, above all else, a priceless, private low-key collection, affirming the victory of personal battles for survival in what others have considered 'a low-key affair'.

Notes

1. Troger (1987), p. 285.
2. Fourteen interviewees came through personal recommendation and were initially contacted through letters promising complete confidentiality. Some were interviewed in pairs at their request, and others individually. Most were taped interviews, but a few women preferred to write down their experiences. Two women still live in Hong Kong, one in Australia and the rest in England. Two, sadly, have died since our interviews in 1991–2. There were 2,500 internees in Stanley. Nine hundred were predominantly British women, others were Dutch, Belgian, American and Eurasian. Many were over thirty years of age.
3. Thomson (1990), p. 25.
4. Ibid., p. 128.
5. Higonnet claims that 'the discourse of war and militarism stresses masculine qualities which permeate the whole society' (Higonnet et

al. (1987), p. 4). I believe the gendering of war is intrinsically linked with war memories. However, there is no room in this chapter to discuss the ramifications of the images, language and psychology related to this. I intend to explore this area further in my Ph.D. thesis, 'A comparative study of Far Eastern internment, 1942–5'.

6. Hausen (1987).
7. For more details of the evacuation plan see Archer and Federowich (1996).
8. Perras (1995). Ferris (1993). The author would like to point out that this chapter is concerned with the memories of internees in Hong Kong. On the issue of Hong Kong's role in the defence of the Far East see Bell (1996). Here Bell argues that faith in the superiority of the Royal Navy and the certainty of Hong Kong's relief was dominant in British minds.
9. Interviewee A. The interview records and other source materials cited are in the possession of Bernice Archer.
10. Interviewee B.
11. Interviewee C.
12. Major-General H. L. Ismay, CB, DSO, First Lord of the Admiralty, appointed Senior Staff Officer in charge of the General Staff, 1 May 1940, quoted in Endacott (1978), p. 59.
13. Report by C. C. Roberts, October 1945, in his private papers, held by John Swire and Sons Ltd., London.
14. Private diary of ex-internee.
15. For more details see Clarke (1946).
16. Interviewee D.
17. Interviewee C.
18. Interviewee E.
19. Thomson (1990), p. 26.
20. Psychologist Peter Hodgkinson in Sheridan and Kenning (1993), p. 267. This book covers first-hand accounts by, and details of the symptoms and treatment of survivors of, recent disasters during the 1980s.
21. Most of the interviewees claimed this.
22. Poem by Herbert Read, quoted in Bergonzi (1965), p. 74.
23. Stericker (1942–5).
24. Private diary of ex-internee.
25. Unpublished memoir of ex-internee.
26. Interviewee F.
27. Rosenthall (1991), p. 37.
28. Young (1993), p. 7.
29. Ibid., preface, p. viii.
30. Kettle (1993).

31. Young (1993), preface, p. viii.
32. Tonkin (1992), p. 94.
33. Letter to the author from the son of an interviewee who recently died.
34. Thomson (1990), p. 27.
35. Hausen (1987), p. 140.

Bibliography

Primary Sources

Unpublished letters and diaries by internees in the possession of the author
Taped interviewees with internees.
Report by C. C. Roberts, October 1945, in his private papers, held by
John Swire and Sons Ltd., London.
Stericker, John (1942–5), 'Captive Colony: the story of Stanley Internment
Camp, Hong Kong', chapter VII, p. 13. Unpublished manuscript held
in the University of Hong Kong Library.

Secondary Sources

Archer, Bernice and Federowitch, Kent (1996), 'The experience of women
and children in Stanley Internment Camp, Hong Kong 1942–5',
Women's History Review, forthcoming.
Bell, Christopher M. (1996), '"Our most exposed outpost": Hong Kong
and the British Far East Strategy, 1921–1941', *The Journal of Military
History*, pp. 61–88.
Bergonzi, B. (1965), *Heroes' Twilight,* London: Constable.
Clarke, Selwyn S. (1946), *Selwyn S. Clarke: Report on the Medical and
Health Conditions in Hong Kong, 1st January 1942–31st August 1945,*
London: HMSO.
Endacott, G. B. (1978), *Hong Kong Eclipse,* Hong Kong: Oxford Uni-
versity Press.
Ferris, John (1993), 'Worthy of some better enemy? The British estimate
of the Imperial Japanese Army 1919–41 and the fall of Singapore',
Canadian Journal of History, vol. 38, pp. 223–56.
Hausen, Karin (1987), 'The German nation's obligation to the heroes'
widows and World War I', in M. Higonnet et al. (eds), *Behind the
Lines*, Yale: Yale University Press, pp. 126–40.
Higonnet, M. *et al.* (eds) (1987), *Behind the Lines*, Yale: Yale University
Press.
Kettle, Martin (1993), 'A flowering of emotion', writing about Armistice
Day and the Red Poppy, *Guardian*, 6 November.
Perras, Galen Roger (1995), '"Our position in the Far East would be

stronger without this unsatisfactory commitment": Britain and the reinforcement of Hong Kong, 1941', *Canadian Journal of History*, August, pp. 231–59.

Rosenthall, Gabriele (1991), 'German war memories', *Oral History*, Autumn, pp. 34–41.

Sheridan, Geraldine and Kenning, Thomas (1993), *Survivors*, London: Pan Books.

Thomson, Alistair (1990), 'Anzac memories: putting popular memory theory into practice in Australia', *Oral History*, Spring, pp. 25–39.

Tonkin, Elizabeth (1992) *Narrating Our Pasts*, Cambridge: Cambridge University Press

Troger, Annemarie (1987), 'German women's memories of World War II', in M. Higonnet et al. (eds), *Behind the Lines*, Yale: Yale University Press, pp. 285–99.

Young, James E. (1993), *The Texture of Memory: Holocaust Memorials and Meaning,* Yale: Yale University Press.

4

Facing 'the Finger of Scorn': Veterans' Memories of Ireland after the Great War

Jane Leonard

Introduction

A major problem in researching the post-war experiences of servicemen is that many of the obvious sources – diaries, correspondence, memoirs and unit histories – conclude abruptly with peace and demobilization. A similar impression of 11 November 1918 as a last stop on a train journey is often conveyed in recorded interviews with veterans, who are unwilling to switch from combat adventures to their pedestrian or poverty-stricken peacetime lives. Irish veterans, who returned in 1919 to find a different and disorientating war in progress, had an additional reluctance to recollect this period.

This chapter is largely based on interviews conducted with Irish ex-servicemen during the 1980s and 1990s. None are still alive. The chapter aims to chart their memories of life in southern Ireland during the immediate post-war years and to identify which topics continued to evoke ambivalent and uneasy memories.[1] While oral history archives in Britain, such as the Imperial War Museum's Department of Sound Records and the Liddle Collection at Leeds University, hold several interviews with Irish veterans, these mostly concentrate on their wartime experiences and have not been used for this chapter.

Several studies of *southern* Irish participation in the Great War have been published in the last decade.[2] Few make use of oral history, as with most publications on this period in Irish history. Two exceptions are Uinseann MacEoin's study of radical republicanism and John Brewer's work on the Royal Irish Constabulary. It is regrettable that no oral history of the Irish Free State army and police during the 1920s was undertaken. A substantial series of interviews with veterans of the 1916 to 1923 revolutionary and civil war period was conducted by the Irish Bureau of Military History, which operated from the 1930s to the 1960s. These transcripts, which should considerably illuminate this period, remain closed to researchers.[3]

Recent studies of the *northern* Irish wartime experience have made considerable use of oral history. These include Philip Orr's compelling account of the 36th (Ulster) Division. However, the interviews with veterans used in these studies have largely focused on wartime trench experiences and on pre-war membership of the Ulster Volunteer Force.[4]

A brief outline of Irish participation in the war and of Ireland's altered political condition by its end will set this chapter in context. Recent research indicates that approximately 200,000 Irishmen resident in Ireland served in the war. Some 27,000 became fatalities and about 100,000 returned to Ireland between the Armistice and May 1920 (when records of demobilization ceased). The remaining 73,000 Irishmen either stayed in Great Britain as civilians or re-servicemen, emigrated or had been invalided out of the forces prior to the Armistice.[5]

Recruitment in Ireland was unusual in that conscription was never imposed. A further distinction between Irish recruits and those elsewhere in the United Kingdom was that they included members of two pre-war political militias, the Ulster Volunteer Force (UVF) and the Irish Volunteers. These bodies were established in 1913, and were intended respectively to stop or safeguard the introduction of Home Rule into Ireland. When the World War interrupted these preparations for civil war, many members of the UVF joined the 36th (Ulster) Division, while the Irish Volunteers split on the issue of supporting the British war effort. Those who supported the Home Rule Party's endorsement of the war joined the 10th and 16th (Irish) Divisions. While the War Office permitted the 36th (Ulster) Division to inherit the officering and ethos of the pre-war UVF, it restricted attempts to give the two southern divisions a nationalist identity. The unease of Irish nationalists in the British forces with this imbalance deepened with the Easter Rising in 1916, Sinn Fein's growing popularity during 1917 and 1918, and its massive victory over the Home Rule Party in the general election of December 1918. While returning veterans of the 36th (Ulster) Division were welcomed by functions in town halls, Protestant churches and Orange Halls, the return of survivors of the 10th and 16th (Irish) Divisions was largely unmarked by their communities.[6]

During the 1970s and the 1980s, Great War survivors elsewhere, such as the Anzac veterans interviewed by Alistair Thomson, grew more loquacious as popular interest in the war (and consequently their heroic status) increased.[7] The interviews used in this chapter were mostly held during the 1980s, in a period when official and popular ambivalence persisted about Irish participation in both world wars. Since these interviews took place, attitudes towards war commemoration have changed. The revulsion caused by the Enniskillen Remembrance Sunday bomb in 1987 and the moves towards ceasefires and negotiations in Northern Ireland have stimulated communities throughout the Republic of Ireland to restore (or erect new) war memorials and to publish histories of the war's local impact. At official level, the state has restored and completed the Irish National War Memorial Park in Dublin. The attendance of government representatives at the main Remembrance Sunday service in Dublin no longer generates controversy. In 1995, the Irish government's participation in war commemoration included the issue of postage stamps and the holding of ecumenical services to mark the conclusion of the Second World War.[8]

These interviews largely predated this rehabilitation of Irish participation in the world wars. Many of those interviewed were embarrassed or hesitant when asked about their motivations in enlisting, their subsequent political allegiances and their attitudes in old age to having served in the war. Widows and families of veterans were awkward and puzzled when their own recollections revealed the scale of Armistice Day celebrations and the active presence of the British Legion in inter-war Ireland.

Wartime Politics and Initial Reception on Coming Home

Those who served or convalesced in Ireland during the period after the 1916 Easter Rising were aware of the changing political situation. Following a period of convalescence from injuries received on the Somme, John Tierney was posted to a garrison battalion of the Leinster Regiment. He was stationed in Tipperary town, where he passed the time reading Sinn Fein periodicals:

> Life was easy here and a good deal of political views were expressed. There was a good deal of leftist politics in this place. We had nothing much to do, of course, and living easily ... We got associated with some of the republican elements there at the time and I used to buy copies of *Nationality*. The atmosphere got somewhat explosive, you see, in Ireland, generally at that time ... so we were all shipped to England. We were sent to Portsmouth.[9]

Another interviewee, Terence Poulter, then a second lieutenant in the Royal Dublin Fusiliers, recalled that his battalion was shipped to Grimsby in the autumn of 1917. From their barracks beside the Royal Canal in Dublin, his soldiers were discovered tossing their rifles to Sinn Fein contacts on passing barges. No Irish units were felt to be immune from 'republican elements' and all Irish reserve battalions and depots were transferred to England and Scotland that winter. When the Armistice came in 1918, demobilization centres for troops intending to return to Ireland were similarly located outside the country. This meant that rifles and uniforms were safely surrendered.[10]

Growing public solidarity with Sinn Fein meant that servicemen often experienced hostility and rejection. Sam Hutchinson spent most of 1918 as a convalescent patient in a Ministry of Pensions hospital in Dublin. Service patients, in their distinctive blue uniforms, were jeered and taunted on their daily walks around the city. 'The finger of scorn was pointed at us', he recalled. Some veterans never forgave this early rejection. Jack Campbell, a pre-war regular in the Black Watch, spent much of 1919 in another Dublin hospital:

> When I came back, I couldn't get out of Dublin quick enough. I tell you this. I got discharged, as I told you, from the King George V Hospital on the 28th August. One evening I was in uniform. I was walking down Westmoreland Street . . . . I noticed two ladies, well I won't call them ladies. Two women and two men were coming towards me and when they got alongside me, the two women stepped over in front of me and spit [*sic*] on me. That was their way of saying they didn't like the British soldiers. They didn't ask me if I was Irish or Dutch or what. I thought to myself, I don't know. There was no work here and certainly there wasn't any work for the ex-British servicemen 'cause they weren't liked . . . I got out of Dublin quick and went over to England. And I didn't come back to Dublin until I was retired and seventy years old . . .The couple of ladies spitting on me didn't leave any doubt in my mind where I wanted to go. Wanted to go back, you know, where I had respect.[11]

Unemployment and Intimidation

Unemployment among veterans in Ireland was far higher than elsewhere in the United Kingdom. Many employers heeded Sinn Fein's warnings not to hire veterans. Schemes such as the King's National Roll, listing firms which hired disabled ex-soldiers, operated in Ulster but not in the rest of the country. Unemployment among southern veterans remained high after the establishment of the Irish Free State in 1922. Applicants to the Irish Grants Committee (established by the British government in the mid-1920s to assess and compensate material losses caused by the Anglo-Irish Treaty of 1921) included many southern veterans. Michael O'Mahoney, who emigrated to Canada when the IRA expelled him from Limerick in 1920, was unable to find work when he returned to Ireland. He complained: 'Only for volunteering my services in the Great War I would still be employed in pre-war occupation as you know there is not any use for men that served in the British army.' Similarly, Michael Shannon, a former tailor in County Clare, found that he 'was never insulted until I returned from the war and cannot get work since I been [*sic*] an ex-soldier I am not wanted anywhere'.[12]

Intimidation of veterans by the IRA and Sinn Fein took many forms. Those allocated cottages and smallholdings under the 1919 Irish Land (Soldiers and Sailors) Act were threatened and boycotted. In some cases, their new homes were vandalized or set on fire. Cultural boycotts included the refusal to let former hurlers and Gaelic football players rejoin the Gaelic Athletic Association if they had served in the war. Some Sinn Fein-controlled local councils refused to enrol ex-servicemen in vocational colleges or to admit them as patients in workhouses and hospitals.

The extremes of intimidation included beating, mutilation, punishment shooting, prolonged kidnapping, expulsion from Ireland and murder. During the period from 1919 to 1924, upwards of 120 ex-servicemen were killed either by the IRA or by the anti-Treaty republican side during the Civil War. Some of these veterans were undoubtedly intelligence agents for the police and military forces. However, the vast majority appear to have been killed simply as a retrospective punishment for their service in the Great War. As ex-members of the British forces, they formed a marginalized and unwelcome group in Irish society.[13]

Interviewees were reluctant to discuss these murkier aspects of post-war Ireland. Many said that they were unaware of intimidation. Fred Thackaberry, employed as a government printer in Dublin Castle after the war, maintained that innocent ex-servicemen were not targeted by the IRA: 'If the IRA shot ex-soldiers, it was not because they were ex-soldiers. It was because of their activities.'[14]

Socializing with serving soldiers and policemen in post-war Ireland, even if only to reminisce about the Western Front, was risky. Jack Moyney, an ex-Irish Guardsman who had won the Victoria Cross, was a railway porter in Roscrea after the war. He offered a blunt explanation of why he shunned the company of local British troops: 'I wouldn't get mixed up with them at all. That time, if you talked to them, they'd say you were giving information or something like that. So I kept away from them.'[15]

Attitudes to the IRA

Veterans were forthright in recalling personal encounters with the IRA and in offering opinions of the IRA's soldiering abilities. The homes of ex-officers were obvious targets for arms raids. Terence Poulter relished describing how he and his brother foiled one raid on their home in Dublin:

We had a house on the Milltown Road. We lived right opposite Shamrock Rovers after the war. That was father's home. And the brother and I. He was on crutches. The brother Edgar. He had his whole knee blown out the week before the Armistice. The house on Milltown Road. We had three revolvers, a rifle, a box of ammunition. All our army equipment was in the house and these fellows knew that. They were determined to get them. But this night Edgar and I came up. We'd been out down in Salthill or somewhere. We heard the gate go and nobody came out, so we thought, 'it's somebody playing a practical joke'. We went up and opened the gate. There was a fellow standing inside the gate. Edgar puts up his crutch and, says he, 'come on, put them up, put them up'. The fellow had in his hand a revolver with a barrel about that length. He dropped the revolver and put his hands up over his head. At that time, the hall door opened, and the gang were inside trying to find the revolvers and the rifles. But there wasn't one in the house. I'd hidden them only the day before. I'd wrapped them up in newspapers and put them up the greenhouse flue.[16]

Prompted either by patriotism or pragmatism, some veterans did join or assist the IRA. John Bond and his three brothers found work after the war in the local quarry owned by Sean Wall, commander of the East Limerick IRA brigade. In return, they acted as training instructors in the evenings. John Bond, who rejoined the British army in 1920, was scathing about the IRA's poor survival skills: 'The IRA, they didn't know one end of a rifle from another. They were hopeless. They didn't know how to take cover or anything. Or they didn't know if they were going anywhere, what the land was like, whether there was water there.'[17]

Two interviewees were reluctant to disclose their later IRA service. One was in receipt of both British and Irish government war pensions and was reluctant that too much honesty about his 1919–21 IRA service would jeopardize his British award. The other veteran was John Tierney, whose wartime introduction to Sinn Fein newspapers has already been quoted. After the war, Tierney became a Home Office clerk in London and leaked sensitive files to his IRA contacts. In 1921, he was arrested and sent to Ballykinlar Internment Camp in County Down. Tierney was very reticent and oblique in confirming his involvement with the IRA. Initially, he told his interviewer that he was in an Irish cultural movement in London. Pressed for this group's actual name, he gradually confided that it was 'the boys', 'the lads', 'the local officers', the local officials' and eventually, 'the IRA'.[18]

Attitudes to Britain and the British Army

Veterans' ambivalence regarding the IRA was mirrored in their attitudes to Britain. A number stressed that they felt as much British as Irish, yet they also expressed resentment of British policy in Ireland. In particular, and ironically, they resented the paramilitary police forces composed of ex-servicemen which were used in Ireland in 1920 and 1921 to augment the regular Royal Irish Constabulary. Patrick Neville, an amputee, recalled with indignation how Black and Tans in Clare mistook the iron of his surgical boot for a concealed gun. The house of another Clare convalescent veteran, Rodney Gallagher, was raided by troops who thought he was an IRA drill instructor: 'They pulled me out of bed, they did, and fired shots at me down that lane there . . .There was a couple of ex-soldiers here, training the boys . . . giving them tips . . . They were blaming the ex-servicemen.' Gallagher's post-war memories were richly ambivalent. Irritated by the raid on his house and well-disposed towards the IRA (like Tierney, he called them 'the boys'), he nonetheless rejoined the British Army once his recovery was complete. News of British reprisals in Ireland continued to aggrieve him: 'We'd be getting letters about the trouble here and they would all gather around you, those that were training with you, to hear about the troubles in the country.'

Gallagher was serving in India with the Royal Garrison Artillery when a battalion of Connaught Rangers, stationed a couple of thousand miles from his unit, mutinied in June 1920. The mutiny, ostensibly prompted by anger at British policy in Ireland, was also caused by poor morale, officering and discomfort with the climate and service conditions. Gallagher recalled how all Irish soldiers in India at the time were given a form to sign, confirming their continued allegiance to the crown. Two years later, still in India, he and other Irish soldiers watched newsreels of the evacuating British Army handing over the Curragh camp in County Kildare to the new Free State army. Gallagher and his friends cheered as 'they hoisted up the Irish flag and pulled down the Union Jack'. He remained in the British army until 1924.[19]

For Michael Kenny, who served with the other battalion of the Connaught Rangers in Silesia in 1920, respect for the mutineers gradually replaced disapproval. In 1970, when the body of James Daly, the solider executed for leading the mutiny, was repatriated to Ireland, Kenny was an active member of the British Legion in Dublin. He officially represented the Connaught Rangers' Old Comrades Association at Daly's re-interral. He saw no ambiguity in representing his old regiment at a ceremony held by the National Graves Association, the body responsible for Irish republican commemorations. Similarly, John Bond saw no conflict between his post-war drilling of the IRA and the fact that (following later service alongside ex-Black and Tans in the Palestine Police) he spent his retirement as a Chelsea Pensioner.[20]

Many veterans expressed mixed feelings of loyalty and disaffection with Britain. Jack Moyney, the Irish Guards VC hero, was proud of his annual invitations to regimental reunions in London. Yet he was blunt about what prompted other ex-soldiers to join the IRA: 'Why wouldn't you? After fighting, for them to come over and start killing your people the. . . .There was plenty of Tans here and Auxiliaries. They were a rough looking gang altogether . . . the scruff of England.'

Only one of those interviewed defended the Black and Tans and Auxiliary units of the Royal Irish Constabulary. Terence Poulter was fiercely loyal about some of his wartime friends who later joined these units. Shortly before I interviewed him, he had had an argument with his rector about British reprisals in Ireland:

> I said, don't you dare call them Black and Tans criminals. They had men pop shots at them, and they were no more criminals than you were. I had quite a heated argument about it. 'Cause the Black and Tans they only did what they had to do . . . they had to eliminate the IRA. That was their job. Because the unfortunate soldier, the English military man, was being massacred and shot from around the corner.[21]

Commemoration

The commemoration of Ireland's role in the Great War has consistently been marked by controversy and conflict. On the actual night of the Armistice, 11 November 1918, Sinn Fein supporters clashed with celebrating soldiers in Dublin. Throughout the inter-war period, Armistice Day in the Irish Free State was marked by bomb and arson attacks by republicans on war memorials, British Legion halls and cinemas showing war films. Parading ex-servicemen were frequently beaten up. Much of this war of commemoration focused on the wearing of poppies. Several veterans described with relish how they dealt with those trying to remove their poppies by placing a razor-blade inside the paper flowers. Poppy-snatching thus incurred slashed fingers.[22] These confrontations were recalled robustly. Asked about the present-day condition of the County Offaly memorial in Tullamore, one ex-soldier confirmed that it was still there, adding ruefully, 'They haven't blown it up . . . that's one of the few things they haven't done.'

The Irish Free State's prevarication during the 1920s and 1930s in sanctioning and siting the Irish National War Memorial Park in Dublin was still producing bitter memories in the 1980s. Initially given various central locations, the memorial park was eventually built at Island-bridge, near Dublin's Phoenix Park. It was never officially opened and the Irish government also refused an invitation to attend the first Armistice Day ceremonies held there in 1937. Andrew Barry, a former Royal Dublin Fusilier and an official of the British Legion, was bitter about this delay and about nationalist perceptions of the park as an imperial monument:

> This is bad news. We had been granted a site in College Green for the national war memorial and it was blocked off straightaway. It was near the police station. Then we were given, as I understand, the Merrion Square and that was too near . . . Then we were given a slice up in the Phoenix Park, a huge slice . . .

That park has never been opened. Never been officially opened and never will because the money was subscribed by the all-Ireland business, by all-Ireland people, during the war or the end of the war. And then it was felt that the North was royalty there and someone else wouldn't have royalty. A beautiful park.[23]

The commemoration of Irish participation in both world wars became beleaguered as the Northern Irish conflict worsened in the early 1970s. Following a series of bomb scares, most of the British Legion's branches in the Republic closed. Passwords and heavy security were used by the remaining Legion clubs while outdoor Remembrance Sunday ceremonies at Islandbridge and elsewhere were abandoned on police advice. Street sales of poppies were halted as were masses said in memory of the Irish war dead. War commemoration was confined to remembrance services inside the anonymous doors of Protestant churches.

More recent events in Northern Ireland, such as the IRA's bombing of a Remembrance Sunday ceremony in Enniskillen in 1987 and the paramilitary ceasefires, have produced a new commitment in the Republic to commemorate the Irish who served in both world wars. This revisionism, whether manifested in the refurbished appearance of war memorials or the speeches and stamps issued by recent governments, did not impinge on the recollections of elderly veterans or of their families. They became apologetic and reticent when their memories of commemoration seemed to them to fit uncomfortably into the standard folk memory about the early decades of the Irish state. As Alistair Thomson and the Popular Memory Group have noted, 'memories are painful if they do not conform with the public norms or versions of the past'.[24] Asked about Armistice Day in an area of Dublin where the British Legion was active, the daughter of an ex-soldier became confused and embarrassed by her private memories:

They used to have poppy collections in Sandymount when I was a child.

[*Author: door to door?*]

No, at the church. I'm almost certain. It's like a dream to me that they did this. Poppies weren't then a forbidden thing in Sandymount. Maybe I'm wrong but it's like a dream to me that I remember going to Mass as a child in the Star of the Sea Church at Sandymount, and seeing people selling poppies . . . . I remember, in later years, feeling that the poppy wasn't the thing to wear . . . I don't think you could get poppies here in later years. So that's what strikes me, that the poppy was part of my childhood . . . I suppose, maybe, with the Troubles and the IRA, you wouldn't be that keen to wear a poppy nowadays. You'd be aggravating the situation.[25]

Conclusion

The common theme in these interviews is ambivalent identity. Veterans did not assimilate easily into the Ireland that evolved after 1918. Suspect for their previous service with the British, even those who joined the IRA or the Free State army found it difficult to integrate. Those who had been directly intimidated by the IRA or who retained a loyalty to Britain found the adjustment to the new order even harder. Of these interviewees, over half either rejoined the British forces or emigrated to England or America in the early 1920s.

Former officers found the adjustment particularly hard. Some appeared not to have tried. The ex-captain of the Royal Dublin Fusiliers, Terence Poulter, combined a nostalgia for garrison culture with a contempt for the new state's administrators and Gaelic culture. He missed the presence of British Army officers at race meetings in Ireland and mocked the new state's attempts to promote the Irish language: 'I mourned the passing of British rule in Ireland . . . I never felt the same under the Irish government. Never felt the same. Lot of yahoos who have no idea how to run a country.'[26]

This rejection of independent Ireland was undoubtedly influenced by the intimidation and alienation experienced by many veterans during the post-Armistice years of revolution and civil war. They matured into middle age and retirement, aware that they were excluded from the national cultural identity forged after independence in 1922. This identity declared, in the words of a popular ballad, that:

> Twas better to die 'neath an Irish sky
> Than at Suvla or Sedd el Bahr.[27]

The Irish who survived Gallipoli and the Western Front 'backed the wrong horse' in joining the British forces, as one of them recalled. The same veteran recognized that his British Army service was compromised by the Easter Rising and the post-war revolution in Ireland, but he regretted that the history textbooks used by his children and grandchildren were silent on the extent of his generation's participation in the war.[28] Much of the reticence and embarrassment that veterans displayed stemmed precisely from conflicting urges to assimilate or dissociate. It is not surprising that the subject of post-war Ireland, where their war service was at best ignored and at worst a liability, so often provoked only their silence.

Notes

1. Of 24 interviews, most were held in Dublin. The remainder were in Munster, the Irish midlands and England. In addition to my own recordings, a number of interviews conducted by Patrick Callan, Peadar MacNamara and Kevin Myers have also been used. I am grateful to them for sharing these sources with me.

2. Denman (1995); Denman (1992); Dooley (1995); Johnstone (1992); Fitzpatrick (1986). A number of interviews are used in Dungan (1995); and in Staunton (1986), an excellent study.

3. MacEoin (1989); Brewer (1990). The Bureau of Military History's records are held by the Irish Department of Defence and should eventually be deposited in the National Archives of Ireland, Dublin.

4. Orr (1987); Mitchell (1991); MacFhionnghaile (1987); *Battlelines*, the magazine of the Somme Association, Belfast, regularly carries interviews with veterans of the 36th (Ulster) Division; life in post-war Ulster was included in an outline questionnaire by Williams (1986).

5. Statistical analyses are given in Fitzpatrick (1996), pp. 379–406; and in Perry (1994). I am grateful to David Fitzpatrick for pointing out that the exclusion of officers from these demobilization records affects calculation of the residual number of veterans.

6. On politics and the Irish Division, see Denman (1992), esp. chs 1, 2, and 6; also Lemisko (1992); and Leonard (1996a).

7. Thomson (1990), pp. 30–1; see also his stimulating book, Thomson (1994).

8. For a survey of official attitudes to commemoration, see Leonard (1996b). Restored memorials include those in Limerick and Port-laoise. Bandon, County Cork, erected a memorial to its Great War dead in the autumn of 1996. Local studies include McGuinn (1994) and Ballincollig Community School (1991).

9. Interview with John Tierney, Dublin, 1980 [interview by Kevin Myers]. *Nationality* was a Sinn Fein newspaper, edited by Arthur Griffith.

10. Interview with Terence Poulter, Dublin, November 1988; on the transfer of Irish battalions from Ireland, see Gill and Gloden (1985), pp. 60–1.

11. Interview with Sam Hutchinson, Dublin, June 1993; interview with Jack Campbell, Dublin, September 1988.

12. The CO762 series in the Public Record Office, London contains over 200 boxes of compensation claims made to the Irish Grants Committee: see CO762/94 and CO762/96 for O'Mahoney and Shannon.

Unemployment among ex-servicemen is analysed in Fitzpatrick (1996), pp. 397–9.

13. Details on intimidation and murder patterns are taken from the London University dissertation which I am completing on 'Ex-servicemen and the formation of the Irish Free State, 1919–32'. Some preliminary findings are given in Leonard (1990).

14. Interview with Fred Thackaberry, Dublin, August 1993.

15. Interview with Jack Moyney, Roscrea, 1980 [interview by Kevin Myers].

16. Interview with Terence Poulter, Dublin, November 1988.

17. Interview with John Bond, London, February 1989.

18. Interview with Michael O'M., Kilkee, November 1988; interview with John Tierney, Dublin, 1980 [interview by Kevin Myers].

19. Interview with Patrick Neville, Ennis, November 1988 [interview by Peadar MacNamara]; interview with Rodney Gallagher, Kilrush, November 1988. The most recent study of the mutiny is Anthony Babington (1991).

20. Interview with Michael Kenny, Dublin, November 1988; interview with John Bond, London, February 1989.

21. Interview with Jack Moyney, Roscrea, 1980 [interview by Kevin Myers]; interview with Terence Poulter, Dublin, November 1988.

22. For more detail on Armistice Day clashes, see Leonard (1996b).

23. Interview with Andrew Barry, Dublin. c. 1983 [interview by Dr Patrick Callan].

24. Thomson (1990), p. 25.

25. Interview with Marjorie K., Dublin, June 1993.

26. Interview with Terence Poulter, Dublin, November 1988.

27. The ballad is called 'The Foggy Dew'.

28. Interview with Sam Hutchinson, Dublin, June 1993.

Bibliography

Babington, Anthony (1991), *The Devil to Pay: The Mutiny of the Connaught Rangers, India, July 1920*, London: Leo Cooper.

Ballincollig Community School (1991), school journal, *Times Past*, special issue on the First World War.

Battlelines, the magazine of the Somme Association, Belfast.

Brewer, John (1990), *An Oral History of the Royal Irish Constabulary*, Belfast: Institute of Irish Studies.

Denman, Terence (1992), *Ireland's Unknown Soldiers: the 16th (Irish) Division in the Great War*, Dublin: Irish Academic Press.

Denman, Terence (1995), *A Lonely Grave: The Life and Death of William Redmond*, Dublin: Irish Academic Press.

Dooley, Tom (1995), *Irishmen or English Soldiers? The Times and World of a Southern Catholic Man Enlisting in the British Army during the First World War*, Liverpool: Liverpool University Press.

Dungan, Myles (1995), *Irish Voices from the Great War*, Dublin: Irish Academic Press.

Fitzpatrick, David (ed.) (1986), *Ireland and the First World War*, Dublin: Trinity History Workshop.

Fitzpatrick, David (1996), 'Militarism in Ireland, 1900–22', in T. Bartlett and K. Jeffrey (eds), *A Military History of Ireland*, Cambridge: Cambridge University Press, pp. 379–406.

Gill, Douglas and Gloden, Dallas (1985), *The Unknown Army*, London: Verso.

Johnstone, Tom (1992), *Orange, Green and Khaki: The Story of the Irish Regiments in the Great War, 1914–18*, Dublin: Gill & Macmillan.

Lemisko, Lynn (1992), 'Politics, performance and morale: 16 Irish Division, 1914–18', unpublished University of Calgary MA thesis.

Leonard, Jane (1990), '"Getting them at last": the IRA and ex-servicemen', in David Fitzpatrick (ed.), *Revolution? Ireland 1917–23*, Dublin: Trinity History Workshop, pp. 118–29.

Leonard, Jane (1996a), 'The reactions of Irish officers in the British army to the Easter Rising of 1916', in Hugh Cecil and Peter Liddle (eds), *Facing Armageddon: the Great War experienced, 1914–18*, London: Pen & Sword, pp. 256–68.

Leonard, Jane (1996b), 'The twinge of memory: Armistice Day in Ireland since 1919', in Richard English and Graham Walker (eds), *Unionism in Modern Ireland*, London: Macmillan, pp. 99–114.

MacEoin, Uinseann (1989), *Survivors*, Dublin: Argenta Publications.

MacFhionnghaile, Niall (1987), *Donegal, Ireland and the First World War*, Letterkenny: An Crann.

McGuinn, James (1994), *Sligo Men in the Great War, 1914–18*, Belturbet: Naughan Press.

Mitchell, Gardiner (1991), *Three Cheers for the Derrys: A History of the 10th Royal Inniskilling Fusiliers in the 1914–18 War*, Derry: Yes! Publications.

Orr, Philip (1987), *The Road to the Somme. Men of the Ulster Division Tell their Story*, Belfast: Blackstaff Press.

Perry, Nick (1994), 'Nationality in the Irish infantry regiments in the First World War', *War and Society*, vol. 12, no. 7, pp. 65–95.

Staunton, Martin (1986), 'The Royal Munster Fusiliers in the Great War, 1914–19', University College Dublin MA thesis.

Thomson, Alistair (1990), 'Anzac memories: putting popular memory theory into practice in Australia', *Oral History*, vol. 18, pp. 25–31.

Thomson, Alistair (1994), *Anzac Memories: Living with the Legend,*

Melbourne: Oxford University Press.

Williams, Fionnuala (1986), 'Enquiry about the Great War 1914–18 and the period leading up to it', *Newsletter of the Ulster Society for Oral History*, vol. 5, pp. 5–9.

5

Rehabilitating the Traumatized War Veteran: The Case of French Conscripts from the Algerian War, 1954–1962
Martin Evans

Between 1954 and 1962 3 million French conscripts fought in the Algerian war.[1] For France this was the longest war of decolonization and in the minds of many conscripts the enormity of this trauma has left an indelible imprint on their lives, marking them out as the 'Algerian generation'. Yet in terms of public remembrance their experience has remained largely forgotten, overshadowed by the memories of the First World War and the Second World War. Taking this official marginalization as a starting point, this chapter explores the nature of conscripts' memories within contemporary France. The first part will examine the role of the largest Algerian ex-servicemen's organization, the FNACA, outlining how, in the face of public neglect and exclusion, it has attempted to foster a new mood of recognition and reconciliation towards Algerian veterans. The second part will then focus on Bertrand Tavernier's *The Undeclared War* (*La Guerre Sans Nom*), a film portrait of Algerian veterans in the Grenoble region, released in 1992 to coincide with the thirtieth anniversary of the end of the war. In doing so it will examine how Tavernier draws upon personal testimonies to emphasize one image above all else: the manner in which the war continues to be a source of terrible social and psychological wounds.

For French conscripts the contours of their memories are firmly rooted in the highly particular nature of the Algerian war. What characterized military service in Algeria first and foremost was diversity of experience. For reservists recalled to fight for six months in 1956; for conscripts whose military service was eventually lengthened to twenty-seven months; for professional soldiers; for the tiny minority of deserters; for those soldiers who rebelled against de Gaulle's pro-independence policy in the putsch of April 1961: no one group participated in the war in the same way, with the result that each group has asserted a different, and often openly conflicting, pattern of remembering. This divergency of memory is intensified by the nature of the war itself which varied greatly according to *when* you were there. Between 1954 and 1960 the war was primarily directed against the Algerian liberation movement. But by 1961 this state of affairs had changed dramatically, with the army under attack, not only from the Algerians, but also from diehard French settlers who were completely opposed to independence. Thus, unlike the First World War, with the figure of the ordinary soldier in the trenches, the Algerian war generated no consensual imagery around which subsequent memories could easily coalesce. For the French historian Jean-Pierre Rioux this absence of consensual imagery is compounded by two further factors. Firstly, the lack of any sacred battlefield which could act as a physical site of private and public remembrance.[2] Because the conflict was essentially an anti-guerrilla war, which took place in what is now a foreign country, the Algerian war produced no equivalents to the Marne or Verdun, no places of pilgrimage which veterans could visit to mourn and remember. The statue to the unknown soldier of the North African campaign, inaugurated by President Valéry Giscard d'Estaing on 16 October 1977 and situated in Lorette (near Arras), is, Rioux notes acidly, little known and little visited. Secondly, Rioux underlines the fact that within the French collective memory the First World War is a fixed event with a clearly defined beginning and a clearly defined end. In contrast the Algerian war has no such clarity. Retrospectively it is now accepted that the war started with the National Liberation Front (FLN) rebellion on 1 November 1954, but when did it end? With the Franco-Algerian ceasefire of 19 March 1962, at the time unanimously disavowed by the settlers? With the OAS–FLN ceasefire on 17 June 1962?[3] Or with the declaration of independence on 3 July 1962? The lack of a temporal coherence, itself reflective of the way in which the assertion of any chronology is the source of ongoing conflict, means, Rioux argues, that it is difficult to insert the Algerian war into public forms of remembrance.

Significantly too, the Algerian conflict was never officially defined by the French authorities as a war. France invaded Algeria in 1830 and in December 1848 its vast territories were annexed not as a colony but as an integral part of France. To have recognized that France was at war with another country would have involved overturning Algeria's status as three French departments and admitting that it constituted a separate nationstate, something no French government was prepared to do. Instead the Algerian rebellion was referred to as 'a law and order problem' and the usage of the term 'war' was explicitly forbidden within the media. Consequently when hostilities ceased in 1962 the position of all Algerian veterans became highly problematic. The first question which imposed itself was whether those who fought in Algeria should be accorded the title of ex-servicemen? And from this fundamental issue flowed a whole host of interrelated problems. Should those who died in Algeria be included on war monuments? Should veterans be invited to participate in official parades? How did they stand in respect to rights to war pensions, allowances for those wounded and provision for widows?

This non-status of Algerian veterans was further exacerbated by a conscious will to forget during the 1960s. With the end of the Algerian war de Gaulle underlined the need to turn the page in a bold and assertive manner. Thus in the new France, resolutely 'hexagonal' and clearly orientated towards the challenges of economic modernization, the conscripts, along with the million 'repatriated' settlers, quickly became untidy reminders of outdated colonial values. Inasmuch as the government recognized any problem of reintegration, it was hoped that the combination of consumerism and full employment would, by rapidly reinserting the veterans into mainstream society, efface any trauma. The nature of this official amnesia is most tellingly revealed by the rituals of remembrance de Gaulle chose to sponsor in the years immediately after 1962. Rather than remember Algeria, the need to legitimize the Fifth Republic established a clear-cut hierarchy of memory whereby Gaullist resistance was the primary focus of remembering. Through impressive state occasions, such as the burial of the Resistance hero Jean Moulin in the Pantheon in 1964, Gaullism constructed an easily recognizable version of Resistance which stressed the unity of the French people behind de Gaulle, a unity which, it was claimed, was now being rediscovered with the Fifth Republic. According to this logic Vichy was conveniently dismissed as an illegal regime imposed by the Nazis, whilst the idea of the Resistance as a subversive, subterranean movement was largely forgotten. Through such imagery the Resistance was seen to represent a store of cohesive memories around which a new, positive national identity could be formed. In sharp contrast the Algerian war was viewed as an embarrassment. It was embarrassing because it had been so divisive. It was embarrassing because it had been a humiliating defeat. And finally it was embarrassing because any evocation of the Algerian issue challenged the democratic legitimacy of the Fifth Republic, since in returning to the Algerian war it would have been difficult to avoid the manner in which de Gaulle used the threat of a military putsch to return to power in May 1958. The fusion of these factors meant that it was impossible to compose a positive memory of the Algerian war. Henceforth it became a taboo subject in the eyes of the Gaullist regime.

Undoubtedly such official non-recognition has been central in defining the shape of Algerian veterans' remembering. Their absence from public remembrance provoked widespread bitterness amongst veterans because, for them, it tellingly underlined their own lack of self-worth within French society. For some, official invisibility intensified individual amnesia: convinced that the war was a shameful event, the desire to forget became a dominant emotion. For others general indifference led in the opposite direction, heightening their need to find alternative forms of remembrance. A small minority of ex-conscripts, such as Philippe Labro and Georges Mattéi, looked towards writing as a way of dramatizing their experience.[4] For these authors, as Phillip Dine has emphasized in his excellent account of French fiction of the Algerian war, literature came to represent a mode of access to the memories denied at a public level by an indifferent mother country.[5] Through the device of the novel they gave a voice to the lost generation of the Algerian war, communicating the complex feelings which had underpinned their combat experience. However, in rightly acknowledging the collective significance of this work it is important not to lose sight of the limitations of fiction as a mechanism of remembering. Ultimately writing was restricted to a tiny minority, middle class for the most part and with privileged access to printing and publication. In this context a more immediate and more widespread expression of a will to remember was the establishment of ex-servicemen's organizations. Through such organizations ex-conscripts came together to combat their marginalization in ways which were both general and specific; general in the sense that they wished to challenge public indifference; specific because they wanted to create their own particular public which would affirm the way *they* wanted to remember the Algerian war.

In numerical terms the most important ex-servicemen's group is the National Federation of North African Ex-Servicemen (FNACA).[6] Founded during the war itself in September 1958, the original organization represented the fusion of three separate groups. Initially it was riven with division. Some saw it as a vehicle for anti-war protest. Others wanted to develop a more traditional ex-servicemen's organization. Tension produced splits, with the latter winning over the former, and in 1963, in an effort to convey a conventional image, the organization changed its name to the FNACA by including ex-servicemen in the title. Further pressure from members for an apolitical role led the FNACA to cut any lingering ties with the Left, especially the Communist Party, and since the mid-1960s the FNACA has tirelessly proclaimed its independence from any ideological perspective. At the outset the FNACA had 21,000 members, a nucleus which mushroomed in the 1970s, when membership was expanded to include those who fought in Tunisia and Morocco. By 1988 membership stood at 310,000. Overall this represents 10 per cent of those who fought in North Africa between 1952 and 1962.

With the cessation of hostilities the FNACA became the most forceful exponent of the ex-conscripts' cause. Neither bellicose nor *revanchist*, it quickly adopted a twofold strategy, combining lobbying over ex-servicemen's rights with pressure for some form of official commemoration of the war. In both cases what united FNACA members was anger at the neglect suffered by Algerian veterans compared with the recognition accorded to those who fought in the world wars. Within this sense of discrimination members found a shared identity which cut across social and political differences. In the years that followed 1962 no theme was more insistent than the need for equality of rights concerning war pensions and allowances for the wounded. For the FNACA these specific issues were symbolic of a broader need officially to recognize Algerian veterans by according them ex-servicemen status. Nevertheless, in the face of FNACA protestations, de Gaulle remained inflexible, consistently opposing such a move, firstly because it would have meant admitting that a war had taken place, and secondly because, given that 3 million men fought in Algeria, it would have burdened the state with considerable extra expense. Only in the wake of de Gaulle's resignation in 1969 did the FNACA find a climate more sympathetic to their cause with the result that in 1974, in the face of continued pressure, the French government finally accorded Algerian veterans ex-servicemen status.

From the outset the issue of ex-servicemen status was intimately connected to the FNACA campaign to have the Algerian war officially remembered. As early as 1963 FNACA members were calling for the date of the Algerian ceasefire (19 March 1962) to be commemorated annually, in the same way that 11 November and 8 May were for First World War and Second World War veterans respectively. In this way the FNACA wanted the government to recognize publicly Algerian ex-conscripts as the third generation of combat veterans with their own particular calendar of remembrance.[7] Anger at official indifference led the FNACA to press home their cause through a carefully coordinated plan of action. On the second anniversary of the ceasefire in 1964 FNACA members organized a ceremony at the Tomb of the Unknown Soldier in Paris, whilst in the provinces wreaths were laid at war monuments and a one-minute silence observed. The failure of national government to respond in any meaningful way prompted the FNACA to mount a grassroots campaign calling for individual municipalities to name a street after the 19 March 1962 ceasefire.[8] Through this movement from below the FNACA hoped to compensate for the absence of a state-sponsored memory imposed from above, accumulating a network of local sites around which alternative forms of remembering could coalesce. In concrete terms it was a strategy which met with limited success, as at a local level the Right proved just as resistant to any institutionalization of remembrance, however modest in form. By 1988 a mere 1,700 out of 38,000 municipalities, in the main on the Left, had named a street in this way. Such a poor response was indicative not only of indifference but also of outright hostility. The most vehement opposition came from French settler and pro-colonial Algeria ex-servicemen's organizations, for whom 19 March 1962 will forever remain a shameful date, the moment when France betrayed French Algeria to the Algerian rebels. The yearly commemorations organized by the FNACA led to violent confrontations, a trend which became more pronounced with the rise of the extreme Right during the 1980s. In March 1988 the unofficial FNACA ceremony at the Tomb of the Unknown Soldier was openly attacked by a large-scale National Front counter-demonstration.

The victory of the Socialists in May 1981 brought with it high expectations on the part of the FNACA. It was hoped that the new regime under François Mitterrand would lead to a redefinition of official attitudes, transforming the manner in which Algerian veterans were viewed by the rest of society. But when no gesture of public recognition was forthcoming the sense of disappointment was acute, with the result that the FNACA looked towards new ways of bringing their plight to public attention. Through the establishment of an archive of former conscripts' oral testimonies, the setting up of a special group to examine how their experience was taught within schools and the organization of a touring exhibition, the FNACA set out to challenge continuing government amnesia and present an accurate account of what took place in Algeria. In 1986 the FNACA raised its profile further by attending the second world conference of ex-service people, resisters and victims of war. Central to this participation was a meeting with the Algerian delegation designed publicly to promote reconciliation between the two countries. Predictably, it was a gesture greeted with widespread hostility on the part of the extreme Right, leading the latter to reiterate the accusation that the FNACA was nothing more than a Communist Party front motivated by anti-patriotic instincts.

For FNACA veterans what underpinned this work was the desire to communicate the relevance of their memories to young people through the assertion of a particular set of values and understandings concerning the Algerian war. From the perspective of the 1980s their military service in Algeria was now recast as a chastening experience. Manipulated by cynical politicians, condemned to fight in a war not of their choosing, the manner in which conscripts were sacrificed during the Algerian war, the FNACA argued, should act as a permanent warning to future generations. In this sense their memories are not marginal to contemporary concerns, still less wasted or worthless. By demonstrating the dire consequences of war they pass on powerful lessons for young people. Above all, they underline the need to avoid conflict through the promotion of peace and understanding between different races and cultures. Through the adoption of this self-consciously didactic position, the FNACA hoped to construct a distinctive memory of the war that was empowering and affirming for ex-conscripts. Presenting an alternative to the familiar narrative of the war hero, rejecting the stereotype of ex-conscripts as misfits or pariahs, the basis of this remembering was a new image of masculine self-worth which, in opposing war and embracing peace, communicated a clear-cut code of values. As such it was an image which facilitated a healing process not only between generations but within veterans themselves. By giving a positive meaning to their remembrance, it helped many to come to terms with a question at the core of their experience: what thirty years ago had they fought for in Algeria?

This shift in identity indicated the extent to which the 1980s represented a different social and emotional context for remembering. By this point FNACA veterans were in their mid- to late fifties and the sensation that their working careers were nearing an end encouraged many to look back over their lives in a meaningful manner. Inevitably this intensification of the will to remember returned them to Algeria, producing a greater desire to talk in detail about their war experience. Now, benefiting as they saw it from a greater distance on events, veterans were motivated by a determination to overcome misrepresentation and 'set the record straight'. Significantly too, many members were extremely sensitive to the rise of the extreme Right-wing National Front party, in particular the way in which the latter's spectacular electoral successes had led commentators to explain away support for Le Pen in terms of the pernicious legacy of the Algerian war. In recalling their experience FNACA members wished to underline not only their attachment to republican and democratic values, but also their desire to make a stand against racism, thereby challenging the image of Algerian veterans as embittered Right-wing extremists. This reshaping of memory was most clearly expressed in a collection of FNACA testimonies, published in 1987 to coincide with the twenty-fifth anniversary of the end of the war.[9] Through these testimonies the FNACA veterans set out to present a record of their everyday experience, and what emerged was a complex picture, in which long periods of boredom and isolation were punctuated by moments of intense fear and anguish. Within the epilogue, written in a pungent and forceful manner, the FNACA used the testimonies to assert its opposition to racism and anti-semitism; its belief in democratic principles; and its support for the United Nations. The collection concluded with the FNACA message produced for the 1985 International Year of Youth, a UN-sponsored initiative. Here young people were told:

At the age of legitimate hopes, you possess these riches: *never to have known War*. Yet, Peace is not definitively won. It calls for vigilance and courage. At a time when we are witnessing a rise in intolerance with its trail of violence, do not forget that hatred, racism and xenophobia lead to catastrophe, to War. Make yourself sensitive to a problem which will determine your Future, in order to live in a world where there are no more Ex-Servicemen. Such is the sense of our message.[10]

As part of this broader attempt to rehabilitate the Algerian veteran, the FNACA commissioned a group of psychiatrists to conduct the first-ever inquiry into the psychological disorders caused by the war. Published in 1985, the final report catalogued in detail the after-effects suffered by veterans, showing how large numbers had come back from Algeria in a disturbed condition, unable to cope with day-to-day life. Depression, insomnia, nervousness, frequent nightmares, violent mood swings: the report found that these were common phenomena amongst ex-conscripts. In relating these symptoms veterans underlined the extent to which the Algerian war had been a watershed experience. Thereafter they felt emotionally estranged, incapable of sustaining any close relationship. Writing in 1989 Bernard Sigg, one of the psychiatrists from the inquiry, explained these memories in terms of the fact that the Algerian war was not a conventional war, but a counter-insurgency operation, where the conscripts were engaged in a battle against the local population, analogous to the Americans in Vietnam or the Russians in Afghanistan.[11] Confronted with a clandestine resistance movement using bombing and assassination to create a climate of insecurity, the conscripts lived in a perpetual state of tension. The cumulative effect of this anxiety was a deep-felt neurosis which, on returning to civilian life, often translated itself into a depressive condition. For Sigg these conclusions, by demonstrating beyond doubt the existence of a medical illness related to service in the Algerian war, were a savage indictment of government neglect, and here Sigg talked about the significance of the Vietnam comparison. In America, Sigg argued, the army had long recognized a pattern of psychological problems affecting Vietnam veterans. In their case, he continued, the authorities were more willing to accept the need for a comprehensive programme of therapy, designed to overcome veterans' suffering and facilitate reintegration into mainstream society. Sigg now called on the French government to face up to its own responsibilities by caring for traumatized ex-conscripts in a similar manner.

Sigg's arguments indicated the extent to which the treatment of Vietnam veterans became a point of reference for the FNACA during the 1980s. The FNACA followed closely the inauguration of the Vietnam memorial in Washington. Likewise it took a strong interest in films such as Michael Cimino's *The Deer Hunter* and Oliver Stone's *Platoon*, applauding the way in which they portrayed the lot of the ordinary soldier in an honest and open fashion. What impressed the FNACA was how these initiatives were collectively indicative of a climate of compassion and understanding for Vietnam veterans, a climate so lacking in their own case. The FNACA was particularly mindful of the image conveyed within the Vietnam films of the veteran as a helpless victim of government policy. Lost, helpless, confused: they had been put in a situation which they did not understand and was not their fault. Claiming victimhood in this way struck a powerful chord, and during the 1980s FNACA discourse became infused with similar imagery. In lobbying the government the FNACA now argued that Algerian veterans, as a body which had suffered a long history of discrimination, constituted a distinctive minority group in special need of consideration.

The assertion of victimhood is at the centre of Bertrand Tavernier's documentary portrait of Algerian veterans, *The Undeclared War,* released in 1992 to coincide with the thirtieth anniversary of the end of the war.[12] In agreeing to the project, Tavernier underlined, he was not interested in producing a conventional history of the period. What drew him to the subject was a desire to make a film about the place of the Algerian war within France today.[13] Through a probing documentary style he wanted to explore the twin themes of memory and trauma, revealing the emotional wounds bequeathed by the conflict. Getting veterans to confide in this manner involved an enormous amount of groundwork, and in this respect Georges Mattéi, as the person who carried out the initial research, played a pivotal part.[14] It was Mattéi who chose to locate the film in the region around Grenoble in the French Alps, firstly because it had the largest association of the FNACA, numbering some 10,000, and secondly because, as a veteran of the war who had fought with a unit from this region, this gave him the specialized knowledge necessary to test the veracity of what he was being told.[15] Similarly it was Mattéi, in conjunction with another Algerian war veteran, François Sikirdji, who took a key role in securing the cooperation of the FNACA, and here the fact that he himself was a veteran was again enormously significant. It meant that he was perceived not as an outsider who might distort their memories, but as an insider who understood what they had been through then and what they were coping with now. Undoubtedly, Mattéi feels, this helped overcome inhibitions and was a crucial factor in determining the quality of the final filmed interviews.

The originality of the *The Undeclared War* lies in the fact that it contains no archive footage from the time. Instead Tavernier chose to structure the film around twenty-nine retrospective interviews, all of which took place in intimate settings such as the home, the workplace or the local bar. To underline the interviewees' authenticity, he made continual usage not only of personal photographs, drawn upon as *aide-memoires* to help the veterans faithfully reconstruct their memories, but also excerpts from radio programmes and popular music of the period. This tone of realism was further reinforced through footage of veterans' meetings, ceremonies and dinner dances, as well as scenes of the desolate Algerian landscape, the latter to convey the solitary context in which they fought and the former to underline the present-day role of the FNACA. In talking to veterans Tavernier was particularly attentive to the need to give them room for self-expression. For him the role of the interviewer, Patrick Rotman, was as a facilitator, allowing veterans to relate their experiences in their own words, and with their own priorities and interests. Tavernier wanted a grassroots perspective, and within this approach the film finds a unity of purpose, exposing the limitations of any single history or image of the conscript experience. The outcome is a slow, measured style which, in lasting four hours, draws viewers in emotionally, permitting them to identify with the plight of the veterans. In this way Tavernier wanted the film to provoke a widespread reflection amongst his compatriots, touching the French conscience about the Algerian conflict in the way that Marcel Ophuls's film *The Sorrow and the Pity* had in respect to the Vichy period.

To communicate the hidden suffering of veterans, Tavernier edited the final footage with immense care. The opening sequence, in which a succession of interviewees admit their personal amnesia over the war, establishes the central concern of the film: the way in which the Algerian conflict has been the focus of an enormous taboo. Thereafter Tavernier, in chronological order from 1956 to 1962, explores painful stories of loss, hardship and death, and here two moments in particular exemplify the general thrust of the film. The first is the interview with Serge Puygrenier where he recounts how he lost his leg in action. What characterizes this scene is mounting anger and discomfort. Puygrenier tells how the loss of the leg has left him feeling like a freak, unable to do normal activities like swimming in the sea. Sitting beside him, his wife emphasizes the psychological toll of dealing with his disability. Recently made redundant, and with little prospect of finding work, it means that every day they are forced to relive the Algerian war. The second instance is the interview with René Donazzolo. Here he recalls how at one point, surrounded by Algerians and with no ammunition, he thought that he was going to die. The one thing that saved him was an artillery barrage which forced the Algerians to retreat. In retelling the story he is eventually overcome with emotion, breaking down into tears, at which point Patrick Rotman calls upon the cameraperson to cut filming. When he regains his composure, Donazzolo explains that he has never talked about this experience before, not even within his family. What is striking in both cases is the voyeurism of the camera as it deliberately dwells on uncomfortable body language. In this sense what is *not* said is just as significant as what is said. In revealing the difficulty they have in communicating their memories in words, it indicates the depth of the trauma and the extent to which it has set them apart from French society.

Hatred of politicians of whatever political hue is a strong subtext within the film. This hostility is based on the notion that politicians condemned a whole generation to waste the best years of their lives in a pointless conflict. Then, in refusing to face up to the legacy of the war, they left the same generation to carry an intolerable burden of shame and guilt. The result of this neglect, the film argues, is a masculinity in crisis, broken by the war and in dire need of help. To underline this image the film does not address how the war affected girlfriends, wives and mothers.[16] Nor is the violence done to Algerians a central issue. While veterans readily admit that torture existed, it is dealt with as one issue amongst many. To have done otherwise and accepted the mistreatment of Algerians as a defining image would have challenged Tavernier's message, presenting the conscripts as the perpetrators, rather than the victims, of violence. Ignoring the Algerian perspective allows Tavernier to annex the Algerian war as a uniquely French trauma, and nowhere is this more evident than in the concluding shots of the film, when Tavernier follows an outing of traumatized veterans from a Grenoble psychiatric hospital. Over a piano one veteran recounts how he saw dozens of Algerians executed. Witnessing torture, he explains, made him physically ill, so much so that he cannot bear recalling it. At this point Tavernier does not cut to consider the fate of those being tortured. He does not ponder how the war traumatized Algerian society. Instead he focuses on the obvious distress of the FNACA veteran and with this single scene underlines the enduring message of *The Undeclared War*, that is, how the Algerian war constitutes a past which is permanently present, continuing to victimize French conscripts thirty years on.

Notes

1. According to official statistics French military casualties during the Algerian war comprised 15,583 killed in action, 7,918 killed by accident and 200,000 wounded.
2. Rioux (1990).
3. The Secret Army Organization (OAS) was a group of diehard settlers dedicated to the cause of French Algeria.
4. Labro (1982); Mattéi (1982). Other novels include Stil (1978); Zimmermann (1988).

5. Dine (1994). For a general assessment of the memory of the Algerian war within France see Stora (1992). See also Evans (1997).
6. On the role of ex-servicemen's organizations and the Algerian war see Liauzu (1990).
7. The FNACA saw themselves as the third generation because the Algerian war had involved conscripts. In contrast the Indo-China conflict was restricted to professional soldiers and volunteers.
8. On this point see Rouyard (1990).
9. FNACA (1987). For testimonies of conscripts see also Vittori (1977).
10. FNACA (1987), p. 776.
11. Sigg (1989). The book also contains a summary of the report on the psychological disorders suffered by conscripts commissioned by the FNACA.
12. See also the book based on the film, Rotman and Tavernier (1992).
13. On this see Frodon (1992) and Chalandon (1992).
14. Interview with Georges Mattéi, 17 July 1995, Paris.
15. A further reason why the Grenoble region was chosen was because it was the site of a large-scale anti-war protest, opposing the recall of reservists to fight in Algeria, on 18 May 1956.
16. The experience of girlfriends, wives and mothers surfaces twice in the film. Once with Puygrenier and his wife, and then again when Tavernier traces the impact of the death of one conscript, Henri Giraud, on his immediate family.

Bibliography

Chalandon, Sorj (1992), 'Algerie: la memoire des soldats du rang', *Liberation*, 19 February, pp. 22–3.

Dine, Philip (1994), *Images of the Algerian War: French Fiction and Film, 1954–1962*, Oxford: Clarendon Press.

Evans, Martin (1997), *The Memory of Resistance: French Opposition to the Algerian War, 1954–1962*, Oxford: Berg.

FNACA (1987), *Enfin ils parlent. Temoignages 1952–1962*, Paris: FNACA.

Frodon, Jean-Michel (1962), 'La guerre sans nom, un film de Bertrand Tavernier et Patrick Rotman: le voyage dans la memoire', *Le Monde*, 20 February, pp. 25–6.

Labro, Philippe (1982), *Deux feux mal eteint,* Paris: Gallimard.

Liauzu, Claude (1990), 'Le contingent entre silence et discours ancien combattant', in Jean-Pierre Rioux (ed.), *La Guerre d'Algérie et les français*, Paris: Fayard.

Mattéi, Georges (1982), *La Guerre des guesses,* Paris: Balland.

Rioux, Jean-Pierre (1990), 'La flamme et les buchers', in Jean-Pierre

Rioux (ed.), *La Guerre d'Algérie et les français*, Paris: Fayard.

Rotman, Patrick and Tavernier, Bertrand (1992), *La guerre sans nom: les appeles d'Algerie 1952–1962*, Paris: Seuil.

Rouyard, Frederic (1990), 'La bataille du 19 mars', in Jean-Pierre Rioux (ed.), *La Guerre d'Algérie et les français*, Paris: Fayard.

Sigg, Bernard (1989), *Le Silence et la Honte*, Paris: Messidor/Editions Sociales.

Stil, André (1978), *Trois pas dans une guerre,* Paris: Grasset.

Stora, Benjamin (1992), *La gangrène et l'oubli*, Paris: La Découverte.

Vittori, Jean-Pierre (1977), *Nous, les appelés d'Algérie*, Paris: Stock.

Zimmermann, Daniel (1988), *Nouvelles de la zone interdite*, Paris: L'Instant.

Part III

Museums

—6—

Making Histories: Experiencing the Blitz in London's Museums in the 1990s
Lucy Noakes

Presenting the Past

> Look around you in this extraordinary country and contemplate the various Shows and Diversions of the People and then say whether their temper or Mind at various periods of our history may not be collected from them?[1]

This chapter focuses on the public production of the past. In the drive to make the past 'come alive' which informs so many of today's *public* histories — books, films, television programmes, theme parks and museums — the Blitz is often privileged over other events of the war years. Two recent representations of the Second World War in London museums, the 'Blitz Experience' in the Imperial War Museum, and the Winston Churchill Britain at War Theme Museum near London Bridge, both focus on the Blitz in their histories of the war.

Why is this? Both exhibitions attempt to represent the experience of the *people's war* rather than information about diplomatic or political manoeuvring or military tactics in wartime, yet the Blitz was by no means an experience common to all British people in the way, for example, that rationing was. Air raids were concentrated on the large towns and cities, particularly sites of strategic importance such as Portsmouth, Southampton, Coventry and London. The smaller 'tip-and-run' attacks only occurred over the easily accessible coasts of southern and eastern England.[2] Furthermore, the London Blitz was an experience peculiar to those living in London in 1940–1, and the bulk of the bombing was concentrated on a few boroughs, most notably those in the east of the city such as Stepney.[3] The Blitz, it would appear, is being moved from its position during the war as an important but by no means universal *experience* to the centre of public *memories* of the war.

There are several possible reasons for this. In part, it is because the Blitz is both exciting and easily accessible. One does not need a detailed knowledge of diplomatic missions or military tactics to appreciate the horror of being bombed. As large numbers of the visitors to both of these exhibitions are parties of schoolchildren, excitement and immediacy are an important part of their appeal. Moreover, the Blitz was an active, dramatic part of the war which affected women at least as much as men. As women were far more likely to remain in Britain, and in the home, than men, their chances of experiencing aerial bombardment were that much higher.[4] Thus perhaps women visitors to the exhibitions are able to identify with representations of the Blitz in a way which could be problematic if the experience focused on the armed services. The Blitz is likely to remain central to the personal memories of those who experienced it as a time of heightened emotions and personal and national importance. Its central position on the public stage reinforces its importance in these more private memories, and helps to position the personal experience as a part of public, national history. Representations of the Blitz are also, of course, representations of large-scale bombing of civilians, a key, defining, twentieth-century phenomenon with which we are all familiar, if not through experience, then through its many cultural manifestations such as Picasso's *Guernica*, films such as Boorman's *Hope and Glory* and Coppola's *Apocalypse Now*, and scenes on the television of Baghdad, Basra and Sarajevo. The Blitz is Britain's claim to inclusion in these events.

Perhaps more importantly though, the Blitz has become an important part of public memories of the war because public images and memories of it overwhelmingly present a unified picture of Britain at war; a time when 'we' were all soldiers in the front line. The common myth of the Blitz, as outlined in Angus Calder's book of the same name,[5] is that it was a time when the nation, led by Churchill and under bombardment from Hitler, overcame its internal divisions and aligned itself behind the values of 'freedom', 'democracy' and the 'rights of the individual'. If the Second World War can be seen as a key moment in our national identity and national history, then the Blitz is a key moment in the war. This chapter is an examination of how this particular history is reproduced in two London museums in the 1990s.

Both of the museum exhibitions mentioned above essentially tell this story: the Blitz was a levelling, egalitarian time when the nation, divided by the class conflict of the 1930s, became 'the people'; a time when everyone pulled together and 'we' were all in it together. This image of the Blitz is one which is given a particular legitimization by its inclusion and foregrounding in museum displays. Museums are powerful sites of cultural transmission and public education; they are an embodiment of knowledge and power, important hegemonic instruments. The state museum is an important site not only for the exhibition of objects, but also for the exhibition of national beliefs; it is a place where the 'imagined community' of the nation becomes visible.[6] The large national museums established in the eighteenth and nineteenth centuries were intended not only as display sites for the wealth and power of the imperial British nation, but also as authoritative sites of public education. The Museums Act of 1845 heralded an explosion in the creation of museums; almost 300 were founded in Britain between 1850 and 1914, many of them in the urban, industrial centres of the North of England.[7] The same period saw a growth in the number of large state museums in London. As the British Museum's collections grew in size and scope they were divided: the National Gallery was founded in 1824, the National Portrait Gallery in 1856, the Science Museum in 1883, the Tate Gallery in 1896 and the Victoria and Albert Museum of Design and Manufacture in 1899.[8] This growth in the numbers of museums coincided with the growing economic, cultural and political power of the middle classes. Admission to the museums was free, and it was hoped that the urban working class, the site of so much bourgeois anxiety, would be 'improved' by entering the museums and looking at the exhibits. Like the municipal libraries which were also founded at this time, the museums were intended as sites of both entertainment and education for the working class; by actively displacing sites of culture and education which had been created by a politically radical working class, such as the Halls of Science, the museums and libraries of the nineteenth century came to dominate public cultural education.[9] Museums became authoritative sites for the exhibition of the ideal nation.

The authority of museums was embodied in the form, as well as the content of these buildings. Their architectural form often deliberately recalled past ceremonial buildings such as palaces and temples, sites of authority, ceremony and worship. They were often sited in the middle of towns and cities, close to the town hall, the site of local civic power. London museums and galleries in particular were able to signify, through both their position in the capital and their physical appearance, close links with both the British state and with past institutions of power, knowledge and ceremony.[10] The museum or gallery, particularly the large, central state museum or gallery, was a place where ideas of the nation could be both legitimized and made visible.

The Imperial War Museum was founded in 1917, and formally established by an Act of Parliament in 1920,[11] with the specific aim of giving the British public an overview of the Great War of 1914–18. Whilst the museum was originally intended as a private enterprise, the War Cabinet and officials from both the armed services and the Ministry of Munitions soon had representatives on its Central Committee, and the official aim of the museum became 'to collect and preserve for British inspection objects illustrating the British share in the war'.[12] The museum was officially opened by King George V in 1920 at the Crystal Palace, moving from there to a temporary home at the South Kensington Imperial Institute, and in 1935 to its present home at the former Bethlam Hospital at Southwark.

From its inception, the Imperial War Museum was a consciously 'national' museum, with the aim of creating a sense of inclusion and membership of the nation amongst its members. As many members of the nation as possible were to be included in the museum's presentation of a nation at war, including munitions workers and Land Army girls. These goals were made explicit in the King's dedicatory speech at the official opening of the museum in 1920, when he explained that it stood 'not for a group of trophies won from a beaten army nor for a symbol of the pride of victory, but as an embodiment and lasting memorial of common effort and common sacrifice'.[13] The museum, despite its name, thus represented the First World War less as a great imperial victory for Britain, and more as a time of national unity, shared suffering and shared effort. The institution was surrounded from its inception by the imagery and language of common sacrifice and effort.[14]

This view of the war might perhaps have been the antithesis of the feelings and views of some of the museum's early visitors, who may well have been wondering just *what* they had fought and suffered for. The imagined visitors to the Imperial War Museum may have entered the building having only experienced *their* war, and perhaps carrying with them feelings of bitterness and anger, but, having viewed the exhibits, emerged with a picture of the *nation's* war, and a subsequent understanding and acceptance of the aims and values that they, along with the rest of the nation, had been fighting for. The ideal visitor to the museum would thus become the ideal citizen.

Of course, this ideal visitor, the passive 'subject' who absorbs the message of the museum or gallery without question rarely, if ever, exists. Our experience of museums, like our experience of everything else in life, is shaped by a variety of factors, gender, class, sexuality, religious and political beliefs being amongst them. If a museum is a text, then we all make our own readings of it, and an individual may also visit a museum and 'read' it differently at different points in his or her life. Nevertheless, the inclusion of an object from the past, or a representation of the past, in a museum is an important means of legitimizing it, of bestowing on it an aura of importance. When objects appear in museums, they become part of 'our' history.

The Imperial War Museum and the Winston Churchill Britain at War Theme Museum (hereafter referred to as the Winston Churchill Museum) are, in many ways, very different sorts of institutions. The Imperial War Museum is a national, state-sponsored museum, following in the traditions of the institutions discussed above and set up largely to educate its visitors in an inclusive sense of national history and identity. Until recently, admission to the museum was free, and its main purpose was to function as a site of officially informed education about British wars in the twentieth century. The Winston Churchill Museum, however, was conceived primarily as a commercial enterprise. Sited next door to the London Dungeon (a museum of crime and punishment featuring realistically gruesome waxwork models of murder victims), its aim seems to be to attract as many paying visitors as possible, and this is partly done by the emphasis in both its publicity material and displays on the most exciting and immediately accessible events of the war years.

However, what these institutions share is the special place of museums in the construction of a public sense of the past. Museums provide one of the principal means by which people can gain access to the past and a special historic legitimacy is conferred upon events and objects when they are included in museums. The past which is displayed in museums becomes known to the museum's visitors, and its place in a museum display ensures that it is embodied with a special significance, an importance which comes from its site within an institution which signifies knowledge and authority. When they become the subject of numerous or particularly important museum exhibitions and displays, aspects of the past can change their meaning. They cease to be just a part of *history* and instead have the potential to become a part of our shared, national, *heritage*.

It is important here to distinguish clearly between heritage and history. If 'history' can be seen as an attempt to represent the past, then 'heritage' is an attempt to take aspects of that past, and inscribe them as especially significant in the collective history of a group of people, be it a class, region or nation.[15] Heritage, then, is closely linked with our need for a sense of the past, a sense of continuity, belonging and identity. This is often represented through a commercialization of the past in 'heritage centres' and 'heritage experiences', the primary concern of which is to make money.[16] In the shift from history to heritage, certain aspects of the event, period or lifestyle being remembered will be prioritized over others, sometimes leading to a sanitized or romanticized view of the past. Of course, it is not just museums and heritage centres which have the power to create heritage; this happens when an aspect of history is foregrounded across a whole range of public sites of communication. However, the special role of museums, their place in our society as sites of authority and official knowledge, means that they have an ability to imbue the subjects of their exhibitions with a particular significance. It is this process which happens in the two representations of the Blitz discussed here.

Because of its inclusion in the Imperial War Museum's Second World War display, and especially because of the prominence it is given there, the Blitz is situated within the museum as an important part of the nation's heritage. However, like the main displays in the Winston Churchill Museum, the 'Blitz Experience' does not display a collection of objects from the past which have been designated as valuable and important enough to be preserved and displayed. Although both museums do display some artefacts from the Second World War, the Imperial War Museum more so than the Winston Churchill Museum, these objects are not a part of their 'Blitz Experiences'. Rather than build a display around historical objects, the curators have created a particular version of the past for people to visit and, importantly, to interact with. In this way, these displays differ fundamentally from more traditional museum displays, which rely upon the existence, discovery and acquisition of objects and artefacts in their presentation of the past.

The main objective of these displays is to present a theme, not to preserve and display a collection of objects. Yet paradoxically, the process of interpretation and recreation becomes less, rather than more, visible. In a 'traditional' museum display the objects on display are often in a glass case, chosen, classified and labelled by the visitors' knowledgeable intermediaries, the curators. In a display without artefacts, and without labels, this process of choice and interpretation becomes hidden. Because these themed museum 'experiences' or heritage displays begin with the choice of a period, event or lifestyle as particularly significant and worthy of commemoration rather than beginning with the discovery or acquisition of artefacts, they have the ability to tell us more about current preoccupations with the past than do the older, object-reliant, forms of museum display. Rather than *preserving* the past, they *create* it.

Within these themed displays, as within heritage centres, the past becomes a place which we can visit. We, the visitors to the past, are often guided through it by actors representing its inhabitants, telling us 'their' story. By making the historian or curator, the interpreter of the past, invisible, the themed display, or experience, gives a particular credence and legitimization to one particular version of events which cannot be achieved to the same extent in the more traditional museum display. The version of past events which they present can be one which sanitizes or omits contested or problematic aspects of the past. It is this process which can be seen in both the Imperial War Museum's 'Blitz Experience' and the Winston Churchill Museum.

Experiencing the Blitz

In 1989 the newly renovated Imperial War Museum welcomed the first visitors to the new 'Blitz Experience'. Publicized as an opportunity for the inhabitants of the late twentieth century to experience the sights, smells and sounds of the Blitz on London of 1940–1, the 'Blitz Experience' formed the new, interactive centrepiece of the museum's Second World War display.[17] Through the 'Blitz Experience', the Blitz is presented as a central part of the body of knowledge which the Second World War exhibition is meant to impart to its visitors. It is the highlight of the display.

The 'Blitz Experience' is situated near the exit from the Second World War display. Visitors are ushered into it by a guide, entering through a small, dark doorway to find themselves in a reconstruction of a London brick-built shelter. The visitors, or shelterers as they are now, are urged on into the shelter by the taped voice of 'George', a local air raid warden, and unmistakable as a working-class man from east London. As the shelter fills more voices appear on the tape, all with strong London accents. Some talk about their day whilst others complain of lack of sleep. As the bombs begin to fall, George leads them in a hearty rendition of 'Roll Out the Barrel'. As the bombs get closer George's daughter Val becomes hysterical, her screams gradually drowning out the singing. A bomb drops uncomfortably close and the shelter reverberates. Everything goes quiet.

The shelterers are then helped outside by the museum guide, whose flashlight plays around the devastated street that they are now standing in. In front of them lies an upturned pram, its front wheel still spinning. Behind this are the ruins of a house. Before the new shelterers become *too* worried about the fates of the occupants of the pram and the house, the voices on the tape reassure each other that the owners of the house were 'bombed out' in the previous week, and so are no longer in residence. It is property which has been destroyed here, not lives. Next the flashlight picks out a bombed pub, and groans can be heard coming from beneath the rubble. This is Albert, the publican, whom, we are told, has always refused to come into the shelter, preferring to sleep behind his bar. The voices reassure Albert until, a few seconds later, the Heavy Rescue Squad appear to dig him out and carry him away on a stretcher, explaining to George's anxious wife Edith that he will be alright. None of this is seen, but is heard on tape. The background to this drama is a diorama of London on fire, dominated by the recurring symbol of London in the Blitz, St Paul's Cathedral. A gasworks in the distance of the diorama explodes and collapses, presumably killing a young warden George has been speaking to who was on his way there. As the shelterers are led through the remains of the street they see the front of a bomb-blasted shop, identified as George's, and hear his son, Harry, crying for his toys. An upper-class WVS woman is heard repeatedly offering tea to the now bombed-out family, and in a nice touch of class antagonism, Edith tells George that 'if she offers me a cup of tea once more I'm going to take that tea urn and ram it down 'er throat!' However, George goes on to tell the visiting shelterers that it was this WVS woman 'what sorted us out in the end with a place at a rest centre'. As the shelterers move towards the exit and the 1990s, George tells them that this was one of the worst nights of London's Blitz. He confides that what kept them going was the knowledge that 'we was all in it together.' As the shelterers leave blitzed London to become museum visitors once more, their last 'experience' of the Blitz is George's fading voice saying 'Don't forget us'.

In late 1992 this representation of London's Blitz was joined by the Winston Churchill Museum in Tooley Street. The publicity for the museum promises potential visitors that it 'makes World War Two come alive' and that visitors will 'experience the sights, sounds and smells of the London Blitz with amazing realistic effects'.[18] Like the Blitz Experience, and like many other privately owned heritage centres, the Winston Churchill Museum does not set out to assemble and display a collection of objects from the past which have been designated as important enough, valuable enough, to be preserved and displayed. Although the museum does display some artefacts from the war, such as cigarette cards, clothes and toys, they are not the main reason for its existence. The display of these objects forms one of three main parts of the Museum, the other two being recreations of a London tube shelter, and of a blitzed street. Two-thirds of the museum are thus devoted to the interactive, themed, 'experience'.

There are two outstanding features of this museum which are particularly relevant to a study of public histories, public stories, about the Second World War. These are, once again, the foregrounding of the 1940–1 Blitz on London as a central, formative experience of the nation at war, and secondly, the emphasis placed, both within the museum's displays and in its title, on Winston Churchill's role as war leader; the intertwining of his personal biography with the history of 'the people' during the Second World War.

As with the 'Blitz Experience', the visitor is encouraged to understand the Blitz by 'experiencing' it, by interacting with it. The visitor is actively encouraged to share the experience of Britain at war, to 'see it . . . feel it . . . breathe it . . . be part of those momentous days'.[19] Descending in a rickety lift, the visitor emerges into a reconstruction of a Tube shelter, where she or he can sit on 'original bales of wartime blankets'[20] to watch a collage of wartime newsreels covering the period from the 'phoney war' of 1939 to the 1942 battle of El Alamein, often described as the turning point of the war for Britain, the British Army's first real victory against the Third Reich. Again, the set-piece shelter is a large communal shelter, although the highest estimate of the total Tube population on any one night was 177,000, less than 5 per cent of London's population.[21] Representations of the Blitz which focus on these large public shelters reinforce the idea that the Blitz was a time when the nation was unified by a common sense of purpose and experience. It is a sanitized version of a minority experience presented as a majority experience, and bears little resemblance to the Tube shelter recalled by a former shelterer in Calder's *The People's War*, who described a place where 'the stench was frightful, urine and excrement mixed with strong carbolic, sweat, and dirty, unwashed humanity'.[22] In contrast this shelter is fairly pleasant: there are chairs, bunk beds, a tea urn and even a well-stocked bookcase. The walls are covered with well-known posters from the war: 'Keep Mum, She's Not So Dumb', 'Careless Talk Costs Lives', and 'Dig for Victory'. All of these slogans would probably be recognized by a majority of adult British visitors to the museum. They act as powerful signifiers of a shared national past; a recognizable part of the dominant popular memory of the war.

Emerging from the Tube shelter, the visitor next walks along a corridor lined with photos of London during the Blitz and newspaper headlines of the time. At the end of this corridor the visitor can choose to enter an Anderson shelter, where she or he can listen to the recorded sounds of an air raid, look at an exhibition called 'The Home Front' which focuses entirely on women's experiences of the war, or pass straight on through 'The Rainbow Bar' (where dummies of a British woman and an American soldier are jitterbugging) to the centrepiece of the museum, the 'Blitz Experience'.

This exhibition differs significantly from the 'Blitz Experience' at the Imperial War Museum. There are no voice-overs and no taped narrative to guide the visitor; instead she or he is left to pick his or her own way through a devastated department store and street. The whole experience is far more disorientating than the Blitz Experience; the large room it is housed in is dark, the floor is uneven and the visitors make their way round the exhibition at their own pace, able to return for a second look at some things whilst bypassing others. There is no George here to guide the visitor, no reminder that 'We was all in it together'. However, like the other display, physical damage to people is minimal; the central figure in the display is a fireman carrying a girl to safety. What are perhaps first thought to be bodies turn out on closer inspection to be mannequins from the bombed shop. Again, the main damage is suffered by property, not people.

Winston Churchill is a central figure in the museum. The museum has chosen as its logo a line drawing of Churchill's famous 'V for Victory' salute and his presence is inescapable within the displays. Whilst the Imperial War Museum emphasizes 'the people's war', the Winston Churchill Museum makes explicit links between Churchill as the nation's leader and the nation as a whole. Illustrations of people during the London Blitz all have quotes from Churchill as their captions: 'Never has so much been owed by so many to so few', 'We shall defend our island whatever the cost may be', 'Give us the tools and we shall finish the job'. The majority of the photographs show people 'carrying on' during the Blitz; postmen picking their way over rubble, shopkeepers opening bombed-out shops, people queuing up for tea from mobile WVS canteens. Churchill is linked with the war in a seamless narrative which has little space for hardship and suffering, and none at all for dissent or dissatis-faction.

Obviously these very public, official memories of the Blitz are partial recollections, foregrounding some images at the expense of others. The injury, death, fear and destruction which dominate some personal memories of the Blitz are overshadowed by images of togetherness and community. This 'writing-out' of problematic memories of the period is by no means unique to these displays, and is perhaps best illustrated by an examination of the problems that one group of people had when trying to find a public site for *their* memories.

On 3 March 1993, the East London Borough of Bethnal Green marked, for the first time, a wartime anniversary. A plaque was unveiled on the staircase of Bethnal Green Tube Station to commemorate the deaths of 173 people there during an air raid on 3 March 1943. The dead were not the direct victims of a bombing raid, but died of suffocation after a woman carrying a baby tripped near the bottom of the steps and fell in the darkness, causing those behind her to fall as well. People had rushed into the shelter after a salvo of new, unfamiliar anti-aircraft rockets from nearby Victoria Park had made them panic. The official Home Office statement said that 'There was built an immovable and interrelated mass of bodies, five, six or more deep.'[23] A local magistrate commented that 'the staircase was ... converted from a corridor to a charnel house in from ten to fifteen seconds'.[24] The Home Secretary, Herbert Morrison, urged stoic-ism on the community, telling them that they were 'a people tested and hardened by the experience of the Blitz and as well able to bear loss bravely as any people in the world'.[25] The tragedy was not reported in the press for two days and when it did appear Bethnal Green was not named, and there was no mention of the possibility of panic amongst the shelterers. The disaster had no official commemoration, no real space in the public representations of the war, and so it became margin-alized, a largely unwritten part of wartime history, and certainly not a part of 'our heritage', only really remembered by those whom it personally affected.

This marginalization of the Bethnal Green Tube tragedy made it ever more difficult for the survivors and bereaved to speak about it. Fifty years on, the unveiling of the commemorative plaque meant that some of them spoke for the first time in public about their memories. One woman remembered visiting the mortuary to find the body of her mother, whose hair had turned white overnight, and that of her two-year-old nephew who had died without a visible mark on him. Another told of trying to hold onto her best friend's hand in the crush, letting go only to find her the next day in the mortuary with her baby brother. Yet another woman said she had never used Bethnal Green station since; another how she ritually counted every one of the steps that people fell down when she used it.[26] There is no mention of this tragedy in either of the museum displays, just as there is no mention of the times when bombs fell on Balham Tube, injuring 600 people, at Bank, killing 100, or at Marble Arch, killing 20.[27] Memories like this, of death, tragedy and grief, have little space in the 'Blitz Experiences'. When they *are* present they are both marginalized and sanitized, surpassed by more positive images of the period.

When looking at the process of public remembering it is important to discover what has been forgotten, in order better to understand what has been remembered. Remembering, both public and private, is a process of sifting, as some events and images are discarded or put aside whilst others are carefully saved. However, the museum displays, like the wider public memories of the war, do not *entirely* forget memories such as these. If this was the case, they would not win such a wide audience; the absence of any suffering at all would mark them out as unrealistic representations of the period. Instead, problematic memories and images of the Blitz can be present, but tend to be sanitized and modified, overwhelmed by more positive images of the war. This process can be illustrated by the script for the Imperial War Museum's 'Blitz Experience'.

Whilst the 'Blitz Experience' privileges notions of community togetherness and national unity over images of fear and destruction, these more problematic images and memories are still present. Behind the singing of 'Roll Out the Barrel', the warden's daughter can be heard screaming hysterically. Houses are destroyed and people are injured. A young, unnamed warden of whom we hear once is killed when the gasworks explodes. George's shop is hit and he and his family have to move into temporary accommodation. He tells the visitors that 'some parts of London was prepared for the Blitz. Well, ours certainly wasn't . . . it was the most miserable winter I've ever known.' However, these memories of fear, injury, death, discomfort and official incompetence are small in comparison to the more popular memories given prominence here: memories such as the community singing in the shelter, 'cockney' humour and the notion which is central to the 'Blitz Experience': 'We was all in it together'.

The fifth draft of the script for the 'Blitz Experience', the one which was being used for the display in 1993, illustrates the process by which problematic images and memories become marginalized and sometimes eventually disappear. The original script for the 'Blitz Experience' contained references to the physical destruction of *people* by bombs, the lack of sanitation, light and heat in the public shelters, and the fact that some shelters were built quickly without adequate cement, collapsing easily if a bomb fell nearby, and causing many casualties and deaths.[28] Gone is George's original description of shelters with 'no lavatory – just a bucket. Cold, dark, damp'.[29] Gone too is Val's story about a shelter in which all the occupants died: 'They said it weren't built with any cement. Just collapsed it did. I saw them – bits of bodies everywhere.'[30] Missing as well is Val's description of the infamous Tilbury Shelter in the East End, where 'there's s'posed to be over 14,000 people living'.[31] In the eventual script, all these references were cut; they cannot be made to fit with a picture of the Blitz which privileges images of good-humoured cockneys, community spirit and national unity over and above the images of death, injury and destruction which feature in many individual memories of the period. There is very little space for these memories on the public stage.

There are many similarities in the processes of public and private remembering discussed here, both essentially being processes by which the past is shaped by the present; processes of selection, reordering and reconstruction. They are, of course, often interdependent on each other: the museum displays discussed here would not work if they were entirely unrepresentative of people's experiences and memories of the period; one of the reasons why people have felt it difficult to talk publicly about the Bethnal Green disaster is because of its lack of commemoration in the public sphere. Perhaps most importantly, memory is never fixed, but always open to further reinterpretation and reshaping according to present events and preoccupations. The conclusion will outline what these very public sites of memory can tell us about Britain in the 1990s.

Conclusions: Remembering the Blitz

Ideas about the past are central to conceptions of British nationhood. Representations of the Second World War such as those discussed here work to remind us that 'We' can all 'pull together' if needs be; emphasizing notions of togetherness and community in the face of adversity. They present a picture of the nation in which 'the people' are central. Yet 'the people' of the 'Blitz Experience' and the Winston Churchill Museum are a people denuded of almost all class antagonism and of all revolutionary potential. In 1940, far from being an immediately unifying experience, the Blitz had the potential to increase the class divisions seen in the 1930s: one local Essex dignitary reacted to the influx of Londoners fleeing the bombs by declaring 'I won't have these people billeted on our people',[32] and the Communist Party organized an invasion of the Savoy Hotel's luxurious private shelter in protest at the lack of safe public shelters in the East End. This divisive aspect of the early days of the Blitz, when bombing was almost exclusively concentrated on the socially marginal working-class and immigrant areas of the East End, have all but disappeared from today's public representations of the Blitz. George in the 'Blitz Experience' tells visitors 'We was all in it together', whilst the display in the Winston Churchill Museum links quotes of Churchill with photographs of 'the people' to produce a seamless picture of a united Britain. Today's public memory of the war, the memory which dominates the museum displays discussed here, speaks to us of a nation unproblematically united in battle.

This public memory of the war is one which is specific to Britain in the 1980s and 1990s. It is a concept of the past which is central to ideas of British nationhood which have become closely associated with the New Right, and which was seen in particularly sharp relief during the Falklands/Malvinas War of 1982, during which links were drawn, both in political discourse and in much of the media, between the national aims of both wars, a national unity which overrode any internal divisions, and a Conservative leadership.[33] The democratizing, modernizing people's war, which led to the landslide electoral victory for a reforming Labour government in 1945, has been claimed and reshaped by the contemporary Right as a key moment in Britain's national past; the last time that Britain was still 'Great'.

The authoritative nature of museums, and the absence of visible interpreters of the past in the 'Blitz Experience' and the Winston Churchill Museum, makes them particularly powerful producers of a public past. The images of the Blitz seen here could be experienced by visitors as absolute and unquestionable; the aim being to produce an 'experience' which is as 'real' as possible. Oppositional or problematic images of the Blitz are overwhelmed by more positive images; images which serve to support the New Right's construction of British national identity as something natural and unchanging, untouched by 'modern' impositions such as the politics of gender, race or class.

In a nation which has experienced massive social economic and political changes over the past fifteen years the Blitz, a time of huge disruption and uncertainty, has come to act as a symbol of unity and continuity. It is this memory of the nation at war which is reinforced in these displays and passed on to visitors, including children and foreign tourists. The displays of the 'Blitz Experience' perhaps tell us more about our state of mind today then they do about Britain in the Second World War.

Notes

1. From the nineteenth-century scrapbook of a 'Mr W.A. of Peckham', cited in C. Sorenson, 'Theme parks and time machines', in Verso (1989), p. 61.
2. Remaining bombs were also often 'dumped' over coastal towns by German pilots returning to the Continent after bombing large towns and cities.
3. Calder (1969), p. 164.
4. Until 1943, more civilians than members of the armed forces were killed in the war. A total of 60,950 people died as a result of the bombing campaigns, of whom about half were women. Summerfield and Braybon (1987), pp. 2–3.
5. Calder (1991).
6. The idea of imagined communities used here is drawn from Anderson (1983).
7. Hewison (1987), pp. 86–7.
8. Ibid., p. 86.
9. Yeo and Yeo (1988), p. 236.
10. Duncan and Wallach (1980).
11. Condell (1985), p. 34.
12. *The Times*, 26 March 1917, p. 20, cited in Condell (1985), p. 23.
13. 'The King's Dedicatory Speech, Crystal Palace, 9 June 1920', cited in Condell (1985), p. 149.
14. Foster (1936), p. 215.
15. I recognize that this is a vastly simplified definition of history, practitioners of which of course choose to focus on particular areas and claim a special significance for their particular field of research. However, for the purposes of this chapter, it is necessary to define history in this way *specifically* in relation to heritage. History differs from heritage in the ways in which it is presented to and known by the public, and in the general significance given to particular aspects of the past. Consumption, perhaps, is the key difference between heritage and history.
16. Merriman (1991), p. 8.
17. Publicity leaflet for the Imperial War Museum, subtitled 'Part of Your Family's History'.
18. Publicity leaflet for the Winston Churchill Britain at War Theme Museum, 1992.
19. Ibid.
20. Ibid.
21. Calder (1969), p. 157. These figures are given for 27 September 1940,

near the beginning of the Blitz when the highest numbers of people were attempting to shelter from bombing.

22. Ibid., p. 183.
23. Dunne (1943), p. 5.
24. Cited in *The Times*, 1 March 1993.
25. Ibid.
26. Ibid., and the *Independent*, 4 March 1993.
27. Calder (1969), pp. 338–9 and p. 183.
28. Ibid., p. 113.
29. 'Blitz Experience Script' fifth draft, undated, Imperial War Museum, p. 3.
30. Ibid., p. 7.
31. Ibid., p. 11. This shelter, where thousands of people sheltered every night is vividly described by a Mass Observation team which visited it in September 1940:

> A dense block of people, nothing else. By 7.30 p.m. every bit of floor space taken up. Deckchairs, blankets, stools, seats, pillows . . . people lying everywhere. The floor was awash with urine. Only two lavatories for 5,000 women, none for men . . . overcome by smell. People are sleeping on piles of rubbish . . . the passages are loaded with filth. Lights dim or non-existent . . . they sit, in darkness, head of one against feet of the next . . . there is no room to move and hardly any to stretch. Some horses are still stabled there, and their mess mingles with that of the humans. (cited in Calder (1969), p. 117)

32. Calder (1969), p. 166.
33. For a detailed discussion of the memories of the Second World War dominant within political discourse in 1982, see Barnett (1982).

Bibliography

Primary Sources

Publicity leaflets for the Imperial War Museum and the Winston Churchill Britain at War Theme Museum, 1989 and 1992.
Fifth draft of 'Blitz Experience' script, Imperial War Museum.
The Times.
The Independent.

Secondary Sources

Anderson, B. (1983), *Imagined Communities*, London: Verso.
Barnett, A. (1982), *Iron Britannia*, London: Allison & Busby.

Calder, A. (1969), *The People's War 1939–1945*, London: Cape.

Calder, A. (1991), *The Myth of the Blitz*, London: Cape.

Condell, D. (1985), 'The Imperial War Museum 1917–1920. A study of the institution and its presentation of the First World War', unpublished Mphil dissertation, Imperial War Museum.

Dawson, G. and West, B. (1984), 'Our finest hour? The popular memory of World War Two and the struggle over national identity', in G. Hurd (ed.), *National Fictions: World War Two in British Films and Television*, London: BFI Books.

Duncan, C. and Wallach, A. (1980), 'The Universal Survey Museum', in *Art History*, vol. 3, no. 4, pp. 448–69.

Dunne, L. R. (1943), Magistrate of the Police Courts of the Metropolis, *Home Office Enquiry into an Accident at the London Tube Station*, London: Home Office.

Hewison, R. (1987), *The Heritage Industry. Britain in a Climate of Decline*, London: Methuen.

Merriman, N. (1991), *Beyond the Glass Case: The Past, the Heritage and the Public in Britain*, Leicester: Leicester University Press.

Summerfield, P. and Braybon, G. (1987), *Out of the Cage: Women in the Two World Wars*, London: Pandora.

Verso, P. (ed.) (1989), *The New Museology*, London: Reaktion.

Yeo, E. and Yeo, S. (1988), 'On the uses of community from Owenism to the present', in S. Yeo (ed.), *New Views of Co-operation*, London: Routledge.

7

Love Letters versus Letters Carved in Stone: Gender, Memory and the 'Forces Sweethearts' Exhibition

Margaretta Jolly

The 'Forces Sweethearts' exhibition put on by the Imperial War Museum in 1993 commemorated a very different war experience from that of the outsize guns and mottled tanks that loom in the museum's central gallery. It invited us to peep into heart-shaped cases at mannequins in Great War wedding dresses; the scarlet sequinned strapless of a Marilyn Monroe pin-up; a tumble of trinkets and bouquet upon bouquet of faded letters. Charting wartime romance from the First World War to the Gulf, the exhibition was about the flip side of battle, the home life, dreams and fantasies of those in the services. It was a recognition of 'private' life, which to a large extent is also where those in the services 'escaped' from war. It also put women in the forefront. The exhibition thus potentially waded into interesting and radical waters. Certainly, the exhibition director, Pennie Ritchie Calder, suggested that it was considered as a new, if not quite controversial, departure for the museum's trustees, focusing as it did on 'personal feelings and emotions'. This direction was partly motivated by a need to attract a new sector of the public as well as to 'feminize the museum'.[1] In this it was successful. Coachloads of old ladies made unprecedented visits to Lambeth and takings rocketed at a time when all museums were struggling to keep themselves viable.[2] The exhibition also received a huge amount of media coverage and spawned the best-selling accompanying book written by Joanna Lumley.[3]

However, unsurprisingly perhaps, the exhibition presented an anachronistic and limited conception of love in war. The 'down side' of love in war – abortion, divorce, sexual disease, heartbreak and death – was hugely underplayed. Gay or lesbian sweethearts were entirely absent. This was intentional. As Ritchie Calder put it, the museum wished to 'celebrate' and commemorate rather than provide a representative social history. The increasing critical interest in the way that wars are being commemorated makes such a choice interesting, and this chapter will examine how that 'celebration' of wartime love was constructed and what it meant. In particular, it will focus on the exhibition of letters as a form of memory. Ephemeral, private and partial, they represent the opposite pole from monuments to the fallen in remembering war. But the symbolic properties of those individual texts as love letters, it will be argued, were nevertheless mobilized into a comparable hegemonic memory – one that was comic and redeeming rather than tragic or warning, but no less powerful. What is the relation of this kind of romance narrative to the usual public commemoration of war? How does its version of gender relations structure the public memory of recent wars? These much broader questions will be approached by way of a journey through the exhibition's rosy-lit curving gallery reverberating with the strains of Vera Lynn, with reference to interviews with some of the visitors making that same journey.

The Exhibition as Text

The exhibition was an imaginative set piece, comparable to the museum's Blitz and Trench displays, which plunge the visitor into a complete sensory experience, with lights, sound and even smell effects. It was housed in a twisting, organically shaped corridor of corrugated tin walls, inset with red velvet cases and doused with a dim pink light that seemed to waver along with the wistful crooning of 'We'll Meet Again'. The first room displayed 'The Dream Girls', a survey of pin-ups and military entertainers' paraphernalia. These ranged from Second World War aircraft 'nose art' to a hotwater bottle in the shape of a Varga-style pin-up; Rita Hayworth's cigarette case and compact and the fan mail of the saucy Second World War cartoon strip pin-up Jane; and a homely photo of the Princess of Wales that was very popular in the Falklands War. It also, more controversially, showed some modern pin-ups of a 'page three' genre, which made a definite contrast to the demure water-colours of First World War postcards. One display, for example, told us how model Gail McKenna's topless shot got her voted 'Miss Tabouk' by men serving on an RAF base at Tabouk during the Gulf War in 1991. The editor of the base newssheet, bypassing Saudi Arabian censorship, had arranged for the *Sun* newspaper to send out photos of six models from which the choice was made. Also on display was a letter from Major-General Mike Jackson of the Ministry of Defence, dated 21 September 1992, thanking Miss Ewin for visiting and entertaining a British contingent in the UN Protection Forces and being a 'tremendous morale booster'. He wrote: 'We are doing our best to improve the welfare conditions out there for our troops and it is so important for artists such as yourself to provide that vital link back home.'

Before passing into the next room, visitors could snatch a momentary memory of Second World War love in a moonlit dappled corner, where a man and woman's old fashioned bikes rested side by side, their baskets filled with trench hat, letter, groceries. An old post-box was inset into the brick, another acknowledgement of the vital role that letters played in wartime relationships, and a tribute to the Royal Mail who were sponsoring half the costs of the exhibition at £40,000. You then went into a section titled 'The Real Thing', which told you, according to the press release, of 'the meetings, the partings, the reunions and the heartbreaking stories of the men who didn't come home'. It displayed rings, lockets, poems, sweetheart brooches, pressed flowers and love letters, including the correspondence which has made the *Guinness Book of Records*: 6,000 letters exchanged by a padre and his fiancée in the Second World War. Here, the peepshow cases were fronted by round red velvet stools, which ingeniously evoked both boudoir and Hollywood dressing-room within the womb-like feel of the exhibition as a whole. The visitor passed then through a narrow scooped passage on which was printed a *mélange* of statistics documenting the 'B-side' of wartime romance (as Ritchie Calder described it), numbers not just of letters sent and lengths of servicemen's time overseas, but of deaths, venereal disease, illegitimacy and divorces. Finally one emerged into a pale green corridor representing 'Wartime Weddings'. Oval panels displayed wedding presents, telegrams, photographs, honeymoon hotel bills and orange blossom and, principally, the 'Gowns'. Highly prized and lovingly preserved, their silk and satin, sometimes concocted from curtains and parachute silk in the 'Make Do and Mend' style of the Second World War, were particularly emotive. In between, blurred and faded black and white wedding photos showed couples smiling for the camera in the face of unknown futures. The visitor then stepped out into the cool high vault of the central gallery, returning to the suspended, still and strangely abstract technologies of planes and guns.

From Pin-ups to 'The Real Thing'

The exhibition was conceived in 1986 by Pennie Ritchie Calder, the museum's exhibitions director. She had come across a photo of Cherry Richards, the first officially condoned army pin-up, on the cover of the army magazine *Soldier* of 18 August 1945. Interested in her 'girl-next-door' look and her home-made bathing costume (originally an old vest), Ritchie Calder wondered what had become of her. Inspired by the picture, she thought of doing a whole exhibition of pin-ups, and then of expanding this to wartime romance. But from the start the transition from pin-ups to what the museum had positioned as 'real' romance was awkward. Feminism has shown the whole relation of images of women to actual heterosexual relationships to be profoundly complex and controversial, and the exhibition appeared to show an interesting naiveté about simply juxtaposing them. At its most obvious, the pin-ups display risked seeming simply sexist. The designers were certainly aware of this to the extent that they urged servicewomen to send in their pin-ups. But they got no response – 'Soldier Girls Guard Secrets' said the *Wolverhampton Express and Star*,[4] and the *Shropshire Star* told us that:

> Generations of bashful women soldiers are refusing to 'kiss and tell' about the men of their dreams. While their male counterparts are happy to talk about their fantasy women, the female troops are maintaining a determined silence. The I.W.M. is urging all servicemen and women who served in conflicts from WW1 through to the Gulf to reveal their morale-boosting secrets for a special Forces Sweethearts exhibition. But organizer Pennie Ritchie Calder said that while there had been a good response from the men, not one woman had responded to her appeal. 'They do seem to be terribly modest about declaring their interests in men,' she said today. 'It would be nice to know who they talked about when the lights went out at night.'[5]

The apparently one-sided 'Dream Girls' display was therefore justified as historically accurate. But the criterion of historical accuracy was only partially considered, since the organizers also deliberately suppressed material that might have offended visitors, such as 'American pin-ups from the Korean War' which are 'just too explicit' or too obvious a display of condoms. There was also a noticeable dearth of references to non-white soldiers or sweethearts, particularly given the large number of interracial relationships during the Second World War, as well as any reference to 'fraternisation with the enemy'. Perhaps most inconsistent was the lack of any representation of lesbians and gay sweethearts. This was partly due to the fact that no material was sent in (although Ritchie Calder said they hadn't advertised in the lesbian and gay press, and there is now a considerable amount of published as well as archival material on twentieth-century gay history),[6] but more fundamentally because:

> We thought that if we then started looking at the whole question of homosexuality . . . we might upset the sensibilities of visitors or those in authority . . .. We took the easy option and probably the less courageous option . . . but . . . I think it would have led to it being . . . judged as a different sort of exhibition to the one we'd intended because everybody would have leapt on that bandwagon . . . they would have said 'Lesbians rule at the Imperial War Museum!' and I think that would have just meant the whole thing would have from the start been taken completely the wrong way.[7]

Discussion with a group of elderly women about the issue in the exhibition confirmed Ritchie Calder's view – producing comments like: 'it didn't exist'; 'well, it did exist but we didn't talk about it'; 'this is an exhibition about then, not now'; and most revealingly: 'this is turning into a sex-talk!'[8]

Clearly the trouble is about sexuality. While the notion of romance obviously involves a certain displacement of the sexual, it can be suggested that lesbian and gay relationships were not included because they are perceived as sexual rather than romantic.[9] More generally, military culture tends to encourage a regression to stereotypical ideas of femininity, in which the notions of 'home' and 'front' are synonymous with the dichotomy between women and men, and also between 'wife' and prostitute 'camp-followers'. The opposition between home and front has always been more a construct than a reality, and with today's military technology is even more clearly so. But that fundamental opposition between masculine and feminine, and within that, 'women for love' and 'women for sexual release', remains crucial to military ideology. At the same time, both these oppositions are highly unstable themselves, and at one level, compete against each other. The exhibition's attempt to separate sex and romance structurally in separate rooms, while uniting them under the single notion of 'Forces Sweethearts', testifies to this instability. Managing that transition from 'male-defined' 'pin-up' to 'female-defined' 'Real Thing' was far from easy, as the censorship of the 'explicitly' sexual showed. The quest to find out what happened to the 1944 pin-up Cherry Richards, whose 'girl-next-doorish' woollen vest swimming costume started the whole thing off, seems to me another level at which the divide was 'managed'. The press was given the story that 'Cherry' had been twenty when the picture was taken and came from Doncaster. Eventually she was found living on a housing estate in Yorkshire, 'Still a stunner!' After the original photo was taken she had been deluged with fan mail and offers of marriage but, already married for three years, she did not go on with the career and 'her home and family became the most important things in her life'.[10] Thus the pin-up was symbolically domesticated through romantic quest.[11]

The choice of Joanna Lumley as the author of the exhibition's accompanying book represented another working-out of this tension. Ritchie Calder described how the trustees' original idea of Jilly Cooper, who had already written a book on animals in war, did not come to fruition. Lumley, the second choice, proved ideal. Free from the titillating, if not sleazy, associations of Cooper, she was perfect as a pin-up herself, but 'in the nicest possible way', and possessed of both an upper-class army background and a 'mumsy' sincerity,[12] or as the *Tatler* put it more nastily: 'She is more a cheesecake version of Maggie Smith than a sex siren.'[13]

Of course, the sexual segregation that still underlies military ideology today has meant that pin-ups have always tended to represent domestic as well as sexual fantasies for male soldiers, as the offers of marriage Cherry Richards received from readers of *Soldier* show; though the reasons for this are complex, and perhaps are more true for the lower ranks, since their sexuality is far more controlled by commandants' policies on leave, sexual disease, prostitution and homosexuality. At any rate, the reaction of some visitors to the pin-ups section of the exhibition testified to the continuing liveliness of the issue.[14] Women interviewed without exception expressed discomfort at the increasing sexualization of the pin-ups over the century, although they accepted the idea of pin-ups' normality or even necessity for 'male morale'. Men's reactions ranged from slight embarrassment to disclaiming any personal interest, while also looking back to a more 'innocent era'.

Letters, Women and True-Life Love Stories

So what of 'The Real Thing'? Tribute should first of all be made to the museum for collecting the mementoes, stories and letters that fill not just this section of the exhibition, but their excellent archives. Many of the letters are not only moving but fascinating: as Lumley says, 'blubhissima' stuff!'[15] However it is not these items' historical value that will be assessed, but their effect on the visitor and the way they work in the exhibition and book. Most of the material dates from the Second World War, not only because that provided the bulk of contributions from the public, but because of the era's distinctive phenomenon of 'courtship by mail'; its new opportunities for unexpected meetings with the opposite sex, particularly with the stationing of foreign troops in Britain; and the much longer periods when men were without leave. The story of Denis and Edith is a typical Second World War 'plot'. Lumley deftly narrates it using short extracts from Denis's diary (nothing if not brief), and Edith's reminiscences. In the summer of 1940, he was a fighter pilot and she a bomber and fighter plotter in the operations room at Debden. On 29 September, his diary entry reads: 'Did nothing during the day but there was the usual band in the Mess and when they packed up I completed the party at the Sergeants' Mess. Met Edith Heap and fell in love with her at sight. I rather cut Margaret Cameron and I am not so popular with her as I was!!!' The speed of his attachment to Edith is innocently comic against his prosaic style. The innocence is underlined by Edith's account of their trip to Cambridge where he was very worried about the hotel only having a double room (though not a double bed) and their immediate engagement over a bottle of bubbly at the Red Lion: 'oh place of sublime happiness', remembers Edith. But the story turns dramatically bittersweet when Edith, on watch a couple of weeks later, heard a cry of 'Blue 4 going down into the sea'. Nobody else knew who the pilot was – but she did.[16]

We don't actually know from the book what Edith did in later life, or whether she remained single. But her story reminds us that part of the 'writing to the moment' effect of letters and diaries is not just their immediacy, but their innocence of the future. The later reader is given the immense power of superior knowledge of what happened later, even of the 'ending' of the writer's life, while by contrast, the writer becomes an unconscious prisoner of time. This aesthetic makes for an inevitable pathos, which the museum uses to great effect. This is particularly true of the case of a series of letters that get special attention in the book because they are so extremely innocent and full of faith in a future that wasn't to be, and because they seem in that way emblematic of the First World War. Lumley gives us the background:[17]

> 1916. Will Martin and Emily Chitticks were sweethearts, but not yet officially engaged. Will was serving with the Royal 1st Devon Yeomanry in Essex and Norfolk. He had been brought up by this aunt, disliked his own mother who had treated him badly and longed for the day when he and Emily could have a home of their own.

The letters of both are unpretentious, shyly teasing – she prodding him to 'mention' their engagement 'to Dad', he saying he might be able to summon up the courage if he did it by letter, and hoping the ring he sent her fits. He does not mention his work or surroundings until the last letter (of those reproduced), in which he tells her that he has volunteered to go across to France:

> I can scarcely understand why so many people fall in love and appreciate me so much. It is quite a new sensation to be thought so much of, but I am glad for your sake. I hope you will always have occasion to be proud of me, dear . . . By the way, dear, they asked for volunteers to go to Devonport to train with the 3rd Devons as infantry, and of course go across eventually. I have volunteered for it, but I shall have to pass a medical examination first . . . It is nothing to worry about, dear. Now, Sweetheart, I will close with fondest love & lots of kisses, from
> Your Loving Sweetheart
> xxxx Will xxxx

The next letter is from his Commanding Officer, Mr Caleb, 'regretting to inform her . . .', and her own letters were returned marked 'Killed in Action'. By the time Caleb got her reply saying that she was proud that Will had done his duty, he too had been killed. The story has an extra pathos and mystery to it. Even though she didn't yet know that her fiancé had been killed, for some reason Emily suddenly started writing in red ink the day after he died. She left a note requesting that his letters be buried with her, but it was only found years after her own death – too late for even that reunion.[18]

These kinds of letters, in which we see the 'private man' in the soldier, defined by feelings not action, and by the individual women he loves, not by the army he serves, whether happily or not, make one rage at the futility of men's sacrifice in war, particularly when the content of the letter is as far from violence as Will's. It seems almost impossible to unify the man and the soldier in many of them, and it is this which moves the spectator as much as pity for their fates. Indeed, it is that classic contradiction in the masculine military identity that gives them, and the exhibition, their punch.[19] The exhibition shows us the soldier, and this is arguably more so of the ordinary working-class soldier, confiding his personal feelings to his sweetheart (or his mother or, sometimes, even his daughter), and how those women typically come to represent the locus of his private hopes and fears cathected around the idea of 'home' and, to a lesser extent, around 'desire'.[20] These personal records, then, are the drama of that military split between private and public, femininity and masculinity. To that extent, they testify to the pain that ideology can mean in men's and women's actual experiences of war and, in a simple sense, are evidence of how central women are to the military institution. Cynthia Enloe in her brilliant book *Does Khaki Become You: The Militarization of Women's Lives*, summarizes:

> Soldiers' lives are hard. Even away from the dangers of the battlefield, they are subject to and possibly made discontented by hierarchical command structures and perpetual uprooting. Yet commanders need men who will soldier with a sense of fervour and a willingness to sacrifice. 'Morale' preoccupies officers, and a good commander is one who can create 'good morale' in the ranks. To portray the soldier's regiment as a 'family' which cares for him and to whom he owes loyalty is one solution. But without women, this is a difficult enterprize. If women can be made to play the role of wives, daughters, mothers, and 'sweethearts', waving their men off to war, writing them letters of encouragement and devotion in the field, reminding them that women's and children's safety depends on men's bravery, *then* women can be an invaluable resource to commanders.[21]

Enloe shows how military strategists have always crucially depended on women's labour as wives, prostitutes, defence workers, mothers and more. But the essence of military ideology is to deny that dependence on women. In relation to the sexual and emotional lives of soldiers, this sets up an oppressive opposition between their identification with the army and other men, and that with women. Enloe summarizes the military authorities' perpetual question: 'How can women whom military men have relationships with be controlled so as to minimize women's influence on military operations while at the *same time* maintain the morale and re-enlistments of the men themselves?'[22]

In wartime, pin-ups and even more so letters from home are on one level part of that attempt to govern the dichotomy between femininity and masculinity, individual and collective identity: but to that extent they are always disturbed as well as disturbing. The huge efforts of military authorities to ensure good postal services between home and front are therefore accompanied by a highly ideological agenda about the do's and don'ts of writing to the forces. This was particularly true in the Second World War, in the ubiquitous discourse in the popular press on keeping up morale 'by mail'. A central feature of the discourse concerned reassuring soldiers of women's loyalty, and specifically, of their fidelity. Of course, infidelity by both men and women was common and is one of the issues examined in 'The Real Thing'. But again, while men's infidelity is condoned, chastity is reinforced for women as a patriotic as well as a personal duty. The significant sexualization of mainstream images of women during the Second World War makes this especially paradoxical, and is implied in the strangely contradictory advice to women to both be 'sincere' in their letters and yet not to mention anything that might depress an absent man – summed up in one magazine's rather facetious proposal that the first commandment on writing to your serviceman is 'Don't Mention Other Men!'[23] Vera Lynn's weekly radio show 'Sincerely Yours – a letter in words and music', started in 1941, perhaps epitomized the connection between femininity, fidelity, sincerity, letter-writing and male morale, just as she herself epitomized the ideal 'Forces Sweetheart'.

It is thus not surprising that the dramatic tension between public and private identities in the men's letters is very differently played out in the women's letters that are displayed and archived. There is often no comparable struggle of identity, such as between loyalty and a desire to explore new freedoms in their partner's absence.[24] This can seem particularly paradoxical when war has been the occasion for new opportunities for women in the public sphere, especially through the mass employment of women in the Second World War. But women's letters typically testify to the continuity of their identification first and foremost with their partner and their family. Indeed the classic difficulty for the Forces Sweetheart is about maintaining an identity through writing that is over-defined through her relationship with a man that is absent and 'othered'. This is not wholly disempowering. Women's insistence in their letters upon their need and desire for the other can at times subvert the 'good girl–bad girl' opposition. Indeed, women are typically encouraged to identify patriotic duty with their personal loyalty to soldiers specifically to combat what military authorities perceive as women's dangerously individual pull on male soldiers away from military identification. A letter from Lucille DesCoteau, an eighteen-year-old American girl, to General MacArthur, is a striking example of where these tensions are held in check:[25]

> Lowell, Mass. July 30, 1943.
> Dear and Brave General MacArthur:
> Before you read any further, please ask yourself this question, 'Am I General Douglas MacArthur?' If you are an assistant or mail summarizer, you need not read any further. I am sure that you are doing your best in trying to help the greatest man God ever created, but if your answer is 'no' to that question, please deliver this letter *right away* to General MacArthur because this letter is very important – make sure that *he* gets it right away.
> Dear General, by this time you must have my letter, and I beg you, please do not tear it and throw it in the waste basket. Because, in this letter, *I want to pour out my heart to you – my own life, I think, could never equal the value of what this letter can perhaps do*, [my italics] so you see how much it means. I know it is very bold and forward of me to write to you – a great General – but *my heart is pushing the pen right along and will not let it stop.* [my italics] So, if you don't think you have time right this minute, then put it aside until you do find a few moments – but please read it . . .
> My childhood sweetheart and fiancé, Staff Sgt Joseph Roland Dennis Simoneau, enlisted in the Army in 1939. Brave, wasn't he? He lied about his age because he wanted so much to be helping his Country. But, he turned 18 two months later. I will never forget that night – 5 years ago young as we were – I was in my first year of high school – I was fourteen years old – he was seventeen, but we knew our hearts. He said to me, 'Lou, we are too young for love – we must pass this stage of growing up before we can really appreciate what love is; you must continue to be a good girl and I must make a man of myself – we must learn not to be selfish. I want and desire you so much, Lou, and I will work so hard. I will go to school and study hard, and become someone, and I will do everything my Superiors in the Army request of me.' And with those words, he left me . . . And now I am putting in 48 hours and sometimes 55 hours a week working in a War Plant. I still use every minute of my spare time praying for him. He was reported 'missing in action' shortly after the surrender. And, I lived in doubt until three weeks ago when he was reported a Jap[anese] prisoner at a Java camp by the Japanese Red Cross . . .
> But it is him I am fighting for. I do not care if he never wants me when and *if* he does ever return. All I want is mercy for him . . .

The letter is uncomfortable as much as it is moving. On the one hand, we have the traditional epistolary tropes of sincerity, artlessness, emotion: her heart not her mind writes, 'pushing her pen along'. It is as if in her disarmingly personal address, she transfers the language of love to the General. But this jibes with the rhetorical framing of her love story, in which Joseph's address to her suddenly distances herself from the writing 'I' and tinges the letter with self-consciousness. At the same time, that self-objectification, as the private language of desire negotiates the public language of patriotism, like her job at the war plant, manifestly does not offer her an alternative identification to that of lover. She is willing to give her life for her lover's even if he doesn't want her when he returns; her own life's value is less than the possible effect of the letter. Of course, letters by their very nature symbolize fidelity, but what strikes home is that while war may paradoxically reveal the private man, it doesn't reveal the private woman, since she is already naturalized as such.

These kinds of constraints should warn us against reading letters as simple reflections of 'The Real Thing', especially given the deliberate cultivation of 'sincerity' in Second World War culture. But if we read war letters not as empirical historical records, but as expressions of history's fantasies, we may retrieve their radical energy, which the exhibition clearly harnesses. Mavis and Gerald Bunyan's correspondence brings out an important aspect of this: the physical quality of letters. The couple were separated for two and a half years when Gerald was posted to the Far East during the Second World War, during which time they exchanged 1,259 letters. Gerald writes on 13 July 1945:

> Today, my lovely, there was no mail from you and I was so disappointed. It is greedy of me really 'cos they come through so quickly. Letters! Letters! Letters! They are all we have and they should be kisses – sweetly intimate kisses arising from our physical love. I seem tongue-tied and cannot find words enough to mirror the thoughts of my heart. If we were together, my adorable girl, my hands could 'talk' with caresses and we would converse in the most beautiful way in the world. It is something between you and I, darling, something that nobody can ever share.[26]

Letters are not just the means of communication but a physical token of the absent other, that gives them a fetishistic quality, easily recognizable by the importance of their physical aspects: the handwriting; the envelope; the way they are hoarded or tied in ribbons. Although Gerald writes that he is 'tongue-tied', unable to 'mirror' his thoughts, the letter itself begins to 'talk' physically as he finishes: 'This letter must be a jumble darling 'cos my thoughts have just trickled off the nib, as they came.' It is not just men who fetishize letters and photos.[27] Here is Mavis's description of receiving a longed-for photo of Gerald:

> I have been such a happy girl all day, beloved. It is a good thing that the pictures do not wear out with being looked at. I cannot describe the feeling it gave me, but as I first looked at it, it was as though you were suddenly in the room with me and my heart seemed to turn somersaults inside me. I almost felt as though, if I put my fingers to your lips, I would feel them so soft and warm. I wanted to touch your face, run my fingers through your hair, as I have done so often in other days. You said it wasn't a good photograph but I think it is the best one there ever was of you.[28]

The much less sexual, more romantic language in which she describes her desire for him may typify differences in the sexes' education, but perhaps ultimately more fundamental is the way her letters demonstrate the more personalized nature of women's fantasies compared to men's. Gerald writes his passionate letter after returning from a showing of the film *Bathing Beauties* in which he declares the 'many "luscious" girls had no effect on me except to increase my longing for you almost to breaking point', but his contrast is self-conscious. This is perhaps the exhibition's most inadvertent admission, as its divide between the pin-ups of male fantasy and 'The Real Thing' sets up the letters and personal photos as the contrasting monument to female sexuality. The irony is that in the military context, such typically female individualized desire gains a public status and even danger.

Letters' capacity to arouse fantasies of the other's presence are at their most bittersweet when a letter arrives after the sender has died. As the poet Roy Fuller put it beautifully in 'War Letters': 'A pair might cease to live / While the indestructible letter, / Turned lies, flew to the other'.[29] In this sense, the letter is transformed into a bizarre monument, its usually ephemeral writing suddenly sinisterly 'indestructible' compared to human mortality. While, on the one hand, this makes for an ironic parody of the artistic paradigm of the transcendence of writing, the inherent drama of that most extreme contradiction between the sense of presence and the knowledge of absence ensures that this 'genre' of wartime letter is often reproduced in anthologies and exhibitions. 'Forces Sweethearts' was no exception – indeed, Ritchie Calder's comment that these 'stand on their own' as exhibits suggests precisely the way they fulfil a criterion of aesthetic structure. Lumley's book contains several letters that were written to be sent in the event of death, ranging from Frederick Baker's sober last instructions to his four-year-old daughter for when she was older, to the generous last love letter from a young submariner, Ivor Gwyn Williams:

18.4.41
Dearest Betty,
Betty, my darling, I think that you won't mind me calling you that for the last time, as I expect by now my sister has informed you that I have died in fighting for our and other countries, but I may say, darling, that my last thoughts were of my family and you, and I love you while there is a breath in my body.
I take this last opportunity of wishing you the happiest married life which it is possible for two people to have. And only wish that it was I. Also give my wishes for a happy and long life to your Mother, Father and all your friends and Relations, and with these few last words I close, wishing you all the very best,
Your most Loving Friend,
Gwyn.[30]

Like the marvellous long diary-letter kept by Freddy Bloom for her husband during her three years in Changi women's civilian prison, these kinds of letters symbolize faith in the other in the face of absence and the impossibility of reply, to an extreme degree. But to the extent that all letters create presence out of absence, they all evoke the difficulty of communication, and the profound duplicity of self-representation. Indeed, an attempt has been made throughout this chapter to highlight the different levels at which their meaning is determined not by the writer, but by the interaction between reader and text. Letters, both as fetish and as a form of memory, work in ways that exceed their definition as a simple technology of communication, in ways that we can call aesthetic.[31] This takes us back to the central aesthetic of the exhibition, which is that of pathos. The word that visitors continually used to describe their impressions was 'poignant'. But, as we shall see, the radical energy of the contradictions that define that emotion is kept firmly under control.

Wartime Marriages: Redemption through Romance

Modern historiography increasingly shows us that we cannot separate the content of history from the form of its telling. Hayden White in particular has drawn our attention to the ways in which, since the Enlightenment, Western understanding of history itself depends upon its being 'narrativized' and infused with the structures of literary genres.[32] While any exhibition must be designed to appeal as well as communicate, this is another reminder that we must not take 'The Real Thing' at face value. The final section of the exhibition, 'Wartime Marriages', like the endings of all stories, was where the genre of this history was decided. A romance itself as well as a history of romance, the closing parade of gowns and photos left us in no doubt. Of course, it was usually to consecrate a continuing relationship that people sent in mementoes in the first place, and visitors certainly enjoyed that 'upbeat' finale. In discussion with one young married couple, the woman said that 'the happy endings are the point of it', and knowing that people 'kept their love alive in war . . . makes it more emotional, more poetic'. The point I wish to make, however, is that if the main task of the museum is to represent the tragedy of repeated wars, this exhibition was comic despite its poignancy, the ending of marriage implying a ritualistic cycle of renewal as against the final ending of death. Unlike tragedy, comedy classically defines itself in opposition to history and its tropes of exhaustiveness, objectivity, tentative closure. Instead, it permits a move away from realism to fantasy; representation to celebration. But as we have seen, these potentially radical terms of comic redemption were limited to legalized love and reunion of the divided sexes. Seeing the exhibition in this light (and the repetition in the press coverage) can crystallize the general sense in which it is difficult to historicize sexuality and love, but also how part of that difficulty is the suppression of women, lesbians and gays as historical subjects. If happy ever after is the only possible ending for a romance, in 'Forces Sweethearts' it is also the moment at which women's history, with story, evaporates.

Conclusion: Genres, Memory and History

It can, therefore, be suggested that the museum's attempt to hold together pin-up and reality in one narrative, that of the 'Forces Sweetheart', is part of a wider confusion between a celebration of romance and a representation of women's war histories. The physical design of the exhibition as not just a realm of fantasy, but a specifically femininized sanctuary was one manifestation of this. Another was the way that personal letters were mobilized as a kind of woman's 'answer' to the man's pin-up, each aesthetic unified by the stock narrative closure of marriage at the end. But this confusion is perhaps most of all due to the context of so little representation of women's war experiences and attention to gendering of men's war history in other parts of the museum. It thus reads as women's history, but in doing so, suggests that women's history is of a different 'genre', in a very literal sense, from men's history. Genre, in other words (though it may be highly popular) becomes implicated in the tendency to essentialize sexual difference in war. Despite Ritchie Calder's emphasis that the exhibition was never meant to be sociological but light entertainment,[33] there is a deeper point to be made about the way that the relation of comic romance to historical tragedy parallels the false separation of women's and men's histories, private and public, letters and monuments, memory and history. These oppositions need to be undone and explored not only if we are to celebrate romance more inclusively, but if we are ever to make women full subjects of history, as well as of redemptive, but secondary, romance.

Notes

1. Interview with P. R. Calder, exhibition organizer, 1993.
2. The exhibition cost £80,000. Takings are difficult to judge, since admission tickets were to the museum as a whole. However, income earned from admissions during the period of the exhibition was vastly

greater than this figure; visitor figures increased, sometimes dramatically; an array of exhibition products including Lumley's book were
very profitable; and there was great media interest. Information from
J. Burchell, Imperial War Museum Marketing Assistant, letter to the
author, 18 October 1993.

3. Lumley (1993).
4. 'Soldier girls guard secrets', *Wolverhampton Express and Star,* 28
   December 1991.
5. *Shropshire Star*, 28 December 1991.
6. For example, Faderman (1992); Flanner (1988); Lesbian History Group
   (1989); The Hall-Carpenter Archives (1990); Weiss and Schiller (1988).
7. Calder, interview.
8. St Pancras Living History Group, personal interview, October 1993.
9. In fact there was a mention of homosexuality in the exhibition, though
   clearly unintentionally. The news-sheet of the RAF base at Tabouk
   in 1991, which featured the vote for Miss Tabouk, also included a
   cartoon of an old woman and a man wearing a 'Proud to be Gay'
   badge in a destroyed landscape, she saying, 'Well, I guess it's up to
   you and I to get the old civilisation rolling again, eh?'
10. *Daily Mail*, 8 June 1991.
11. A reversal of the traditional military 'purging' of women whom the
    authorities consider are inhibiting efficiency, by claiming they are
    prostitutes. See Enloe (1988).
12. Olive Pritchett, 'Making both love and war', *Sunday Telegraph,* 31
    January 1993.
13. Catherine Ostler, 'She is more a cheesecake version of Maggie Smith
    than a sex siren', *Tatler,* March 1992.
14. I interviewed nine women and five men as they walked round the
    exhibition. I do not pretend that this is representative, and I acknow-
    ledge that gender cannot be isolated from other social factors in
    determining their reactions.
15. Lumley (1993), p. 41.
16. Ibid., p. 44.
17. Ibid., p. 92.
18. Ibid., p. 97.
19. This is the same contradiction that motivates much classic male war
    literature.
20. It would seem that the working-class soldier, especially if a conscript,
    has less invested in identifying with the army. But Susan Schweik
    has argued that educated literary men's alienation from war was sig-
    nificantly more true in the Second than in the First World War, because
    of the changed nature of total war, communication and heterosexual
    relationships. See S. Schweik (1986).

21. Enloe (1988), p. 5.
22. Ibid., p. 57.
23. Speare (1942), pp. 15, 22–4, 26–7.
24. This is interestingly continuous with Linda Kauffman's study of the way that female 'amorous epistolary desire' functions in the literary epistolary tradition. See Kauffman (1986).
25. Lumley (1993), pp. 90–1. It is also reprinted in Litoff and Smith (1991).
26. Lumley (1993), p. 80.
27. An interesting parallel is suggested in Emily Apter's recent argument that collecting memorabilia is a specifically female form of fetishism, in both psychoanalytic and Marxist conceptions of fetishism. See Apter (1991).
28. Lumley (1993), p. 83.
29. Fuller, 'War Letters', in Blythe (1993), p. 63.
30. Lumley (1993), p. 151.
31. See Janet Altman's discussion of the letter as a 'privileged physical trace of temporal experience' in her fascinating book *Epistolarity: Approaches to a Form* (1986).
32. White (1989).
33. Calder, interview.

Bibliography

Primary Sources

Interview with P. R. Calder, exhibition organizer, 1993.
Speare, D. (1942), 'Don't Mention Other Men', *Colliers*, 19 December.
Daily Mail, 8 June 1991.
Shropshire Star, 28 December 1991.
Pritchett, Olive (1993), 'Making both love and war', *The Sunday Telegraph*, 31 January.
Ostler, Catherine (1992), 'She is more a cheesecake version of Maggie Smith than a sex siren', *Tatler*, March.
'Soldier girls guard secrets', *Wolverhampton Express and Star*, 28 December 1991.

Secondary Sources

Altman, Janet (1986), *Epistolarity: Approaches to a Form*, Columbus: Ohio State University Press.
Apter, E. (1991), 'Splitting hairs: female fetishism and post-partum sentimentality in Maupassant's fiction', in L. Hunt (ed.), *Eroticism and*

the Body Politic, Baltimore: Johns Hopkins University Press, pp. 164–90.

Blythe, R. (ed.) (1993), *Private Words: Letters and Diaries from the Second World War*, London: Penguin.

Enloe, C. (1988), *Does Khaki Become You?; the Militarization of Women's Lives*, London: Pandora.

Faderman, L. (1992), *Odd Girls and Twilight Lovers: A History of Lesbian Life in Twentieth-Century America*, New York: Penguin.

Flanner, J. (1988), *Darlinghissima: Letters to a Friend*, edited with a commentary by Natalia Danesai Murray, London: Pandora.

The Hall-Carpenter Archives (1990), *Walking After Midnight: Gay Men's Life Stories*, London: Routledge.

Kauffman, L. (1986), *Discourses of Desire: Gender, Genre and Epistolary Fictions*, Ithaca: Cornell University Press.

Lesbian History Group (1989), *Not a Passing Phase: Reclaiming Lesbians in History 1840–1985*, London: The Women's Press.

Litoff, J. B. and Smith, D. C. (1991), *Since You Went Away: Letters from American Women on the Home Front*, New York: Oxford University Press.

Lumley, Joanna (1993), *Forces Sweethearts: Wartime Romance from the First World War to the Gulf*, London: Bloomsbury.

Schweik, S. (1986), 'A Word No Man Can Say For Us', unpublished PhD thesis, University of Yale.

Weiss, A. and Schiller, G. (1988), *Before Stonewall: The Making of a Gay and Lesbian Community*, Seattle: Naiad.

White, W. Hayden (1989), *The Content of the Form: Narrative Discourse and Historical Representation*, Baltimore: Johns Hopkins University Press.

Part IV

Monuments

8

Private Grief and Public Remembrance: British First World War Memorials

Catherine Moriarty

Both private and public memories were generated by memorials built to commemorate the dead of the First World War. The relationship between the two and the various processes called into play were often complex. Public remembrance was dependent on private memory, yet its ultimate objective was to mould and control the latter as a specific stabilized narrative which served to unify national memory.

After the First World War unofficial memorials were raised independently by virtually every community throughout the British Isles. They contrast with the centralized commemorative activities of the Imperial War Graves Commission, which was established in 1917 and whose main task was to build and maintain cemeteries in the battle zones. Official and unofficial memorials mirror the classification of Pierre Nora, who defined 'dominant and dominated sites of memory'.[1] The former (dominant) are spectacular, imposing and, indeed, imposed from above by a national authority or established interest whilst the latter (dominated) are characterized by spontaneity and devotion, 'where one finds the living heart of memory'.[2] This chapter will show how Nora's theoretical work is an invaluable means of analysing the processes and currents of influence at work in the building and reception of a war memorial, but that his distinction cannot be applied at face value to the British experience after the First World War. It would be tempting to term the majority of British First World War memorials as dominated sites of memory; they certainly appeared to be spontaneous and a focus of heartfelt remembrance, yet other determining factors, sometimes overt, sometimes insidious, contributed to their form and meaning. By looking at the organization of their construction and the processes at work during unveiling ceremonies, I hope to show that a highly complex web of private and public memories was called into play. First World War Memorials are composite sites where the commemorative element was only one amid many possible readings.

The sheer speed of memorializing activity towards the end of the war and in the immediate post-war period thwarted the possibility of control by legislative or other means. Rather, each memorial took its form and meaning by utilizing and adapting conventional patterns of communal organization, and was affected by market forces of materials and labour, as well as artistic practice. Choices were made locally rather than determined from above, yet it is important to emphasize that the memorials rarely challenged official interpretations of the war. They complemented forms of remembrance established by the government through the Imperial War Graves Commission, Armistice Day observances and other forms of hegemonic interpretation such as official military histories.

Building a Memorial

The intrinsic need for a communal site of memory was rooted in the decision taken by the War Office in 1915 to ban the repatriation of the war dead.[3] This need was experienced nationwide; in the absence of the dead a focus of grief was required around which surrogate funeral services could be held. Loss became a collective experience, achieved by a meshing of private memories – the many thousands of local memorials provided sites to which memory could attach itself. As Nora has described it, '*Lieux de mémoire* are created by a play of memory and history, an interaction of two factors that results in their reciprocal overdetermination. To begin with, there must be a will to remember.'[4]

The awareness of a need to commemorate the First World War dead developed from about 1915, when press articles and the first parish minutes on the subject started to appear.[5] As casualty lists grew and familiar names were reported killed in local newspapers, it became clear that every community would wish to mark those who would not return. This feeling accelerated when hopes of an early victory began to fade and after the huge losses during 1916. Some memorial inscriptions provide a graphic display of how the news of each death reached the community, listing those who died not alphabetically but by year of death. At Brockham Green, Surrey, the memorial cross in the churchyard lists one name for 1914, four during 1915, nine in 1916, eleven for 1917 and eight for 1918. Such an accumulation of loss mirrors the intensity of the fighting and the mobilization of recent volunteers in the New Armies on the Western Front during 1916 and 1917.

The decision to build a memorial was sometimes made at a public meeting, usually of the parish council; or was suggested by either an ordinary member of the community or a local figure such as the vicar. At Chorley, Lancashire, steps began in 1919, 'when a number of influential local gentlemen in the town informally discussed the question'.[6] Sometimes a letter in the local press generated interest. Often the fact that neighbouring communities had begun to raise funds for a memorial encouraged the desire to create some similar public statement.

Most memorials were organized by a committee which was intended to represent the community as a whole. Members commonly included local worthies of all descriptions: Members of Parliament, local council representatives, prosperous tradesmen, churchmen and busybodies, all of whom were seen, or saw themselves, as representing the interests of particular sections of the community. Sometimes members were elected at a public meeting, but in many instances they were either chosen by the proposer of the scheme or another individual of influence. Some committee members were involved fully throughout the memorializing process whilst others chose to delegate the practicalities to others, often by way of sub-committees. At Tredegar, Gwent, four sub-committees were appointed, entitled 'Estimates and Designs', 'Sites', 'Unveiling' and 'Records'. Most committees consulted the wider public when major decisions were to be made, on the type or site of the memorial for example, by way of public meetings and statements in the local press. A few operated in virtual autonomy and in some cases persuasive individuals did dominate decision-making. The committee often had difficulty reconciling differing wishes and opinions within a community. Occasionally objections manifested themselves in opposing monumental schemes. The role played by the committee and a list of its various members was often mentioned in press accounts of unveiling ceremonies or the programme itself. At the opening of the Birmingham Hall of Memory in July 1925 photographs of the committee dominated the programme.[7] The committee usually had prominent seats at the unveiling, sometimes the chairman actually unveiled the memorial and occasionally the names of committee members were inscribed on the memorial itself.

At the unveiling of the war memorial at Church, Lancashire, the aim of the committee was stated thus: 'the object of the Memorial Committee had been to ensure that there should be a visible reminder of the sacrifice made by the 132 men of Church who gave their lives'.[8] In order to provide such a 'visible reminder' local committees had to make numerous important decisions. They had to consider fundraising, the type of memorial, the site of the memorial, the commissioning, the construction, the inscription and how those named were to be selected, the unveiling ceremony and the memorial's maintenance.

Through the authority of its members the committee made decisions on behalf of the community it represented. Yet it was rarely free to act in complete autonomy, remaining answerable to the general public whose support, as we shall see, was vital for both funding and the memorial's meaning. The public were regularly informed of the committee's intentions and were provided with opportunities to express their views. In some cases this consultation process was merely a formality, but it could provide a space for debate where the wishes and interests of the community at large surfaced.

The choice between a purely symbolic monument and a utilitarian war memorial was a common point of contention. I do not intend to examine the debate in detail here, merely to summarize the main issues at stake. Those advocating a utilitarian memorial argued that a memorial should provide some form of practical benefit for ex-servicemen, the bereaved or the community as a whole. Hospital extensions, extra beds, village halls, playing fields and scholarships were popular choices. Behind many objections to a utilitarian scheme was a fear that the main purpose of the memorial, to commemorate the dead, would be overshadowed or, at worst, in time forgotten. The appropriate spirit of remembrance was also questioned in utilitarian schemes: it would be difficult to emphasize the sanctity of the memorial and would fail to provide a site for reflection.

Many communities opted for a compromise, hoping to provide a functional memorial as well as a monument. Around 5 per cent of communities were able to do so, but in many instances it was not possible to raise the required funds for something like a cottage hospital or almshouses, and the community concentrated their efforts on erecting a symbolic memorial. Yet most utilitarian memorials do not possess the fundamental requirements of sites of memory as specified by Pierre Nora, 'to stop time, to block the work of forgetting, to establish a state of things, to immortalize death, to materialize the immaterial'.[9]

The possibility of forgetting underlies the deeply felt need to create a memorial to posterity. The popular inscription 'Lest We Forget' testifies to this fear in the form of a warning. Great emphasis was placed on the communal act of remembrance, which focused on what the dead had died for and their example of self-sacrifice, rather than on isolated personal memories which would have recalled them as individuals. But often the two strands of memory were intertwined. At Marlow, a large granite cross was unveiled in July 1920 by the Marquis of Lincolnshire. He urged that the dead, 'cannot and must not be forgotten. It would be a shameful day for the country if their great deeds were forgotten, and the men who had fought so gallantly were neglected and uncared for.' The local newspaper described how the Marquis

> impressed upon the boys present not to forget that day, whatever happened in their lives, or to forget the way in which their fathers, brothers and relatives had fought that they might live in peace. If ever they were called upon to do the same, they must do their duty like men, and they would never regret it.[10]

The financing of memorials after the First World War stems from a conjunction of three traditions: the public subscription system; the military practice of contributing to regimental memorials; and the private purchase of a funerary memorial. Occasionally a local landowner, businessman or employer donated the site, paid for the memorial as a whole, or contributed the largest subscription. Public subscription however, was by far the most common method of fundraising. Requests for contributions were published in the local press. These were then added to the committee account via the treasurer, other committee members, or directly to a local bank. In many areas subscription lists were published periodically, but this practice was sometimes denounced on the grounds that the memorial would no longer belong to all the people, but more to some than others. Communal ownership was vital to the memorial's meaning. At Wolverhampton it was stressed that 'the Committee's desire is that every citizen from the most opulent to the very humblest, shall be able to claim a share in helping to rear it, and have a personal interest in it, because of the sacrifice it will symbolise and the memories it will perpetuate'.[11]

That a memorial had been funded by public subscription was of such significance that inscriptions often included the fact. At Oswaldtwistle, Lancashire, for example, the inscription read 'ERECTED BY / PUBLIC SUBSCRIPTION / FOR THE HONOURED MEMORY / OF THE MEN FROM THIS TOWN / WHO GAVE THEIR LIVES / IN THE / GREAT WAR / 1914–1918'.[12] As well as a means of raising funds for a memorial, the public subscription system was a highly symbolic act of communal ownership, approval and cooperation. It is clear that in many instances the bulk of funds required were provided by a handful of wealthy people with a general collection enabling the method of funding to be described as public subscription, yet in other areas the local memorial really was financed by a vast accumulation of small donations. At Ripple, Kent, sixty-five villagers contributed to a memorial cross costing £76. The most common subscription was less than £2: only 19 per cent of the total cost came from donations over £5.[13] At Frimley, Surrey, a more ambitious project for a hospital endowment fund as well as a cross was possible due to several large subscriptions over £100. Here only 17 per cent of the total cost was raised from subscriptions under £10.[14] Thus, the prosperity, population and social composition of an area played a key part in subscription levels.

Analysis of this sort demonstrates that many memorials were financed by small subscriptions from many inhabitants. House-to-house collections were common. The collectors' lists for the memorial at Ashurst, West Sussex, reveal the most common donation to be under a shilling.[15] At Abingdon, Oxfordshire, the collection of funds was organized by Miss Cullen and a 'large volunteer band of ladies'.[16] At Lewes members of the community who had not contributed were sent a letter stating that their name did not appear on the list. Not to contribute would have been regarded as both unpatriotic and an insult to one's neighbours. At Gateshead the method of funding the town's war memorial was included in the unveiling programme:

> The aim of the promoters of the movement was to make the Memorial a people's tribute in the widest sense of the term, and the Committee gratefully acknowledge that the people of Gateshead nobly seconded them in their efforts to accomplish this. It seems worthy of record in this matter to state that in addition to the general body of subscribers the fund represents the contributions of 9,232 people who subscribed through a House to House collection and nearly 20,000 school children have given to the Fund.[17]

Unveiling Ceremonies

Most British war memorials were unveiled between 1920 and 1925. These ceremonies were often the most significant public event which had taken place for years, being attended by entire communities. Shops were closed and other activities suspended. The ceremony was carefully orchestrated with elaborate processions to the memorial. Spectators were precisely marshalled around it. It was important that every facet of the community was represented: schoolchildren, choirs, ex-servicemen, the bereaved and the general public were all allocated their places. Sometimes an enclosure was organized for the bereaved, who had to apply for a certain number of tickets in advance. The proceedings were usually presided over by a civic dignitary who welcomed visitors, and spoke of the history of the memorial and the local war effort. The actual unveiling of the structure, usually covered with a Union Jack, was followed by a religious service, often conducted jointly by the local churches, with hymns and dedicatory prayers sanctifying the memorial and commending the dead to God. In addition, extracts from the standard burial service were often employed, as well as a bugler playing the Last Post shortly followed by Reveille. Periods of silence were common as were solemn readings of the names of the dead. At the end of the ceremony the mayor or parish clerk formally accepted the memorial on behalf of the community, and then the bereaved were allowed to place floral tributes. The ceremony enabled authorities to state how the memorial should be understood and the meaning of any iconography; it was an opportunity for churchmen to give an additional sermon, and for visiting dignitaries to reiterate the meaning of the war and their hope for a better future. Above all, which is what seems to have made a lasting impression on those who witnessed such ceremonies, they were highly emotive and dramatic events. Many accounts report that the spectators were moved to tears. Such an outlet of sorrow,

Figure 8.1

Figure 8.2

V. M. ALDRED.
A. E. ANDERSON.
B. R. BECKETT.
E. BEESTON.
T. BRUCE.
J. D. CARTMELL.
H. CAWTHRAY.
H. CHADWICK.
L. CHAMBERLAIN.
W. I. CLEGG.
W. G. COLE.
L. COLLIER.
J. COLLINGE.
W. CONOLLY.
H. COOK.
S. Y. COOK.
H. D. CROMPTON.
D. DAVIES.
D. DAVIES.
D. W. DAVIES.
H. G. DAVIES.
J. T. DAVIES.
O. G. DAVIES.
S. T. DAVIES.
T. DAVIES.
W. DAVIES.
W. DAVIES.
E. DOYLE.
R. G. EDGAR.

C. EDWARDS.
E. EDWARDS.
E. EDWARDS.
R. EDWARDS.
W. EDWARDS.
L. EVANS.
N. E. EVANS.
N. E. EVANS.
R. R. EVANS.
W. EVANS.
G. E. FLETCHER.
J. FOSTER.
S. GARNESS.
S. GETHING.
E. H. GRIFFITHS.
F. G. HANFORD.
J. S. HARLEY.
C. P. HARROP.
J. L. HARROP.
G. R. HAYWARD.
C. J. HIGGINSON.
H. W. HOMAN.
B. HOWELL.
G. HOWELL.
D. H. HOYLES.
A. H. HUDSON.
A. HUGHES.
D. HUGHES.
J. HUGHES.

Figure 8.3

Figure 8.4

so uncharacteristic of British public life, reveals the force of grief which, for once, was given a place to spill over, to be shared and acknowledged.

At the unveiling of the Ashton-under-Lyne memorial, on 16 September 1922, an invocatory prayer was read which referred to 'this hour of mingled memories'. From this we must infer that the ceremony accompanying the unveiling – the standard mix of interdenominational, civic and military ritual – and indeed the memorial itself, were intended to clarify memory, ordering it in such a way so that the war and the many deaths were given new logic and purpose. The Reverend W. A. Parry, in the act of dedication, prayed that the memorial 'may serve to remind us – as we think of the noble deeds and sacrifices of our brothers – of our own duty to Thee our God, to our Country, to our town, and to one another'.[18] The memorial structure reinforces this hierarchy of thought. The names of 1,512 dead are listed alphabetically on thirty-eight bronze panels which the spectator can easily see by climbing the stepped base. Above these are placed two huge bronze lions representing the British Empire, one in combat with the serpent of evil, the other having triumphantly crushed it. The central Portland Stone column, 35 feet high, is surmounted by a bronze group which depicts a wounded soldier holding a spray of laurels, passing a sword of Justice to a standing female figure representing Peace. The dead thus literally uphold and support the values of Empire, service and honour, and it is through them that these values are to be understood. The penultimate feature of the unveiling ceremony was listed thus: 'the relatives of those whose Names are inscribed on the Tablets will view the Memorial – Children First'.[19] The young, whose memories would be most easily impressed and whose loss was possibly the most inexplicable, were to be the main object of the memorial.

Private grief was acknowledged, yet not dwelt upon. At unveiling ceremonies the audience was urged to convert its grief to pride. At the unveiling of the Horsham War Memorial in November 1921, Major-General Young, Colonel of the Royal Sussex Regiment, said:

> As we stand around this Memorial our thoughts instinctively are centred on the dark years of the war, when so many men of Horsham, with others in the land, passed into the unknown; when every village in Sussex was stricken, and when there was sorrow in almost every home. But I would remind you that with our grief and our sorrow there must always be associated a feeling of pride when we call to mind the splendid spirit of heroism, devotion and self-sacrifice of men of Horsham and men of the county of Sussex.[20]

Similarly at the unveiling of the Lurgan war memorial in Northern Ireland, in May 1928, Senator H. B. Armstrong spoke of how the memorial would

> revive in our minds the miserable and anxious days of the Great War, when we dreaded the approach of the telegraph messenger – a foreboding, alas,

only too often justified – and when, after their short spells of leave from the front we saw our boys off again, with the haunting fear that we should see their faces no more.

Yet his speech swiftly turned to the town's 'civic consciousness and pride in its achievements in local effort'. It had never, he said, 'failed to exhibit a wide, an inspiring patriotism'.[21]

That the memorial was a focus of private grief is undeniable. Unveiling ceremonies were reported at length in local newspapers and sometimes the wording on floral tributes was included as well. The Lewes memorial was unveiled in September 1922 and the *East Sussex News* listed over 200 tributes, the simplicity of the messages contrasting with the rhetoric of the official ceremony.

> In affectionate remembrance of uncle, Percy Fuller, from Arthur and Frank.
> In loving memory of dear Tom.
> To the cherished memory of a loving husband and son, Frederick John Farley, RGA died in Egypt, November 19th, 1917.
> In grateful memory of two who did not come back, J. Burgess and H. Botting from Kenward and Son and fellow workers.
> From your ever-loving wife and dear children and his mate B., Mrs J. Fuller, 18 Spring Gardens.
> Sergeant J. M. Dunning, 'Never Forgotten' from his mother.[22]

Another link between personal grief and public remembrance was the choice of who would perform the act of unveiling. Sometimes a local widow or mother who had lost several sons was chosen. Thus at Scunthorpe the first wreath was laid by Mrs Charlesworth, who had lost four of her eleven sons. At Swanley in Kent Mrs Gedge, who had lost three sons, unveiled the memorial with the following words: 'I unveil this Memorial, erected as an abiding witness of the love of Freedom, Truth, Justice, and Mercy, which moved the heart of this country to enter into war; and also in proud and grateful memory of those from Swanley and District who gave their lives in that great struggle.'[23] Mrs Gedge's loss was therefore appropriated to reiterate ideals. Other mothers would identify with she who had suffered most; if Mrs Gedge could still believe in truth and justice so, it followed, should they. Medal-bedecked children who had lost their fathers were also often a focus of the ceremony. In this way ordinary members of the community became ceremonial lynchpins, linking others who were grieving with the memorial and its meaning.

In other cases a local celebrity was chosen, perhaps the local MP, mayor or lord of the manor who represented the community as individuals and on a wider public platform. A particularly popular choice was a national figure with local connections who could claim to be from the area but also part of national life, such as Lord Lincolnshire who unveiled the Wooburn Green memorial on 6 June 1920. The *Bucks Free Press* reported 'His Lordship was not only the representative of their King, as Lord Lieutenant of the County, but he was a near neighbour, who had known the bitterness of the conflict by the loss of his only son.'[24] Similarly a combination of local widow and famous figure successfully combined both planes of remembrance.

The two-minute silence, introduced at the Whitehall Cenotaph Armistice Day observance in 1919 and used at local ceremonies ever since, and the reiteration of 'We will remember them' (the audience's response to the reading of the passage 'They shall not grow old as we that are left grow old'), 'serves [as Nora describes it] as a concentrated appeal to memory by literally breaking a temporal continuity'.[25] The closing of shops during unveiling ceremonies and the stopping of traffic all contributed to this end. At Tunbridge Wells in February 1923 it was reported that 'the main thoroughfare was temporarily closed to all vehicular traffic, not even the sound of a passing motor car or horse-drawn vehicle could be heard. Complete was the tribute paid by the citizens to those brave and gallant comrades who fell in the great world conflict.'[26] At Egerton outside Manchester the local paper reported that 'during the period of unveiling play was suspended in the cricket match at Eagley, whilst the start of the match at Egerton was delayed until the ceremony was over'.[27]

The word 'memory' appears in many inscriptions, sometimes as a standard introduction to the text, 'IN MEMORY OF THE MEN OF' or given a specific slant, 'HONOURED MEMORY',[28] 'GLORIOUS MEMORY',[29] 'PROUD MEMORY',[30] 'PROUD AND GRATEFUL MEMORY',[31] 'SACRED AND EVERLASTING MEMORY',[32] 'IMMORTAL MEMORY',[33] 'UNDYING MEMORY',[34] 'UNFADING MEMORY'.[35] More significant lapidary arrangements were also popular. The cenotaph at Newport is inscribed with a five-word statement, in large letters: 'THEIR / MEMORY / ENDURETH / FOR EVER'. At Penzance the inscription is headed with the single word, 'REMEMBER'. At Longford, Northern Ireland, the memorial is inscribed 'FORGET THEM NO WE NEVER WILL'.[36] Memory was used to denote the way in which the dead would continue to survive in memory. Memory also referred to the activity of the survivors and the preceding adverbs determined the manner of remembrance. Memory was always described in positive terms: the loss of a loved one was to be viewed as a glorious and meaningful sacrifice rather than as a painful, pointless loss. Thus we never read of 'regretful memory', 'angry memory' or 'broken-hearted memory'.

The names of the dead were a vital component of a memorial. Individually they triggered recollections of one who had been killed; together they provided evidence of the scale of local loss and therefore of the community's pride in the extent of its sacrifice. At Slaidburn in Lancashire a bronze statue of a soldier was unveiled in May 1923 by Bishop Taylor Smith, Chaplain General to the Forces, who said:

> Their names must never be forgotten. It was not enough that they memorialize them on bronze tablets. They must keep their names, not only in their hearts, but teach their meaning to their children, so that they would pass on, from generation to generation, the brave men of Slaidburn ... They who had been privileged to place such a sacrifice as father, husband, brother, sweetheart, or friend upon the altar, [must not] desire to take the sacrifice from the altar, lest they robbed their loved ones and themselves.[37]

In this way private loss was publicly sanctified. To see a name, an ordinary name, inscribed and honoured in a way which had previously only been granted to local worthies was, in itself, regarded as a great honour. The names of the dead were often solemnly read aloud and bestowed with public recognition. A name which brought private sorrow was transformed by commemorative ritual to bring civic pride. Under a list of 132 names on the Finedon war memorial in Northamptonshire is inscribed 'TO KEEP IN MIND THE / GREAT WAR & THOSE / FROM THIS PLACE WHO / GAVE THEIR LIVES / 1914–1919'. The unveiling of the Coleraine memorial in Northern Ireland was reported in the local newspaper:

> As Colonel Knox read out the names everyone stood with bowed head. During the reading of them an occasional sob disturbed the stillness. It was the audible indication of sorrow called up afresh by the mere mention of a name once in daily use in the home, and of re-awakened longing for 'the touch of a vanished hand and the sound of a voice that is still'.[38]

At Colwyn Bay figurative reliefs were included in the three bronze name tablets which were placed on the pedestal supporting a bronze statue of a soldier. The unveiling brochure stated how these illustrative components should be understood. The first panel, entitled 'Military', was described as:

> not in any sense disciplinary, but typifies the care-free spirit in which our citizen soldiers entered upon their new and hazardous life in the War. (Note the various expressions, the comradeship shown by the man sharing his cigarette, the irrepressible humour of the man hanging his helmet upon the rifle of the man in front, and the general easy, yet capable, bearing of all the men.)[39]

The names of those above are, by juxtaposition, embroiled in this narrative. Their own experience, perhaps of conscription, reluctance or fear, overshadowed by the attempt to tell it in glamourizing hindsight.

Another device for moulding memory was to urge recollections of the dead as children, rather than as fighting men. At Boughton Aluph, Kent, a granite memorial cross was unveiled in February 1921. It was sited on the Lees, where, the Reverend Halloran declared 'most of those whose names are inscribed spent their boyhood. Some of them were born in houses close around us, most of them were taught in the school over there and played their happy boyish games around this spot where the memorial stands.'[40] The Burnley war memorial, unveiled in 1926, included a bronze statue of a mother placing a wreath at the base of the central cenotaph. The unveiling programme explained the detail of this figure. 'By her side touching her is the rosemary bush of remembrance and under the rosemary is the cricket bat and ball, for the son is the boy to the mother always – the boy who never grows up in her eyes, and who is loved and remembered best in the days when he was mothered by her.'[41] The use of the present tense encourages the sense of an ongoing act of visualization in which the observer can participate. The memorial becomes a catalyst for giving shape to private memory yet strict instructions encourage that shape to conform with established official history, since we also read that 'The Sculptor has endeavoured to conceive a Memorial that shall breathe nothing of slaughter, but only of duty fulfilled and, by fulfilment of duty, the comfort and thankfulness brought to those who remain.'[42] The bereaved are asked to recall a past before the war, of youth and play, diverting attention from the circumstances and the scale of death. They are to recall images of boyhood, rather than of a man who was killed and indeed was himself trained to kill.

Conclusion

The public usually had a say in what type of memorial they would prefer; they were certainly expected to contribute financially, and to take part in the unveiling ceremony. Without this sense of communal ownership the memorial would effectively be impotent. Public participation in the commemorative ritual was crucial, yet such participation was, to varying degrees, exploited by civic leaders and visiting dignitaries to emphasize the memorial's didactic capacity. Armistice Day ceremonies reinforced the meaning of memorials year by year, and as grieving waned the culture of honouring the dead and following their example of sacrifice persisted apace.

Notes

1. Nora (1989). This article constituted the theoretical introduction to Nora's collaborative three-volume study. As well as monuments (perhaps the most obvious 'sites' of memory), Nora's project considered emblems, rituals, symbols, manuals and mottos; see Nora (1984–93).
2. Ibid., p. 23.
3. Longworth (1985), p. 14.
4. Nora (1989), p. 19.
5. Lawrence Weaver's *Memorials and Monuments* was published in 1915 and it included a preface on the possible forms of commemoration which could be adopted after the war. The *Architectural Review* ran a seven-part series entitled 'Memorials of War' which traced monumental structures from the ancient to the modern.
6. Chorley unveiling ceremony souvenir handbook, 31 May 1924, Imperial War Museum.
7. Birmingham Hall of Memory unveiling ceremony programme, 4 July 1925, Imperial War Museum. Pictures of the committee also appeared in the Chorley programme, see above.
8. *Accrington Observer and Times,* 18 September 1923. National Inventory of War Memorials, Imperial War Museum (hereafter NIWM), record no. 2065.
9. Nora (1989), p. 19.
10. *Maidenhead and Marlow Journal*, 30 July 1920.
11. Wolverhampton unveiling ceremony programme, 2 November 1922, Imperial War Museum.
12. NIWM 2100.
13. Ripple war memorial accounts, Imperial War Museum. The population numbered 295 in 1921.
14. Frimley war memorial accounts, Imperial War Museum. The population numbered 13,676 in 1921.
15. West Sussex Record Office, PAR 11/4/4.
16. *North Berkshire Herald*, 17 September 1921, letter from Mayor to Editor. NIWM 2201.
17. Gateshead unveiling ceremony programme, 14 May 1922, Imperial War Museum.
18. Ashton-under-Lyne unveiling ceremony programme, 16 September 1922, Imperial War Museum.
19. Ibid.
20. *West Sussex County Times and Standard*, 19 November 1921.
21. *Lurgan Mail*, 26 May 1928.
22. *East Sussex Gazette*, 8 September 1922.
23. NIWM 1149.

24. Thorpe (1993), p. 14.
25. Nora (1989), p. 19. For a full history of Armistice Day see Gregory (1994).
26. NIWM 1540.
27. NIWM 1817.
28. For example Risca, Gwent and Shanklin, Isle of Wight.
29. Broadstairs, Kent.
30. Scottish rugby memorial, Edinburgh.
31. St Ives, Cornwall.
32. Risca Colliery, Gwent.
33. London Troops, Royal Exchange, London.
34. Sutton, Humberside.
35. Beetham, Cumbria.
36. I am grateful to Keith Jeffery for this information.
37. *Clitheroe Advertiser and Times*, 25 May 1923.
38. *Coleraine Chronicle*, 18 November 1922.
39. Colwyn Bay Book of Remembrance, 11 November 1922, Imperial War Museum.
40. *Kentish Express and Ashford News*, 12 February 1921.
41. *Burnley Express,* 11 December 1926.
42. Ibid. For a more detailed description of this memorial see Moriarty (1995), p. 19.

Bibliography

This chapter is based on transcriptions, press cuttings, pamphlets and photographs held in the National Inventory of War Memorials, a recording project established in 1989 and jointly managed by the Imperial War Museum and the Royal Commission on the Historical Monuments of England.

Gregory, A. (1994), *The Silence of Memory*, Oxford: Berg.

Longworth, P. (1985), *The Unending Vigil. A History of the Common-wealth War Graves Commission 1917–1984*, London (first published by Constable, 1967).

Moriarty, C. (1995), 'The Absent Dead and Figurative First World War Memorials', *Transactions of the Ancient Monuments Society*, vol. 39, pp. 7–40.

Nora, P. (1984–93), *Les Lieux de Mémoire* (vol. 1, *La République*; vol. 2, *La Nation*; vol. 3, *La France*), Paris: Gallimard.

Nora, P. (1989), 'Between Memory and History: *Les Lieux de Mémoire*', *Representations*, vol. 26, pp. 7–25.

Richardson, A. and Phillips, P. R. (1915a), 'Memorials of War – I Ancient', *Architectural Review*, vol. 37, pp. 27–30.

Richardson, A. and Phillips, P. R. (1915b), 'Memorials of War – II Renaissance', *Architectural Review,* vol. 37, pp. 46–50.

Richardson, A. and Phillips, P. R. (1915c), 'Memorials of War – III Napoleonic', *Architectural Review,* vol. 37, pp. 64–71.

Richardson, A. and Phillips, P. R. (1915d), 'Memorials of War – IV Modern', *Architectural Review,* vol. 37, pp. 95–104.

Richardson, A. and Phillips, P. R. (1915e), 'Memorials of War – V Modern French', *Architectural Review,* vol. 38, pp. 7–12, 21–5.

Richardson, A. and Phillips, P. R. (1915f), 'Memorials of War – VI Modern Italian', *Architectural Review,* vol. 38, pp. 73–8.

Richardson, A. and Phillips, P. R. (1915g), 'Memorials of War – VII American', *Architectural Review,* vol. 38, pp. 107–13.

Thorpe, B. (1993), *The Men of Wooburn War Memorial*, privately published by the author.

Weaver, Sir L. (1915), *Memorials and Monuments Old and New: Two Hundred Subjects Chosen from Seven Centuries*, London: Country Life.

9

Memory, Memorials and Commemoration of War Memorials in Lorraine, 1908–1988
William Kidd

This chapter has two main objectives: to identify ideological and historical factors which influenced and to a significant extent determined the nature of sculptural representation and commemoration of war in Lorraine, and to illustrate these in a sample of memorials presented in what is both a chronological and typological perspective.[1] For reasons that will be obvious, these factors applied also to Alsace, but the study focuses on one of the pair, and indeed on one *département*, the Moselle, with a couple of examples from Alsace and the adjacent Meurthe-et-Moselle to support its general thesis. That thesis is not original, but precisely because of its familiarity, war memorial iconography in Alsace-Lorraine has attracted little attention from scholars.[2] The chosen starting point – 1908 – saw the inauguration of the *Souvenir Français* memorial at Noisseville. The year 1988 is a provisional terminus, although the symmetry suggested in the title is not wholly arbitrary. President Valéry Giscard d'Estaing's controversial proposal in 1975 to discontinue France's 8 May (VE-Day) celebrations provoked a national debate on memory and commemoration and in Lorraine gave fresh impetus to the construction of Second World War and Resistance memorials.

1870–1914

From Gambetta's famous Saint-Quentin speech in November 1871, with its resonant '*n'en parlons jamais, pensons-y toujours*',[3] through the creation of *Le Souvenir Français* by Xavier Niessen in 1887, to the entry of victorious French troops into Metz on 26 November 1918, the problem of memory – its expression or repression – was inseparable from the legacy of defeat and the loss of Alsace-Lorraine. The desire to recapture the 'lost provinces', symbolized in the black-draped statue of Strasbourg on the Place de la Concorde in Paris, was part of the continuing political agenda of the Third Republic, sometimes invisibly present and unspoken, sometimes flaring into life (as in the Boulanger crisis of 1889), occasionally uniting parties and groups otherwise opposed, often dividing the nation: *revanchard* arguments about the prestige of the army underlay the Dreyfus affair which lasted from 1894 until 1906.

The earliest 1870 war memorials erected in Lorraine were battlefield memorials to the fallen of particular engagements. Spicheren–Forbach (1871) is a typical nineteenth-century neo-classical obelisk in red granite, surmounted by a funeral urn, with pyramids of coffins at each side of the square base. The front face lists the battle honours and bears the inscription '*A la mémoire des soldats français morts pour leur patrie*'. These features are replicated on a smaller scale at Vallières, Saint-Privat, and Metz-Chambière. The memorial in the city's eastern cemetery is surmounted by a cross, organized in a complex group with the instruments of war: a cuirassier's breast-plate and helmet, ordinance, shot-basket, rifle, flag, etc. Again, one face of the plinth is dedicated '*Aux soldats français morts pour leur patrie, 1870–1871*'.

The Noisseville memorial, commissioned by *Le Souvenir Français*, paid for '*par souscription publique*' and inaugurated on 4 October 1908 in the presence of an estimated 120,000 spectators,[4] marks a major date in the history of commemoration in the region, and may be considered a template against which to measure subsequent iconographical developments. Entitled '*La Lorraine en deuil pleurant au pied d'un fantassin français blessé*', the work is a complex edifice in red granite, 4 metres high, with three bronze sculpted figures arranged on two levels. On the upper pedestal, a helmeted allegorical figure supports a wounded French soldier, still erect but falling backwards into the folds of the flag; at his feet, a seated, pensive girl in local costume embodies the loss of the territory and the abiding presence of memory, *le souvenir*. The lower plinth is decorated with a cross of Lorraine, an established regional emblem before its adoption two conflicts later as the symbol of *la France libre*, and bears the dedication '*Aux soldats français tombés glorieusement au champ d'honneur*'. Loss is remembered, but defeat is 'gloriously' transcended. The greater intimacy and realistic detail of the female figure (rough country shoes) undercuts the idealization of the upper group, and facilitates the personal identification which, with the more metaphorical ideological note, is part of the memorial's public/private duality.

The *comité d'honneur* for Noisseville, whose primary stimulus came from the local *Souvenir Français* leader Jean Pierre Jean (1872–1942), was Franco-German in composition, and included elected representatives and local 'notables' with transnational industrial and financial interests such as Charles de Wendel. '*Par souci d'apaisement*', the project also received official approval from Count Zeppelin, Prefect of Metz, on behalf of the occupying authorities.[5] But the very numbers attending the inauguration established Noisseville as a place of patriotic pilgrimage, with the Wissembourg memorial in Alsace erected a year later, and marked an :ncrease in French nationalist fervour in the years immediately before the First World War. So much was this so that in 1912, following vigorous anti-French pressure in the pan-Germanist press, the local *Souvenir Français* section changed its name to *Le Souvenir Alsacien-Lorrain* in a vain attempt to minimize the risks of dissolution, which quickly followed in January 1913. As in other cases before and since, Noisseville's significance, its creative and ideological 'lateness', refer as much to conflict to come as to the memory of war thirty-seven years earlier.

Some of the Franco-Prussian War memorials erected elsewhere in France, notably in the west and south-west (Nantes, La Rochelle, Figeac) during the 1890s and early 1900s, articulate a more ideologically stamped expression of remembrance: at Bergerac, a bare-breasted allegorical female warrior-figure is flanked by a uniformed infantryman *en franc-tireur* and a wounded soldier holding aloft the flag; the whole edifice is powerfully reminiscent of the republican idiom of Delacroix and Rudé. By their dates and by their iconographical specificity, such memorials were conceived as much to assert and reinforce republican identity as to commemorate the dead whose defeat ended the Second Empire and ultimately permitted the establishment of the current regime. As late as 1913, a mounted variant on Antoine Mercié's '*Gloria victis*' of 1873 (defeat transcended) was dedicated at Bordeaux, employing the phrase which was to become established usage on 1914–18 memorials: '*aux **enfants** de la Gironde morts pour la patrie*'. These memorials were however usually regional or departmental in scope; it was the industrialization of warfare during the First World War, and the need to commemorate millions of dead in all the belligerent countries, which 'democratized' memorial practice and production, and led in France to their creation in over 36,000 individual 'communes'.

1918–1939

The liberation of Lorraine in November 1918 ended a period of German annexation which had lasted since 1871, a historical circumstance which meant that during the First World War the province's sons were more likely to have fought in the armies of the Wilhelmine Reich than those of the Third Republic with which it was reunited. Accordingly, when it came to commemorating the fallen (to say nothing of celebrating the return to the bosom of the mother country, an event largely overshadowed by the enormity of the human cost), the iconographical signifiers universally available elsewhere in France were wholly inappropriate. This was especially true of military sculptures such as the helmeted *poilu* with greatcoat, puttees and fixed bayonet, often treading a German *Pickelhaube* underfoot which, as exemplified in Eugene Benet's factory-produced '*Combattant victorieux*', found memorial favour with hundreds of communes in other parts of the country.[6] After 1918, the descendant of the Noisseville soldier had to be occluded, omitted altogether or somehow dehistoricized; the serial *poilus* erected in Clouange (subsequently destroyed by the Germans in 1940) and Audun-le-Tiche, another *commune limitrophe* in the western and historically francophone sector of the Moselle, are exceptional in this respect. Similar difficulties arose with other too overtly national or nation-alist emblems, including the patriotic cockerel (*gallus gallus*), of which I have to date identified two examples only in a sample of 120 memorials. By the same token, the dedication '*aux enfants de (. . .) morts pour la France*' would not serve, notably in communes where geographical and linguistic factors conspired to underline the arbitrariness of the national frontiers redrawn after 1918. Local tradition, however, and non-militaristic elements of the sculptural lexicon, offered a number of solutions, albeit with a necessarily reduced range of expression.

In Grosbliederstroph, separated only by a branch of the Saar from its German homologue Kleinbliedersdorf ('Grosblie' and 'Kleinblie' in local parlance), the memorial dedicated '*A la mémoire de nos morts*' is a squat classical obelisk adorned with a centurion's helmet, Roman sword and round shield. The more complex memorial at Uckange (1922) incorporates a cross of Lorraine, a grieving local girl, victor's laurels and funeral urns. The dedication '*A la mémoire des enfants d'Uckange et de nos libérateurs victimes de la grande guerre*' acknowledges liberation, but unites those who fought on the 'right 'and 'wrong 'sides and makes them both victims, not perpetrators, of the injustice of war. The memorial at Puttelange-aux-Lacs, erected in 1924 and subsequently destroyed, was also a composite construction which simultaneously commemorated victory, sacrifice, *le souvenir* and local identity. It consisted of an obelisk and a free-standing female figure in regional costume, with a stylized lion *couchant* (a lion *rampant* figures in the town's coat of arms), and flanking field artillery pieces. Apart from the lion, salvaged for the new (post-1945 memorial), the edifice survives only in old photographs. Replying to questions about the memorial, M. Lang volunteered the information that the sculptor, Scherer of Buzonville, was reputed to have used a local model for his subject, thereby enabling Puttelangeois between the wars to invest the memorial with even greater personal significance. It is a charming story, and a plausible one, but it raises at least one question – the date of commis-sioning – about the memorial at Koenigsmacker-Metrich, near Cattenhom: same female figure, same lion (facing other way), same sculptor.

Joseph Zeiser of Sarreguemines, whose brother Johann, also a sculptor, worked on the German side of the restored frontier after 1918, created

Figure 9.1

Figure 9.2

Figure 9.3

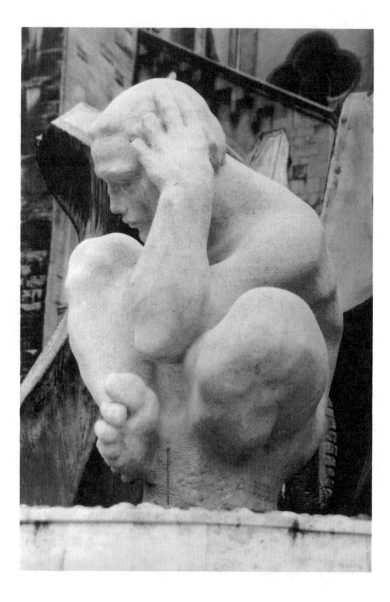

Figure 9.4

the memorials at Merlebach, a sombre obelisk in *grès rouge des Vosges*, and Alsting, whose First World War dead included men killed in the German armies in the Carpathians. Here Zeiser adopted the dehistoricizing device of the dying Roman legionary, half-sitting, half-lying below the outspread wings of an angel holding a crucifix. This rather artisanal village *pietà*, the more poignant for its eschewal of neo-classical sophistication – it appears modelled in cement rather than sculpted from stone – reminds us of another dimension of the commemorative problem: if too conspicuously 'French' military figures had to be avoided, so too had iconographical detail (such as Roman *fasces*, the initials 'RF'), and notably female allegorical figures, too easily identified with the Republic, itself identified with the secular schools legislation of 1881 and the separation of Church and State of 1903–5 which, by virtue of its annexation, Alsace-Lorraine had escaped. After 1918, the Concordat of 1801 remained in force, despite Radical Party determination to extend secularism to the liberated territories in 1924, and survived a second German annexation to remain in force to this day. Antoine Prost's assertion, therefore, that '*quand un poilu mourant tourne vers elle son regard (. . .) la statuaire des monuments aux morts connaît seulement la France républicaine ou la République française*',[7] valid as a generalization for the rest of the country (and even then subject to qualification in, for example, the Breton *départements*),[8] is doubly inapplicable to Alsace-Lorraine. A good example of the non-republican character of statuary in the region is provided by Sarreguemines with its two female figures, an upper bronze '*Renommée*' holding a wreath in each hand (even-handedness towards the fallen of both uniforms), and a lower stone statue representing the town itself.

But one aspect of the exemption from republican legislation also offered a solution to the problem of commemoration and representation, that of erecting memorials of a specifically and unambiguously religious type not found elsewhere in France (unless within the strict boundary of the cemetery or the *enclos paroissial*). As well as the *pietà* at Alsting (which is in the churchyard, as it happens), Lorraine memorials offer innumerable angels, crucifixes, Sacred Hearts, symbolic and 'real' female figures, bearing victor's crowns and signifying spiritual comfort and transcendence, and – perhaps – the possibility of ultimate reconciliation. Examples are to be found at Spicheren (Sacred Heart), in the industrial town of L'Hôpital (an angel in a prominent roadside emplacement), and in Hombourg-Haut, whose memorial angel is set back from a pre-existing *calvaire* close to the old village gate, at the convergence of its two principal streets. Patriotism and religion, patriotism through religion, local and national identity, could finally be expressed in that quintessential warrior *lorraine* Joan of Arc, sufficiently dehistoricized to be (relatively) unproblematic five centuries after defeating the (English) enemy, and conveniently canonized in 1920. One example among many of a factory-produced Joan, armour-clad, holding the flag, eyes turned heavenwards '*en sublime*' is at Longeville-lès-Saint-Avold: '*Souvenez-vous dans vos prières des enfants de Longeville-lès-Saint-Avold victimes de la guerre*'.

As in the rest of France, the majority of First World War memorials in Lorraine were inaugurated in the period 1920–4, though some were considerably later. Sarreguemines, commissioned in 1922, was not erected until 1933, for reasons to do with local political complications and the legality of the original '*concours*' which produced not one but three laureates (one of them Emmanuel Hannaux, responsible for the figures at Noisseville). The inauguration on 22 October 1933 took place therefore in a very different historical context, as post-war commemoration shaded into pre-war anxiety and the domestic political situation lurched into more serious instability. Longwy-Haut (1932) and Longwy-Bas (1933) belong to the same period, as do Drivier's moving Strasbourg *pietà* (1934) in which the twisted naked bodies of *two* victims, arms intertwined, evoke the Franco-German '*frères ennemis*'. Metz, a more complex and imposing if less artistically satisfying edifice in yellow *pierre de Jaumont*, was inaugurated as late as 11 August 1935 by President Lebrun. Here an upper panel represented the continuation of the family (mother, infant, elderly parents) after the death of the father/child commemorated in the *pietà* group below. The memorial was dedicated in the now habitual usage '*Aux enfants de Metz morts victimes de la guerre*', but two bas-relief side panels representing unmistakably French infantry figures added a problematically nationalist note.[9] When, following victory in a new conflict, the Germans re-annexed the city in the summer of 1940, these were removed, and the original dedication replaced by the frankly reappropriationist '*Sie sterben für das Reich*'. After 1945, the memorial was further reduced to its present dimensions and acquired its present dedication '*Aux Morts de la Guerre*', ending a process of reduction and simplification and arguably – but the outsider given to value judgements treads warily – of aesthetic *purification*, which contrasts with the tendency to progressive accretion and accumulation often discernible elsewhere.

Post-1945

It was natural, following a second liberation, that memorials to the previous conflict should serve as a focal point and *lieu de mémoire* for local celebration. In September 1944, the American generals Patton and Walker were photographed at Hayange, with Raymond Mondon, General de Gaulle's representative (and later mayor of Metz) and a group of inhabitants, including women and children dressed in local costume.[10] As in 1918, however, a particular problem presented itself: how to commemorate men who, having served in the French forces in 1939–40, were then forcibly incorporated (*les malgré nous*) into the Wehrmacht in 1942. This group numbered some 100,000 from Alsace and 30,000 from Lorraine, of which combined total 40,000 lost their lives.[11] If the shorter time-span of the second annexation (1940–4 as compared to 1871–1918) attenuated the problem, and anti-Nazism offered a convenient device to express or to mask anti-Germanism, a distinction not uncommon elsewhere in France in post-1945 memorials, the problem was further complicated now by the emergence of the Resistance,[12] some of whose combatants were non-French, and the concomitant of occupation and collaboration, civil war, *la guerre franco-française*.

Depending on the precise circumstances, the need could be catered for by the simple expedient of adding a plaque to the existing 1914–18 memorial. Longeville's apparently terse '*Guerre 1939–1945: Cinq victimes militaires*' should be read as an allusion to the fact that there were non-military victims, celebrated elsewhere (see below). To one of the faces on its 'Roman' memorial, Grosbliederstroph added a black marble panel bearing the gold outline of a French infantry helmet. Often, however, the 1914–18 memorial had been damaged or destroyed, or was simply no longer appropriate to changed circumstances. In these cases the memorial was replaced after 1945 by a new composite edifice commemorating both or sometimes all three conflicts. Puttelange opted for a modern variant on the dead centurion, Bitche for an elaborate fresco which included medieval warriors as well as *pietà*-like motifs and a liberated female captive still bearing broken chains on her wrists. At Théding, an open book records in stone the names of the dead with the dates 1914–18 and 1939–45, as if in a continuous text of loss and remembrance. Though iconographically not very striking, this memorial is of relatively unusual design (the only one so far encountered), and recalls the much-delayed and ultimately never completed '*Livre d'Or*' of the 1920s and 1930s.[13] The bottom of each page bears the epitaph-injunctions '*Ni Haine ni Oubli / Wieder Hass noch Vergessen*' and '*Que l'Humanité vive en paix / Die Menschheit lebe in Frieden*'.

The coal-and-steel towns of Rombas and Petite-Rosselle adopted more frankly nationalistic designs. At the former, side panels list the battles of 1914–18 and 1939–45, while an iron centrepiece portrays a French infantryman, tank commander and partisan, above a marble plaque expressing '*Hommage à nos Déportés, Résistants, Internés, Patriotes*'. Petite-Rosselle opted for a modern bas-relief *pietà* with a dead warrior (not uniformed), and the words '*Ville de Petite Rosselle à la mémoire de ses enfants morts pour la France au cours des guerres 1914–18 et 1939– 45*'. Located close to the regional mining rescue organization's headquarters, in an area where the mineworkings run under the frontier at various points, the memorial incorporates stone safety lamps and collier's tools at each end of the main face.

At Charly-Oradour, a cluster of small individual stones grouped around a soaring obelisk with a crucifixion in bas-relief commemorate the inhabitants of the village who, like thousands of others, were evacuated from the Moselle in 1939 to safety in the west (the Charente, Deux-Sèvres, Haute-Vienne), only to be murdered by the 'Das Reich' division at Oradour-sur-Glane on 10 June 1944. That the stones list men, women and children from the same families, of every age from seventy years to six months, and that the SS unit responsible for the massacre had included thirteen Alsatian draftees, some of whom stood trial in the early 1950s, is a stark reminder that this was a war in which the distinctions between 'them' and 'us', between combatants and non-combatants, were redefined and in which the innocent suffered in new ways. The agony of man's inhumanity to man, the lack of the usual easy identification with the bereft, and the unstated but powerful summons to avoid the repetition of such enormities, are major features of many memorials in the Moselle.

This is strikingly exemplified by the group of unconnected and undifferentiated stone figures created in 1988 beside the church of Saint-Hubert at Rosbruck. Though the faces are recognizable as faces, their traits are distorted, unquiet, and the figures, armless and limbless, seem to rise from the ground or return to it, unclad, or clad only in the distancing, unfamiliar material from which the sculptor has wrought them, leaving them as if embryonic. Rodin's *La Pensée* comes to mind, but 'finish' is denied. A couplet from Aragon's *Strophes pour se souvenir* of 1955:

> Vous n'avez réclamé la gloire ni les larmes
> Ni l'orgue ni la prière aux agonisants[14]

seems to reject the succour of religion, to refuse significance-creating transcendence. Its very incompleteness, however, invites the beholder familiar with the poem, written to celebrate the foreign partisans of the '*groupe Manouchian*' executed in February 1944, silently to recall the remainder of the stanza which proclaims the dead '*Morts pour la France*'.

The new memorial at Montigny-lès-Metz, inaugurated in November 1972 on the twenty-eighth anniversary of the liberation of the town (it replaced a 1914–18 Joan of Arc), is a good example of how some memorials are not just a place, a 'site' of memory in Pierre Nora's now universally accepted phrase, but a *space*, into which the passer-by is invited to penetrate from different sides, and whose significance is progressively revealed/constructed. At first view, between the parish church in weathered Gothic stone, and a modern, lighter-coloured block of low-rise flats, a

Rodinesque figure – man? child? it could be both or either – squats, one hand on head, as if meditating. Almost at ground level, the inscription '*A nos morts*' proclaims the memorial's purpose, which otherwise would not be immediately apparent to the visitor, while the additional inscription '*ils sont morts au maquis dans les camps. Passant souviens t'en*', elides the 'regular' combatant dead (and the problematic '*malgré nous*') and privileges one aspect of the conflict. But that in turn is subsumed into a more significant message about the ultimate incomprehensibility of events, articulated by an incomplete and asymmetrical backdrop whose dark irregular outline seems to dwarf as well as to shelter the squatting figure.

The final example is the memorial erected in 1976 by Longeville-lès-Saint-Avold and two neighbouring 'communes' to commemorate the murder by an SS unit on the night of 3–4 June 1944 of three local men who tried to escape German conscription (*réfractaires*); those who escaped execution were deported to the camps. Situated in rolling countryside outside the town, in the shadow of a grassy bluff surmounted by the characteristic steel cupola of the pre-war Maginot line fortifications and some recent shrubbery and small trees, it is a simple, indeed rather severe, concrete rectangle with a *croix de Lorraine* and the inscription: '*Aux Résistants et aux Déportés 1939–1945*'. An explanatory panel carries the injunction (in German and English as well as French): '*Vous qui passez en ce lieu, souvenez-vous car leur chemin a été celui du sacrifice et leur combat celui de votre liberté*'. The relative severity of the memorial is softened by the landscape and by the view across a wide area of historically contested frontier. Indeed, the visitor who ventures onto the bluff comes upon a small stone calvary offered in 1916 by the German occupiers of the place, still bullet-marked and bearing the inscription '*Zu Ehren Maria Hilf*'. By its complex historical and geographical specificity, the location could not have been better chosen, therefore, to serve as a composite '*lieu de mémoire*' for two wars and two annexations. Inspection of newspaper archives to obtain details on its inauguration revealed, however, that the Maginot line cupola had not been part of the original site, but had been transported to it by the military engineers from Bambiderstroff, some 10 kilometres distant,[15] proof if proof were needed that all 'sites' of memory are in some sense 'constructed'.

Montigny and Longeville might have been among the last examples in Lorraine of a long series of memorial construction, reconstruction or replacement begun after 1945 and might have continued, along with the progressive *aménagement du territoire* during the modernizing 1960s, had it not been for the intrusion of political issues and a change in the general climate of attitudes towards France's recent past following de Gaulle's departure from office in 1969 and his death a year later. Films such as Marcel Ophuls's *Le Chagrin et la Pitié* (1969), banned from national TV but seen by the cinema-going public, and Louis Malle's *Lacombe Lucien* (1974), contributed to increasingly sceptical examination of what became known as the Resistance 'myth'.

More concretely, President Valéry Giscard d'Estaing's proposal in 1975 to abandon the traditional celebrations on 8 May provoked opposition from *anciens combattants* and ex-Resistance organizations who feared the marginalization and ultimate eclipse of the values for which they had fought,[16] provoking national debate on historical memory and commemoration, and giving fresh stimulus to the construction of Second World War and Resistance memorials. Thirty years after the war, with a new entente between France and Germany symbolized in the EEC and in the bi-annual meetings between the heads of state, a practice begun by de Gaulle himself, the President's motives in seeking to *tourner la page* were perfectly honourable, but he underestimated the opposition his proposal would encounter, notably in Alsace-Lorraine. At its national congress at Reims on 23 and 24 May 1975, the *Union des Cheminots Résistants*, better known under the wartime name *Résistance fer*, passed a motion deploring the President's unilateral action, taken, it argued, *'à la surprise de tous, cette commémoration n'ayant jamais eu pour but de maintenir une quelconque agressivité à l'encontre du peuple allemand'.*[17] In March 1976, the *France Libre* parachute team declined to participate in an event at Sigolsheim to be attended by the President.[18] *Souvenir Français* sections which had been in decline (for example Longwy, inactive since the death of its last president in 1964) were stimulated into new life. Others such as Metz, founded in 1907 and still numbering some 200 members, called at its AGM in May 1976 for a recruiting campaign, and decided to ask the municipality to put the *Poilu de l'Esplanade* on a more substantial plinth, considering *'cette vieille figure messine'* to be insufficiently *'mise en valeur'*,[19] a request repeated two years later by the *Comité de Coordination des Associations Patriotiques de la Moselle*. On this occasion, it was argued that not enough was being done to preserve existing memorials from deterioration, and that ways must be found of associating young people with the *'souvenir du sacrifice consenti par leurs aînés'*. Accordingly, it was suggested that *'les plus importantes agglomérations du département aient une rue ou une place qui porte le nom du 8 mai 1945, pour en perpétuer le souvenir'.*[20] The same meeting demanded that the Metz memorial, the great *pietà* at the corner of the rue Serpenoise (now facing onto a busy urban and interurban through route), be resited *'dans un cadre plus propice à l'organisation de cérémonies et au recueillement'*, a demand not so far acceded to.

In parallel with these initiatives, new memorials were inaugurated in 1979 at Schwendorff; in 1984 at Saint-Julien-lès-Metz (Saint-Julien had a very active *Souvenir Français* section, with over 500 members); at

Erching-Guiderkirch, '*seconde commune sinistrée de France*' in terms of its civilian dead (also 1984); and in 1985 at Verny. Of these, only Saint-Julien's memorial was entirely new, Schwerdorff having originally marked 1914–18 by a chapel dedicated to the Sacred Heart (subsequently allowed to fall into disrepair), and Verny, older inhabitants claimed, having had a commemorative cross beside the church which had vanished without trace. In creating or recreating memorials some sixty or seventy years after the event, these communities were surely doing more than repaying a debt to the past. Memory is both static and dynamic, a process of (re)memorization as well as a reservoir of images; it is socially and politically mediated as well as historically and culturally embedded. As the generations are replaced, and overarching perspectives such as class, religion and ideology are further eroded, memory and commemorative activities have become more important as vectors of personal, local and, if not national at least regional, identity.[21]

Notes

1. Slide illustrations used during the conference presentation of the first version of this chapter were from Stirling University French Photographic Archive (SUFPA).
2. See Prost (1977–9), vol. III, p. 41, in which the author explains why he did not include Alsatian memorials in his survey. Alsace-Lorraine is equally absent from Becker (1989) and Bédarida et al. (1986). To my knowledge, Richez (1984), pp. 267–80, is the only local study available, and omits 1870 and 1914–18 and deals exclusively with Alsace.
3. From *Discours*, vol. 2, pp. 170–89, quoted in Bury (1973), p. 68.
4. Figure given by Jean et al. (1929), p. 13.
5. Ibid.
6. By Prost's estimation, perhaps as many as 900. See Prost (1984), p. 224, n. 16.
7. Prost (1977), p. 149.
8. See Kidd (1995).
9. Metz had previously erected '*le Poilu libérateur*', the so-called *Poilu de l'Esplanade*, which, because it celebrated the victorious liberators and not the city's dead, could be safely French.
10. I am indebted to Michel Grandveau of the local *Souvenir Français* section for this information and accompanying illustrations.

11. Barral (1985), p. 122.
12. In the Moselle, notably the *groupe Mario*, formed at the end of 1941, one of whose leaders, Martin Waechter, is commemorated in the churchyard at Rombas.
13. See Chabord (1973).
14. Aragon (1956), pp. 208–9. Better known as a song by Léo Ferré entitled *L'Affiche rouge*, this poem is the subject of Kidd and Blyth (1997).
15. *Le Républicain Lorrain*, 13 May 1976.
16. This episode highlights, incidentally, the singularity of the other Armistice Day (11 November) and its apparent unsuitability as a focus for French commemoration of the Second World War, in contrast to the United Kingdom where the recent fiftieth anniversary excepted, VE-Day celebrations rapidly fell into disuse, to be subsumed into November's Remembrance Sunday.
17. *Le Républicain Lorrain*, 4 June 1975.
18. Ibid., 25 March 1976.
19. Ibid., 2 June 1976.
20. Ibid., 25 April 1978.
21. On cultural aspects of war memorials in France as a whole, see Kidd (1992).

Bibliography

Aragon, L. (1956), *Le Roman inachevé*, Paris: Gallimard.

Barral, P. (1985), 'La tragédie des malgré nous', in *Résistants et Collaborateurs: les Français dans les années noires*, présenté par François Bédarida, Paris: L'Histoire/Seuil, pp. 120–4.

Becker, A. (1989), *Les Monuments aux morts: patrimoine et mémoire de la grande guerre*, Paris: Editions Errance.

Bédarida, F. et al. (1986), *La Mémoire des Français: quarante ans de commémoration de la Seconde Guerre Mondiale*, Paris: Editions du CNRS.

Bury, J. P. T. (1973), *Gambetta and the Making of the Third Republic*, London: Longman.

Chabord, M. Th. (1973), 'Le Livre d'Or de la Première Guerre Mondiale: un projet sans suite', *Revue Historique de l'Armée*, 29ème année, pp. 76–89.

Jean, J. P. et al. (1929), *Le Livre d'Or du Souvenir Français*, Metz: Le Souvenir Français.

Kidd, W. (1992), 'Identity and iconography: French war memorials 1914–1918 and 1939–45', in R. Chapman and N. Hewitt (eds), *Popular Culture and Mass Communication in Twentieth-Century France*, Lampeter: Edwin Mellen Press, pp. 220–40.

Kidd, W. (1995), 'Les monuments aux morts', *Les Cahiers de l'Iroise*, 166, numéro spécial sur 'Bretons dans la grande guerre', pp. 63–8.

Kidd, W. and Blyth, A. H. (1997), 'Aragon, Léo Ferré et "l'affiche rouge"', in Lionel Follet (ed.), *Aragon, Elsa Triolet et les cultures étrangères (Actes du Colloque de Glasgow, 1992)*, Paris: Annales littéraires de l'Université de Besançon, collection 'Linguistique et Sémiotiques', diffusion les Belles Lettres.

Prost, A. (1977), *Les Anciens Combattants, 1914–1940*, Paris: Julliard, Coll. 'Archives'.

Prost, A. (1977–9), *Les Anciens Combattants et la société française, 1914–1939*, 3 vols, Paris: Presses de la Fondation Nationale des Sciences Politiques.

Prost, A. (1984), 'Les monuments aux morts. Culte républicain? Culte civique? Culte patriotique?', in *Les Lieux de mémoire, t. 1, 'La République'* sous la direction de Pierre Nora, Paris: Gallimard, pp. 195–225.

Richez, J. C. (1984), 'Remarques sur la commémoration de la seconde guerre mondiale en Alsace', in *Mémoire de la Seconde Guerre Mondiale (Actes du Colloque de Metz, 6–8 octobre 1938 présentés par Alfred Wahl)*, Metz: Centre de Recherche Histoire et Civilisation de l'Université de Metz.

Part V

Film

–10–

Popular Film, Popular Memory: The Case of the Second World War

Sue Harper

Ah, the war! The officers was ever so cruel to us, Mest' Harper, tied us to gun-wheels, they did, and rolled us down the hill to the enemy.

This is an unverifiable scrap of popular memory. It was a remark about the First World War by an old man, made to my father in 1948. It was immediately recycled into family lore; 'tied us to gun-wheels, they did' became my family's shorthand for unreasonable demands, or even for an unusually hard day's work. We knew that the old man in question had the usual experience in the trenches, but he appeared to have constructed an image of his own history via mythical and highly dramatized accounts. He had made it seem like a scene from a film; and as such it was more satisfactory to him than reality, because it had structure, perspective and catharsis. It is an instructive example of the way an individual may transform the past in a selective and ordered way, depending on the cultural resources at his or her disposal.

During the 1930s and 1940s, film clearly played a major role in the audience's notions of sexual attractiveness and acceptable social behaviour; it also doubtless had some input into their sense of a national past. The relationship between popular film and social memory is complex, and there are several issues which need to be disentangled from each other. Firstly, what contribution did film make to popular memory? Secondly, were the commercially successful films of the Second World War the ones which became key texts in popular memory? Thirdly, what were the industrial and cultural determinants on those post-1945 representations of the war which did well at the box-office, such as *The Dam Busters* and *The Cruel Sea*?

When we consider the contribution of film to popular memory, we are likely to encounter problems with the term 'popular' rather than with 'memory'. We know that memories are structured and selective, and that they may be accessed through a range of discourses which are private and informal as well as public and institutionalized. Memories may reside in autobiographies and conversations, buildings, rituals, paintings, novels and advertisements but, to be useful to the historian, they need to inhere in texts of some sort; it is difficult to assess them if their existence can only be inferred from their social effects. John Tosh describes some modern historians' preoccupation with discourse-less memory as 'the history of mentalities'.[1] This is a thousand miles away from the old intellectual history, which was idealist and inductive, but the problem for the materialist 'historian of mentalities' is that particular rigour is required to establish the nature of the evidence. One of the legacies of the discrediting of the Althusserian model is that the term 'ideology' can no longer be used by historians with any confidence. In any case, as Althusser (rather than Marx) used it, it was always a 'fuzzy concept'.

But it is possible to argue that popular memory is a 'fuzzy concept' too. Certainly the wilder shores of popular memory abut onto the territory of 'folk memory'. Even if we manage to rid popular memory of its taint of 'folk', it still seems a dangerously sentimental concept. During the 1970s Michel Foucault deployed the term 'popular memory' and for him it had nothing in common with dominant memory: 'It is an actual fact that people – I'm talking about people who are barred from writing, from producing their books themselves, from drawing up their own historical accounts – that these people nevertheless do have a way of recording history, of remembering it, of keeping it fresh and using it.'[2] The problem with this approach to popular memory is that it encourages an exclusive pre-occupation with the unconscious and repressed aspects of the generation of meaning, which may have a narrowing effect in the long run. It is really no different from George Orwell's insight from forty years earlier, namely that official history tends to record saints and emperors and to collude in the invisibility of the lives of slaves. Popular memory as a concept has become far too attached to a particular orthodoxy, which is usually fuelled by a sense of political disappointment. In my opinion, it is important not to canonize the popular, or to present it as the hero in the battle against the forces of darkness. It is one part (a crucial one) of wider patterns of social remembering, and we should ensure that we attribute to it a properly conceived class base, as Lefebvre does in *Critique of Everyday Life*.[3] It would be far more fruitful to deploy the term *mass memory* instead. Mass memory can be treated in precisely the same way as the mass audience; it can be categorized according to different class fractions, it can be periodized and, perhaps most importantly, it can be analysed in terms of its gender composition.

Let us return to our (now rephrased) question: what contribution does film make to mass memory? What is the precise relationship between commercially successful films and the mass audience's sense of national identity and interest? The answer depends upon the extent to which cinema can be defined as a mass medium in the period at issue. From the early 1950s, cinema in Britain progressively became a minority activity. Increasingly, it had to compete with other leisure outlets such as television and DIY; and, as Douglas Gomery drily notes, the post-war baby boom meant that people had chosen 'the psychic advantages of having children' over other forms of fun.[4] The box-office successes were, quite simply, based on smaller returns and smaller audiences than the 1930s and 1940s. This means that after (say) 1957 it is difficult to attribute the same degree of cultural significance to popular films, and it is correspondingly difficult to relate them to mass memory.

Certainly cinema was the most important entertainment industry in the 1930s and 1940s. Its aim was to maximize company profits through audience pleasure. The provision of textual delight for the masses was a politically fraught issue, and a sense of moral panic was certainly inculcated by a number of official and quasi-official bodies during this period. The Historical Association, the British Film Institute and the Ministry of Information (MoI) all expressed intense disquiet about the *type* of national history which mass audiences preferred.[5] These institutions were, quite simply, disgusted that mass audiences preferred florid films like *The Private Life of Henry VIII* and *The Wicked Lady*, and they did their best (to little avail) to persuade them to turn to more respectable pleasures. There was no easy consonance between the views of official bodies and mass audiences, nor is it possible to demonstrate conclusively the effect critics had, whether they were populist, highbrow or middlebrow.

So an analysis of the patterns of mass taste is of paramount importance in establishing the input of film into social memories of the war. It is quite clear that audiences had a wide range of film choices, and were discriminating in their tastes. Rather than dismissing audience pleasures of the 1930s and 1940s as 'false consciousness' (that is, seeing viewers as dupes conned by venal producers and exhibitors), we should ascribe creativity to them. That is to say, some popular films of the period contained various and sometimes contradictory discourses, but audiences were able to decode the messages they bore. They used the films to make sense of their own lives. Gramsci argues that the realm of the individual consciousness contains living fossils or residual deposits from the past, and that one should know oneself as 'the product of the historical process which has left in you an infinity of traces'.[6] Film culture contains such fossils too, and the match between these and the residual substrata in the individual's mind is what produces the shock of recognition caused by some films. The pleasure is in the snug fit, like Cinderella's slipper. It is that which makes them popular. So it is possible to argue that film audiences have (and indeed had then) a distinct liking for *residual* films;

for texts which encouraged that sense of security and ease, that snug fit. When British audiences chose British films, they were therefore often likely to be those which evoked deeply rooted *topoi* in the culture. They tended to avoid film enterprises that were, culturally speaking, shallow-rooted. This meant that audiences, particularly those under the intense daily pressures of war, had an in-built bias against representations of the contemporary. A degree of 'time slippage' was essential before the mass audience could prefer films which dealt with the purely contemporary; or, if contemporary films *were* favoured, it was because they contained a significant proportion of residual elements concealed within them. This is a major determinant on film's input into the national view of the war.

There is lamentably little material on actual viewing figures, and the returns on which *Kinematograph Weekly* based its lists of popular films are not available for scrutiny.[7] However, *Kineweekly* listings do show that popular films included a sizeable proportion of American vehicles with no reference to contemporary events (*Rebecca, Hello Frisco, Hello!, Going My Way, Jane Eyre, Cover Girl, Meet Me in Saint Louis, National Velvet, The Bells of St Mary's*). There were many florid Gainsborough melodramas, many of them in historical costume (*The Man in Grey, Fanny by Gaslight, Love Story, Madonna of the Seven Moons, They Were Sisters, The Wicked Lady, Caravan*). Some non-Gainsborough British melodramas also appeared in the lists (*The Seventh Veil, Waltz Time, Hatter's Castle, Dead of Night, Brief Encounter, Lady Hamilton*). The final category of popular film, perhaps the most crucial for us, was that of contemporary war (*49th Parallel, In Which We Serve, Life and Death of Colonel Blimp, The Way Ahead, Perfect Strangers, The Way to the Stars*).

What is interesting about this final set is that each of them gives symbolic significance and textual space to quite a small class fraction. The only exception to this is *The Way Ahead*, which was released on D-Day and which was in effect made for the MoI. This film insists on welding together disparate class groups in the national interest; all the other films give centre-stage to one particular social group, and permit that class fraction to investigate the war from a very narrow perspective. For *49th Parallel*, the key group is the European intelligentsia; for *In Which We Serve*, it is the upper middle class which is the lodestone; for *Blimp*, the gentry class; for *Perfect Strangers*, the lower middle class; and for *The Way to the Stars,* the middle middle class. The film audience in the 1930s and 1940s was extremely sensitive to class distinction: one Mass-Observation letter-writer managed to distinguish between twenty-six different class fractions, and one lower-middle class respondent nicely defined the *middle* middle class as the one which contains 'the well bred dog, the wife who always notices pregnancies in others, sportsmen who go into religion, cultured homosexuals, people slumming'.[8] We might tentatively suggest that these war films (*Blimp* etc.) won favour at the box-office because they offered a coherent interpretation and a comfortably narrow perspective on the international conflict; the old social order is presented as perfectly competent for the job in hand. Audiences could only tolerate images of the anxiety they were experiencing if that anxiety was neutralized by the confident presentation of a class system in which each group had its own idiolect and coherence. This argument does not of course account for the popularity of low-status anodynes like *The Wicked Lady* or more expensive fare like *Lady Hamilton*. These were popular because they dealt with the new dispensation of war, but in disguise, as it were; and they all foregrounded not class but gender as their major item of concern. This chimed in with the changing audience composition of the war period, which was more predominantly female than before.

But *Kineweekly* lists are impressionistic, and with them one has to remain at the level of surmise. To correct this, there are two sets of detailed box-office data, one for Macclesfield and one for Portsmouth.[9] The latter is a list of audience figures of the Regent cinema, and detailed attention to these produces fascinating insights into mass taste. There are some dissimilarities from the Macclesfield figures. Anything to do with the navy tended to do better in Portsmouth than elsewhere, and local bombing patterns, cinema fires, price increases and the periodic nightly exodus of large numbers of the population early in the war all disrupted Portsmouth film-going. Nonetheless a clear pattern emerges from a comparison of both sets of figures, which come from cinemas serving upper working-class/lower middle-class areas. American films, particularly those of Deanna Durbin, did extremely well. But only American films of a certain type; it is piquant to note that in Portsmouth in 1942 Durbin's *It Started with Eve* did extraordinarily good business. It had the highest admissions figures of all at 22,757, whereas in the same year *Citizen Kane* (the darling of film critics) did worst of all at 8,320. The average viewing figures for that year were 13,930.

The Portsmouth and Macclesfield figures are salutary reminders of the great variety of product offered, and of the volatility and selectivity of audience taste. In Portsmouth, for example, in October/November 1942, the heavily promoted (and MoI-backed) *The Young Mr Pitt* did very badly at 10,401, coming forty-fifth out of the year's fifty-two films, even though it was paired with the sensational *Brooklyn Orchid*. These low figures had nothing to do with war or local anxieties, since only two weeks before, *Pardon My Sarong* (a low-status American comedy) came in at 20,136. In 1943, the MoI-backed film about women factory workers, *Millions Like Us*, did very badly at 8,452, whereas only two weeks later another British film about women workers (nurses), *The Lamp Still Burns*, did very well indeed at 18,388. (The average attendance was 12,841.) It is tempting to conclude that Portsmouth audiences liked films about feisty female workers with a taste for romance, but did not warm to films in which war and grief were paramount and in which women were invited to identify with a protagonist who was dependent and winsome. In 1944, the Regent's favourite film was the American musical *Cover Girl* (24,762 out of the year's average of 14,801), but it was run a close second by Noel Coward's *This Happy Breed* at 23,426. This is of great interest, since the film emphasizes family life and the lower middle class, and avoids much mention of the war. There remains the issue of the Gainsborough melodramas. Without a doubt these were runaway hits at the Regent, producing unparalleled figures. For 1945 (average figures 16,128) the best films were Gainsborough's *Madonna of the Seven Moons* (35,189) and *They Were Sisters* (42,022). Since there is no record at the Regent since 1930 of any other film having more than 28,000 viewers (the exception was *Min and Bill* in 1931), these are truly remarkable figures. After the war, the 1946 figures are similar. The average was 16,716, and *The Wicked Lady* gained 48,309. *Caravan* had 46,156.

Clearly, the evidence of attendance figures suggests that it was a very particular type of film that would constitute the material of mass memory in the Second World War. It was usually a flamboyant and excessive melodrama that pleased the mass audience; if it was a war film, it had to be class-specific. This evidence scotches the notion that popular film, or mass memory based on it, bore any resemblance to real events. If it were the case that the war was literally reflected in the films that people favoured and remembered, then it would have been an event in which everyone wore flounced frocks (albeit with class carefully inscribed) and engaged in rough trade. No, people clearly preferred and remembered films from the war period which resolved their anxieties on a *symbolic* level.

However, we also need to look to other kinds of evidence than attendance figures, and in this regard, the books of J. P. Mayer are useful. Mayer was a sociologist who held elitist views on popular culture; he thought that films like *The Wicked Lady* were roughly commensurate with the bread and circuses provided by the Roman emperors. Nonetheless, his publications, the 1946 *Sociology of Film* and the 1948 *British Cinemas and their Audiences*, are invaluable, since they give us access to the (mainly wartime) remembrances of audiences, however coded and selected the utterances are. In the 1946 book, Mayer asked whether respondents ever modelled their behaviour on that of characters in films, and whether their dreams were affected by the films they saw. The responses show clear patterns. Far more women than men admit to being deeply affected by films, and dreaming of them; those who admit to being strongly influenced by films are further down the social ladder; and war films figure very little in their memory of the war period. When modern films from the war *are* recalled, martial elements are selected out. Consider this on *Mrs Miniver* (an MGM film about the impact of war on a British family) from a nineteen-year-old female clerk: 'I think that the happy companionship and love shown in such films as *Mrs Miniver* is the ideal of everyone. Perhaps they make us expect too much of our boyfriends.' Or this response from another nineteen-year-old girl living at home to *Love Story* (a film about a girl with fatal heart disease and a flyer going blind who decide to return to the fray of war and love): 'the hero was what every girl dreams about, handsome, thoughtful, kind and well mannered, and in meeting one of the opposite sex, it is only natural to try to find those qualities in him'.[10] The films which encapsulate the war years for most respondents are those which present pleasures, sexual and sartorial, which were then beyond their means.

Mayer's 1948 book also contains useful material. There are sharp gender distinctions in taste, which crystallize over the issue of historical versus contemporary films. Female respondents (particularly those lower down the social scale) preferred historical films to those that dealt with modern problems: one hairdresser remembered the war period thus:

> I soon found out that I enjoyed historical films, though I believe that the lovely costumes had a great deal to do with it, for I can often remember the times that I would come home and dream that I was the lovely heroine in a beautiful blue crinoline with a feather in my hair. I used to pray so hard for that crinoline.[11]

When they did recall films about the war, female respondents tended, again, to 'rewrite' them in a way which minimized martial conflict. *The Way to the Stars* was remembered by one female thus: 'Douglas Montgomery was very good as Johnny, but I do not see why he had to die at the end. It seemed entirely unnecessary and did not help the plot at all.'[12] *In Which We Serve* and *The Way Ahead* were recalled because 'the glimpses of home life were suptly [*sic*] real without any decoration'.[13] Male respondents by contrast insisted on the intensity of their identification with war heroes. *The Way to the Stars* was remembered by one nineteen-year-old because 'the very lack of Slush made a lump in your throat . . . these people made you feel good, you lived with them, thought with them, felt as they felt, and in fact for two hours you were not you sitting in the one-and-ninepennies, but were living in that film'.[14] A 25-year-old engineering draughtsman praised British war films because they 'tell a straight, unvarnished tale from life and leave it at that . . . no tragic scenes with babies, tears galore, mock heroics, but an epic slice of life'.[15]

The letter pages from *Picturegoer* and other film magazines during the 1940s repeat these findings: that the remembrance of films was determined by gender. Academic studies endorsed this too. Post-war work at the University of Birmingham indicated very clearly that what adolescents remembered from the war period were the Gainsborough blockbusters, especially *The Wicked Lady*. But the males' response was predicated on rather a coercive moralism, in that the heroine had acquired the vicious habit of pleasure and so met 'her just end for her crimes'.[16] Females remembered that 'the beautiful dresses and hairstyles made me speechless with longing'. And one fourteen-year-old was well aware of the earthy aspects of the tale: 'after she had been married to him for a few weeks she refused to sleep with him. Every night she meets Jackson who is a passionate lover.'[17]

Mass-Observation material from the war period is useful too, though not quite late enough to be conclusive. The directive from November 1943 ('What films have you liked during the last year? Please list six films in order of liking') shows again that the Gainsborough films were firmly placed in audience memories, but that the way they were recalled depended on gender. Women liked the flamboyant style of *The Man in Grey,* but men liked it because it provided a welcome return to the days before sexual equality: 'It is "escapist", and we forget the present to dwell in the past when young ladies were taught just what to say to men who asked for their hand in marriage, even though the latter were scoundrels.'[18]

We should not be tempted into interpreting the cinema as a place which conferred temporary homogeneity on a class society. Mass-Observation material from 1939 indicates that, for many middle-class film-goers, the cinema was disapproved of, since it encouraged undue social mixing. Where you sat, and what you enjoyed, were important markers of class status for many middle-class patrons. And the memories they carried away were similarly marked by the cultural competence of their class.[19]

If we now turn to our second question, that of whether the commercially successful films of the war period were the same ones that became key texts in mass memory, we are faced again with the vexed issue of evidence. The first answer to the question must be 'it depends on whose utterance has been preserved for posterity'. The second answer would probably be 'no'. It would be very nice if there were a properly conducted survey with balanced class coverage, but there is not. What there is, though, is a very interesting and extensive Mass-Observation survey from the 1950s asking which films prompted audiences to tears. This material has been analyzed by Vincent Porter and myself, and our findings show that a major change had taken place in audiences' assessment of the war's emotional impact. Very many respondents, both male and female, remarked that the war had instigated a major increase in their emotional receptivity. Put simply, they were more emotionally 'raw' than they had been before, and thus much more sensitive to the blandishments of film art. Some respondents were thus much more suspicious of films which deliberately addressed their feelings, and melodramas were accordingly much more mistrusted than before. Of greater interest, though, are the writers' assessment from the perspective of the 1950s of what really were the great films. *The Wicked Lady* and the like were virtually eradicated from memory and certainly from admiration. Instead, a new pantheon emerged, of art-house films on the one hand and realist and modern films on the other. Of course, these preferences might be accounted for by the fact that the survey was irredeemably biased towards middle-class respondents. The male replies are the most interesting for our purposes here. The films which most caught them on the raw (and usually uncomfortably so) were feature films and documentaries which dealt precisely with aspects of their own war. Such a shift in memory habits must perforce have had enormous implications for the film industry, since men and women clearly remembered the war differently.[20]

If we now turn to our third question, about the industrial and cultural constraints on post-1945 representations of the war, we need to bear in mind that wartime presentations of the military conflict were predicated on lack of foreknowledge of events. Happy endings in pre-1945 films are always negotiated and conditional, and their narrative structures are totally determined by this. After 1945, cinematic representations of the war could have the luxury of the 'adventure' guise, since the happy ending was a foregone conclusion. The adventure tale has an extremely long pedigree in British culture, and although as a mode its progenitors have always been conceived as Rider Haggard and Buchan, it probably has its roots further back in Stevenson and even in Defoe. In any case, it has always been an unambiguously masculine genre, and this tradition is upheld by the proliferation of war films after 1950.

However, detailed attention to Gifford's *The British Film Catalogue 1895–1985* is necessary before we give too caricatured a version of film output. There were an enormous number of comedy films made in the 1950s (*The Belles of St Trinian's, The Ladykillers*) as well as many social dramas (*Yield to the Night, The Flesh Is Weak*). But it is certainly the case that there was an enormous increase in war films and that these figure significantly in box-office ratings: consider *The Wooden Horse* (1950), *The Cruel Sea* (1953) *The Colditz Story* (1955), *The Dam Busters* (1955), *Cockleshell Heroes* (1955), *Reach for the Sky* (1956), *Bridge on the River Kwai* (1957), *Dunkirk* (1958), *Ice Cold in Alex* (1958). These are films which are still 'bankable' insofar as they are quoted in modern television advertisements, the Holsten Pils and Carling Black Label ones using *The Dam Busters* for example. Indeed, right up until the 1970s, every time a cinema closed in Portsmouth, *The Cruel Sea* was shown as the last film of all: a kind of cinematic Last Post.

We are hampered in our analysis of the 'memory significance' of these films by the paucity of oral evidence. There is some material from actors and film-makers of the period, but it is rather commonsensical: Sir John Mills notes that 'people saw the war as rather heroic, exciting and romantic, and we were still going through a tremendous degree of austerity' and Richard Todd argues that 'Americans had cowboys and Indians and we didn't. The only action films we made with any reality were war films. I suppose there was an element of nostalgia for "our finest hour" as well.'[21] The only collection of memoirs of film-going of the period contains few useful references, and in any case respondents are not a balanced selection.[22] There are a few letters in the contemporary *Picturegoer* about war films, but they are inconclusive.

So the significance of these popular war films has to be a matter of textual interpretation and surmise. What is interesting is that none of these films duplicates the narrowing of class interest noted in pre-1945 war films. Rather, these later films flatten out class difference, and they all argue that gender is a determinant which dominates over class. They all evince a preoccupation with male bonding and, without exception, they all undervalue the female presence. In addition, they all deploy realist visual techniques.[23] Not for these film-makers the expressionist extravaganzas of (say) *Pandora and the Flying Dutchman* or *The Tales of Hoffmann*. The *mise-en-scène* of all these war films is thoroughly consonant with the views of those (largely middle-class and always male) film-goers and critics of the 1940s and early 1950s who had insisted that realism was the only respectable way for art to deal with one's feelings. They were all adapted from popular novels (as the Gainsborough films had been), and they all had a degree of access to military service facilities in the course of their production.

How are we to assess these films, and their popularity? On one level we may interpret them as the producers' response to changing gender compositions in the film audience; that audiences no longer wanted the costume blockbusters, because all the women were, quite properly, at home. On another level we may interpret the war films as a nervous response from an industry under acute stress; the breakdown of the studio system, economic crisis and the threat from television led a range of entrepreneurs to play it safe. According to this model, the war setting serves as a kind of shorthand for a known past, the recounting of which confers security and the ritualized dispersal of anxiety. Another attractive model is that this particular mass medium had appropriated to itself the function of society's mythologist. Film culture had come to operate as a fulcrum of the recent past. It had become the gatekeeper of mass memory.

But mass *male* memory perhaps. One way of reading popular film is that it is part of the nation talking to itself, explaining to its fellows (here the word is used advisedly) that which is unspeakable in everyday discourse. Popular film does not just permit the expression of repressed desires; it also justifies the unpalatable past and makes it comfortable. The 1950s war films are thoroughly consonant with the literary tradition of adventure tales, in which action instead of meditation is the dominant mode. But these films might also be interpreted as fathers speaking to sons about themselves and their experiences. Hence the flattening out of class difference alluded to before: the films need to prioritize gender over class. The desired camaraderie cannot obtain without class differences being elided. It is a delicious irony in film history that this exactly repeats the aims of those wartime MoI films which audiences were so reluctant to see; except that MoI policy and films did give some attention, however grudging, to females.

The view of the war encapsulated in these films is just as partial in its way as the image of the past contained in the Gainsborough melodramas. It is not the war of the Blitz or rationing or sexual bonanzas or the Russian convoys or the black market or evacuation or the blackout or death by fire. The place evoked by such films as *The Cruel Sea* is paradoxically a dry one; it is an arena in which male protagonists may interrogate themselves for weakness and insufficient enterprise, and in which they may gain emotional sustenance from their comrades. These films evoke a male (and possibly pre-war) utopia in which interfering females have been consigned to the invisible kitchen quarters.

During the 1940s, it looks as if audiences preferred and remembered films which encouraged them to conceive of the war as a temporary crisis. Audiences chose to alleviate their sufferings with films which arranged gender elements in a radical manner, and class elements in a retrospective and compartmentalized one. However, the memory of war as contained within such films as *Love Story* and *Perfect Strangers* was short-lived. The field of power – social as well as sexual – had altered in such a way as to necessitate a reorientation of representations of the war. During the 1950s it was selectively rewritten by film culture as a specifically male experience. It did not remain thus for ever, of course. British cinema attempted to redress the balance in later periods; but to pursue that point is outside the scope of this chapter.

Notes

1. Tosh (1991), p. 103.
2. Foucault (1977).
3. Lefebvre (1991).
4. Gomery (1992), p. 88.
5. Harper (1994).
6. Gramsci (1957), p. 59.
7. *Kinematograph Weekly*'s list of box-office successes for the war are as follows, in a curtailed form (in each case the first film mentioned is the overall winner).

    1940: *Rebecca, Convoy, Foreign Correspondent, Ninotchka*

    1941: *49th Parallel, The Great Dictator, Pimpernel Smith, All This and Heaven Too, Lady Hamilton, Major Barbara*

    1942: *Mrs Miniver, The First of the Few, How Green Was My Valley, Reap the Wild Wind, Holiday Inn, Hatter's Castle, The Young Mr Pitt*

    1943: *In Which We Serve, Casablanca, Life And Death of Colonel Blimp, Hello Frisco, Hello, The Man In Grey, The Lamp Still Burns, The Adventures of Tartu*

    1944: *For Whom The Bell Tolls, This Happy Breed, Song of Bernadette, Going My Way, Jane Eyre, Cover Girl, Fanny By Gaslight, The Way Ahead*

    1945: *The Seventh Veil, Madonna of the Seven Moons, Frenchman's Creek, Arsenic and Old Lace, Meet Me in Saint Louis, They Were Sisters, The Princess and the Pirate, I Live in Grosvenor Square, Perfect Strangers, Waterloo Road, The Way to the Stars, Henry V*

    1946: *The Wicked Lady, The Bells of St Mary's, Piccadilly Incident, Brief Encounter, The Captive Heart, Caravan, Mildred Pierce, Courage of Lassie, Caesar and Cleopatra*

8. Mass-Observation Directive, June 1939. The question asked respondents which class they thought they belonged to. The directive also questioned them about their feelings on cinema.
9. See Poole (1987). The Portsmouth material is in the City Records Office at Portsmouth, and is the subject of a forthcoming article by Marjorie Hales and myself.
10. Mayer (1946), pp. 223, 257.
11. Mayer (1948), p. 22.
12. Ibid., p. 167.
13. Ibid., p. 172.

14. Ibid., p. 194.
15. Ibid., p. 222.
16. Wall and Simpson (1949), p. 133.
17. Kesterton (1948), pp. 99, 102.
18. Mass-Observation Directive, November 1943.
19. Mass-Observation Directive, June 1939.
20. Harper and Porter (1996).
21. McFarlane (1992), pp. 173, 219.
22. O'Brien and Eyles (1993). There is nothing either in Breakwell and Hammond (1993).
23. Note the interesting account of the extraordinary lengths the film-makers went to to obtain the realistic effects in *The Dam Busters* in McFarlane (1992), p. 220.

Bibliography

Breakwell, I. and Hammond, P. (eds) (1993), *Seeing in the Dark: A Compendium of Cinemagoing*, London: Serpent's Tail.

Foucault, M. (1977), 'Interview with Michel Foucault', *Edinburgh '77 Magazine*, pp. 21–2.

Gomery, D. (1992), *Shared Pleasures: A History of Movie Presentation in the United States*, London: British Film Institute.

Gramsci, A. (1957), *The Modern Prince and Other Writings*, New York: International Publishers.

Harper, S. (1994), *Picturing the Past: The Rise and Fall of the British Costume Film*, London: British Film Institute.

Harper, S. and Porter, V. (1996), 'Moved to tears: weeping in the cinema in post-war Britain', *Screen*, Summer 1996.

Kesterton, B. (1948), 'The social and emotional effects of the recreational film upon adolescents of 13 and 14 years of age in the West Bromwich area', unpublished University of Birmingham PhD thesis.

Lefebvre, H. (1991), *Critique of Everyday Life*, trans. John Moore, London: Verso. This was first published in 1947.

McFarlane, B. (ed.) (1992), *Sixty Voices: Celebrities Recall the Golden Years of British Cinema,* London: British Film Institute.

Mass-Observation material, Mass-Observation Archive, University of Sussex. Directives, June 1939, November 1943.

Mayer, J. P. (1946), *Sociology of Film*, London: Faber.

Mayer, J. P. (1948), *British Cinemas and their Audiences*, London: Dennis Dobson.

O'Brien, M. and Eyles, A. (1993), *Enter the Dream-House; Memories of Cinemas in South London from the Twenties to the Sixties*, London: British Film Institute.

Poole, J. (1987), 'British cinema attendance in wartime: audience preference at the Majestic, Macclesfield, 1939–46', *Historical Journal of Film, Radio and Television*, vol. 7, no. 1, pp. 15–34.

Tosh, J. (1991), *The Pursuit of History*, London: Longman, 2nd edition. First published in 1984.

Wall, W. D. and Simpson, W. A. (1949), 'The film choices of adolescents', *British Journal of Educational Psychology*, vol. xix, no. 2, pp. 121–36.

11

The Vietnam Film and American Memory
John Hellmann

Ten years ago, *American Myth and the Legacy of Vietnam* (1986) chronicled the profound change in the collective American story that took place in the quarter-century between 1958 and 1983 – the disruption of the public myth in which the United States held up a mirror to its collective identity. That disruption was located in an imaginary geography, a symbolic landscape that Americans projected from the previous landscapes of American myth and called Vietnam. There, in addition to bringing extra-ordinary suffering to the people and ecology of the actual country, Americans looked into the mirror of their projected myth and saw reflected back an image that they have not yet been able to forget. The Vietnam War is remembered by Americans, out of all proportion to its material ramifications for the United States, because it was a symbolic war played out within the framework of American myth.

A myth is the construction in narrative, or story, of a collective memory. That memory involves acts of forgetting and fantasy as much as of pre-serving. By the term 'public myth', therefore, reference is made to the core story – articulated through a succession of specific variations upon it – expressing the dominant ideology of the nation-state. The specific complex of stories working variations on that core story, or myth, make up a mythology.

The most important mythology of the United States, subsuming virtually all the competing myths, has been that of the frontier. The frontier mythology is a complex of narratives constructed in triumphant, if some-times vaguely troubled or regretful, affirmation of the American expansion into the forests of New England, the plains of Texas and New Mexico, and the islands of the South Pacific. In the frontier myth, Americans have remembered their history within a master-narrative shaped by their ideology of individualism, freedom, success and special mission. In that master-narrative or public myth, white Europeans leave Europe, or the eastern city or any other emblem of civilization, to move into a wilderness. There the white European male hero works a double transformation. He regresses in a nostalgic return to a more natural state, becoming almost a white Indian as he sheds the artificialities and corruptions of an excessively civilized state. But he also subdues the wilderness, slaying the Indian savage and working as the agent of an advancing progress. In the nineteenth century the most important vehicle for this mythology was the frontier romance. Early in the twentieth century, as the Western became Hollywood's most popular genre, film took over the role of articulating the frontier mythology.[1]

That mythology was profoundly disrupted in Vietnam. With the co-operation of his friends in the press, John F. Kennedy authored the public image of the Special Forces, the so-called Green Berets, as heroes of his New Frontier. In 1961 and 1962, the two full years of the Kennedy administration, American popular magazines showed their audience a dream vision in which contemporary events in south-east Asia were unfolding in photographs and text repeating the defining elements of American myth. This seemingly real-life 'movie' offered the additional pleasure of revising those disturbing elements still marginally present even in the memory of the Old Frontier encoded in Westerns – the racist dispossession of the native inhabitants. Instead, the contemporary descendants of the Western hero were shown bestowing a liberal protection and improvement upon the native inhabitants of this New Frontier.

What followed is known to us all. After Kennedy's assassination and his successor Lyndon Johnson's escalations of American involvement, one terrible spectacle after another was transmitted by television back home to American living rooms. Vietnam became the place where everyone, as a character says in Robert Stone's novel *Dog Soldiers*, 'finds out who they are'.[2] If the frontier was the mythic landscape in which Americans had found their unique identity, then this New Frontier, which had proved as unwilling to give itself as had the 'virgin' wilderness of Manifest Destiny, spoke some terrible message indeed. Kennedy's rhetorical evocation of a New Frontier, and his promotion of Vietnam as a specific setting of that landscape in which contemporary Americans would simultaneously return to the mythic landscape of their pioneer heritage and redeem that heritage of its sins, had invested Vietnam with an expectation that made its frustration apocalyptic.

A public myth is as necessary as it is inevitable. At its best, such a narrative provides the simplified – but vivid, easily recalled and sense-making – shape in which a nation can accept, understand and move forward from a historical catastrophe. If it affords a viable map to a nation's history, circumstances and resources, it can serve as a guide to its future. The alternative is confusion leading to disintegration, or the allure of dangerous myths, fantasies lacking a true guide to actual historical experience. That way lies regressive madness. The stakes are high.

To clarify this clash between the public myth and the Vietnam memory, to suggest why the most important site for mirroring that clash is film and to indicate how the best of the Vietnam films hold the potential to transform that clash into an opening for a profound transformation of American identity, examination will first be made of an episode from the book *Dispatches* (1977), written by Michael Herr and published prior to the major retrospective films on the war. This brief narrative – only two pages in length – encapsulates the traumatic rupture, the unsought and unwanted knowledge, Vietnam has presented to the American public myth; and it foreshadows the course that film would take in depicting Americans in Vietnam. Its author arrived in Vietnam in the middle of 1967, and spent two years there as a reporter on a loosely structured assignment for *Esquire* magazine. In 1977, a full decade later, he produced a book about that experience which is widely regarded as the finest work of American literature to come out of the Vietnam War. Presented by his publishers as a work of memoir and journalism, Herr himself has said that '*Dispatches* is really a book about the writing of a book.'[3] Herr's assertion can be seen as an apt description of the intense struggle the book dramatizes in its author's attempt to bring the 'facts' of his Vietnam experience into the American stories he brought with him. *Dispatches* is a search within Herr's memory for the new story within those facts. What makes his private memory a collective search for all Americans is the role that he shows American movies played in constructing not only his and other Americans' memories but also the 'facts' that Americans played out in Vietnam.[4]

The episode from *Dispatches* to be discussed has itself inspired moments in two major Vietnam films, and has thus made a major contribution to the construction of collective American memory of the war. It served as the basis for the Do Lung bridge sequence in Francis Ford Coppola's epic *Apocalypse Now* (1979), on which Herr worked as a writer, contributing in particular to Captain Willard's voice-over narration. The thematic elements of the *Dispatches* episode may also be discerned as a crucial source for the vision of Stanley Kubrick's Vietnam film *Full Metal Jacket* (1987), for which Herr received credit as co-author of the screenplay. If this brief passage has had an exceptional influence upon the Vietnam film, that influence represents a deepening of Herr's intervention in the movies' mythic power, for the passage is itself about how American film was bound up in the American experience of Vietnam. It is about how American film was 'projected' onto that country.

The episode is set in Khe Sahn, the isolated American base in the remote north-western highlands of South Vietnam which in 1967 was besieged for many months by North Vietnamese forces. At the opening of this episode, the narrator tells how one night he is awakened from his sleep by a boyish American soldier named Mayhew, who informs him that a few North Vietnamese sappers have just been caught trying to infiltrate the base defences. Herr's night-time visitor – like a messenger come in a dream – tempts Herr with a vision of obtaining his deepest wish as a journalist: 'Come on,' he said to me. 'See if we can get you a story.'[5] Indeed, Herr's description of his walk out towards the perimeter suggests a walk through a dreamscape: 'We walked that way in the dark, figures appearing and disappearing in the mist around us, odd, floating presences.' Herr and Mayhew learn from a lieutenant that they have just missed what the lieutenant calls 'the good part', which occurred when three North Vietnamese were sighted attempting to penetrate the outermost line of perimeter wire. 'Missed the good part' is of course a phrase we associate with movie-watching.

The lieutenant is telling Herr that he has missed something entertaining, the satisfying spectacle of the elusive Vietnamese enemy being exposed and destroyed. Movie-watching is the social equivalent of the individual process of dreaming. We speak of movies as mass dreams, for we recognize that the movie screen is the place where we watch culture-wide anxieties answered with compensating wishes played out in the spectacles before us. This metaphor has its analogy in Khe Sahn itself, which had become a spectacle in 1967 in the American media. As a strategy, the reinforcing of the remote base of Khe Sahn, after North Vietnamese troops began massing around it, was itself a response of the American high command to a growing anxiety. The dream was that the heretofore invisible and elusive enemy would at last be lured into a decisive battle in which superior American firepower would bring the war to the desired conclusion.

Immediately after the lieutenant's movie-watching analogy, the three watching Americans hear a sound from the darkness that brings a dissonant note into Herr's hearing of the desired story: 'We heard then what sounded at first like a little girl crying, a subdued, delicate wailing, and as we listened it became louder and more intense, taking on pain as it grew until it was a full, piercing shriek. The three of us turned to each other, we could almost feel each other shivering.' The description of their 'shivering' in the dark furthers the framing of this scene as one of three young Americans watching an actual scene through the mythological/ideological lenses provided by their childhood experiences at the movies. The 'shivering' of the three young American men, watching from the dark, and the shriek coming out of the darkened screen formed for them by the space out on the perimeter, suggests that they are at a horror movie. But then a figure joins them out of another familiar movie genre, stepping not out of the screen before them but rather from the mysterious space behind, the place where in a movie theatre the technology of projection sends forth its fantasy images. Herr tells us:

A Marine brushed past us. He had a mustache and a piece of camoflaged parachute silk fastened bandana-style around his throat, and on his hip he wore a holster which held an M-79 grenade launcher. For a second I thought I'd hallucinated him. I hadn't heard him approaching, and I tried now to see where he might have come from, but I couldn't.

In a sense, Michael Herr *has* 'hallucinated' this Marine. As a viewer of films and television, Herr has participated in the same mass-culture fantasies that have led the marine to costume himself in Vietnam as a Hollywood gunfighter. The passage continues:

The M-79 had been cut down and fitted with a special stock. It was obviously a well-loved object; you could see the kind of work that had gone into it by the amount of light caught from the flares that glistened on the stock. The Marine looked serious, dead-eyed serious, and his right hand hung above the holster, waiting.

The marine is prepared to draw. American readers of Michael Herr's text know the scene about to unfold. It is the one played out in fateful repetitions throughout the history of the American Western, never more intensely than on the film and television screens of the decade and a half leading up to Herr's standing before this spectacle in Khe Sahn. Indeed, every Saturday night for twenty years, from 1955 to 1975, it was the introductory ritual for the television series *Gunsmoke*, when the hero would stand tall in face-to-face confrontation before responding to the first draw of the gunman at the other end of the street by drawing his own gun and protecting civilization in a single act of justified violence. In 1961, the first year of the Kennedy administration which would send American military 'advisors' into combat in Vietnam, *Gunsmoke* was expanded from thirty minutes to an hour, and was one of thirty television Westerns.[6] Not some chemical substance, but an electrified image is the source of Herr's apparent hallucination.

But the fantasy-ritual of the gunfight, creating a desire that has brought the performing Marine and the watching Michael Herr to Vietnam, is unfolding into a spectacle of horror. For the object of our Western hero's attentions is not before us as a deadly gunfighter who will draw first, an emblem of the savagery that must be subdued through an act of justified violence, but is rather manifested in the image of a shrieking voice that sounds 'like a little girl crying'.

'Wait,' the [Marine] said. 'I'll fix that fucker.'

His hand was resting now on the handle of the weapon. The sobbing began again, and the screaming; we had the pattern now, the North Vietnamese was screaming the same thing over and over, and we didn't need a translator to tell us what it was.

'Put that fucker away,' the Marine said, as though to himself. He drew the weapon, opened the breach and dropped in a round that looked like a great swollen bullet, listening very carefully all the while to the shrieking. He placed the M-79 over his left forearm and aimed for a second before firing. There was an enormous flash on the wire 200 meters away, a spray of orange sparks, and then everything was still except for the roll of some bombs exploding kilometers away and the sound of the M-79 being opened, closed again and returned to the holster. Nothing changed on the Marine's face, nothing, and he moved back into the darkness.

'Get some,' Mayhew said quietly. 'Man, did you *see* that?'

And I said, Yes (lying), it was something, really something.

The lieutenant said he hoped that I was getting some real good stories here. He told me to take it easy and disappeared. Mayhew looked out at the wire again, but the silence of the ground in front of us was really talking to him now. His fingers were limp, touching his face, and he looked like a kid at a scary movie. I poked his arm and we went back to the bunker for some more of that sleep.

Note the extreme duality of focus in this passage. It is presented as fact, not fiction. Herr tells us he saw this, and it happened as he describes it. But he also presents it in a narrative pattern familiar from dream and myth, a symbol-laden story of being summoned from a deep sleep to take a dream journey towards a profound revelation. The messenger promises Herr the story he has come to Vietnam seeking, and when Herr follows, the messenger takes him into a self-conscious enactment of the stories that Americans have projected to mirror their desire, have enacted to fulfil that desire.

But as it unfolds in familiar images and actions, it contains one image, one vehicle of information, that creates dissonance in the familiar genre of the Western, indeed flips it over into the horror genre. That image is the 'shriek' that sounds 'like a little girl crying'. Herr gives us no words that would provide a specific message from the voice that is penetrating the perimeter of the base, here also the perimeter of his consciousness. His American identity, his complicity in the American mission and American fantasies, monitors this information, displacing its full reception. Yet Herr tells us he did not need a 'translator' to know what the voice was telling him. It can be assumed that this means that the voice is crying out in helpless agony, perhaps in a plea for rescue. That presents the deeper, repressed information of Vietnam to his consciousness. The image of 'a little girl crying', literally untrue – since the sound actually emanates from a North Vietnamese soldier who moments before represented a deadly threat – exists only in Herr's consciousness. It is thus a vehicle for information from his own unconscious, his own repressed recognition that his observations in Vietnam are in some way terribly at variance with the American story he has brought there. What is that 'little girl crying'?

The Vietnam Film and American Memory

In 1978, shortly after first reading *Dispatches*, I went to the film that effectively ended the period of collective American amnesia that had followed the withdrawal of American combat forces from Vietnam five years earlier. Because of the social nature of the movie-viewing experience, a film has a tremendous potential for becoming a cultural event. After a full decade of division and conflict over Vietnam, Americans notoriously stopped talking about the war after American combat forces were withdrawn in 1973. Even the television news spectacle of the fall of Saigon in 1975 was quickly put away from American consciousness. *The Deer Hunter* brought Vietnam back to American consciousness. It started the post-war conversation among competing narratives concerning the meaning of the war for Americans. The response that I had to my viewing of *The Deer Hunter*, together with my reading of *Dispatches*, would lead to my writing my book about the connections between Vietnam and American mythology.

I had two compelling responses to my first viewing of *The Deer Hunter*. I was possessed by what seemed an inordinately strong reaction to the opening Vietnam scene, which does not come until over an hour into a three-hour film. In that scene the title hero comes to consciousness on the edge of a village in Vietnam to find a North Vietnamese soldier about to shoot a woman and child. Attempting rescue, the hero turns a flame-thrower on the Vietnamese soldier, but not in time to save the woman and child. Watching this scene, I experienced excitement and horror combined with a disturbing *deja vu*. Over the subsequent days and nights, I kept returning in my mind to a sense that I had been in that place, that I had witnessed this scene before, though I had in fact never been to Vietnam.

My other response was perplexity. *The Deer Hunter* was a much stranger film than I had anticipated. For one thing, it was aggressively unrealistic in obvious ways, violating all kinds of obvious elements of verisimilitude to time and place. For example, the Allegheny Mountains portrayed in the film might be the magnificent peaks I visualized when I listened to 'America the Beautiful', but they were not the ones I had seen in Pennsylvania (they were, in fact, the Cascade Mountains of Washington state, transported the length of a continent by the magic of film). For another, it developed into a series of ritualistic encounters involving hunting and Russian roulette that did not immediately yield their meaning, nor upon reflection have the slightest thing to do with the actual methods of hunting deer or one's plausible odds with a six-chambered pistol pointed at one's head.

I knew of course that the title *The Deer Hunter* alluded to James Fenimore Cooper's frontier romance *The Deerslayer*. *The Deerslayer* is one of that early American author's five 'Leatherstocking Tales', which introduced the prototype for the Western hero. But it took repeated viewings of the film, considerable reflection upon my mysterious *dejà vu*, before the answer presented itself to me. Of course, I had been there. Of course, I had been in the presence of a lone white hero attempting to rescue a mother and child from a dark-skinned man. I had been there as a boy in the 1950s and early 1960s as I sat wide-eyed in front of my television set, been there as I gazed up in the darkness of the cinema, been there as I willingly entered the adventure book propped on my lap, been there as I read and viewed a seemingly endless succession of frontier romances and Westerns. Cooper's *The Deerslayer* turns on a series of captivities and rescues in the dark forests of the colonial frontier. The legendary accounts of Daniel Boone and Cooper's frontier romances began the Western by replacing the earlier narratives of Indian captivity, originating from the colonial Puritans, with tales of rescue and revenge. The defining situation, the core story, of the American frontier myth is the climactic moment in which a white male hero, dressed in buckskin or another emblem of his adaptation to the wilderness, slays a dark-skinned man, signified as the full 'savagery' potential in that wilderness if it is left untamed, to rescue a white woman and child, signifying the newly developing civilization.

The opening Vietnam scene of *The Deer Hunter* both repeats and, like the scene from Michael Herr's book *Dispatches,* nightmarishly alters this core story of the American frontier myth. In this case the woman and child are not being saved, and indeed the woman and child killed by the 'savage' North Vietnamese are at the beginning of the scene fleeing into a shelter as an American helicopter swoops in to drop an incendiary bomb upon their village. The woman and child are threatened by a masculine violence coming from both wilderness and machine, both savagery and civilization. Finally, *The Deer Hunter* turns in its last third from a Western set in Vietnam into a story of the white male hero's struggle to free himself, and his community, from captivity to his former obsession with 'one-shot' affirmation of his purity and control.

Contemplating my *dejà vu*, I realized that there was good reason for the American landscape in *The Deer Hunter* to be aggressively unrealistic. Of course, the Allegheny Mountains of that film are really the inspiring peaks celebrated in American song. The American landscape depicted in *The Deer Hunter* is the idealized landscape of American romance and myth. The artistic strategy of *The Deer Hunter* is to depict Vietnam as made up of the core elements of the landscape of the American mythology of the frontier, but to show those elements – the oppositions between savagery and civilization, hero and villain – rendered subtly confused, and thus the myth disturbingly undermined. If Vietnam is at first used in *The Deer Hunter* as a setting for a re-enactment of the Western, the

American experience in Vietnam alters that re-enactment as an awful experience might alter a familiar dream.

Because film, specifically the Western, played such a crucial role in the performance of the national myth that Americans expected to stage in Vietnam, film has been the most important site for Americans' remembering of the war. There they have re-enacted their memory of the war through the lenses of their original dream of it. Thus the Vietnam film has been by turns a decidedly romantic, surrealistic and cartoonish genre. It has taken these high and low forms because they have in common their pointing to the world of fantasy and dream, and that is the mode through which America journeyed on its way to its Vietnam nightmare.

Since I wrote my chronicle of the fate of the American frontier myth in Vietnam, American film-makers have played a central role in creating two regressive mythologies, the mythology of *Rambo* (1985) and the mythology of *JFK* (1991). One focuses on the obsession with the ghosts of those 'missing in action', requiring a Sylvester Stallone to bring them back, the other with phantom snipers on a grassy knoll, demanding a Kevin Costner to walk down the mean streets of recent American history to find out how they led to the corruption of Vietnam. In either case, what is registered is a profound cognitive rupture between the public myth of the United States and recent historical experience. And in either case, the theme is rescue. But now the new American hero must rescue the lost heroes of the public myth – precisely themselves, precisely Americans' pre-Vietnam idea of themselves.

H. Bruce Franklin, who has brilliantly exposed the cynical political calculations contributing to the MIA myth, has also observed that the myth is rooted in a more profound sickness in American culture: 'For its power springs from sources much deeper than the Vietnam War itself, though intimately related to the motives that led America to wage that war and to the war's aftermath in America.'[7] William Gibson, chronicling the paramilitary culture that the Rambo films helped catalyse, has correctly seen the phenomenon as a determined flight from the revelations that Vietnam should have brought to Americans: 'Unable to find a rational way to face the tasks of rebuilding society and reinventing themselves, men instead sought refuge in myths from both America's frontier past and ancient times.'[8]

In contrast to such regressive tendencies in Hollywood, the best films – *The Deer Hunter, Apocalypse Now* and *Full Metal Jacket* – have sought to bring the memory of Vietnam to bear upon American mythic identity in a profoundly transformative way. In the climactic episode of *Full Metal Jacket,* for example, we find a voice outside the public myth of the United States attempting to be heard, attempting to supply some, as Herr puts it countless times in *Dispatches*, 'new information'. In *Dispatches* Herr dramatizes the extinguishing of the voice of 'a little girl crying' by an American marine costumed in the garb of the American public myth. Herr helped make *Full Metal Jacket*, and the film dramatizes similar scenes of brutal extinguishing of the voices of the gender or racial 'other'. But the film moves towards dramatizing and interpreting Vietnam as what Herr in *Dispatches* called the 'turnaround point' of American history. For in the climax marines find that the sniper who has been successfully tormenting and emasculating them is a young Vietnamese girl. Michael Klein has pointed out that 'When the lone sniper is revealed to us to be a Vietnamese woman, the ideological mold of the conventional combat film is shattered.'[9] As she at last lies wounded beneath the surviving marines, the marines find themselves in a situation that is untenable according to their own mythology. Susan White observes that 'They are clearly confused by this woman who embodies both the repulsive and castrating "otherness" of womanhood and the ephemeral virginal/warrior ideal.'[10]

Joker, the protagonist of the film, shoots her, to which the other marines respond by telling him that he is 'hardcore'. But the extinguishing of her voice within the film hardly eliminates it from echoing in the consciousness of the movie-watcher. The revelation that the avenging sniper is a young Vietnamese woman is the surprising 'turnaround point' of the long progression of furious assaults upon femininity, particularly within the male self, that organizes the plot of *Full Metal Jacket* from boot camp in the United States to the various Vietnam scenes. Joker does not make the journey of self-transformation made by the hero of *The Deer Hunter*, but his failure calls upon the viewer to do so as the only path to avoid, as Joker articulates his own fate in the voice-over at the end of the film, being in 'a world of shit'.

The Deer Hunter, *Apocalypse Now* and *Full Metal Jacket* are such important sites of American memory because they have frankly recalled Vietnam as a planned staging of American myth, thus anticipated to be a pleasing spectacle, which instead reflected back the knowledge of American history repressed from that myth. Vietnam became indeed America's New Frontier, the setting in which the crimes against nature, and those defined by white males as closer to nature, were not validated by victory.

To contemplate the message that the Vietnam experience brings to American consciousness, let us conclude by returning to that defensive wire surrounding the American base at Khe Sahn, where a 'shriek' penetrates the perimeter of Michael Herr's consciousness. It has smuggled towards Herr and his fellow Americans in the form of a Vietnamese soldier. It has come in savage shape. It had meant to do him harm. The form lies close to the earth, held at bay by American defences. But in Herr's dreamlike experience, or perhaps more truly in his mythologizing narrative, it has revealed itself to him as a feminized and infantilized voice of pain. It does not need a translator, because it speaks at a level prior to language, prior to ideology, prior to the construction of the 'other'. It is perhaps exactly that voice, which in the American frontier myth has been projected onto a shrieking savage and a crying woman and infant, marginalized objects of threat and rescue, that speaks to Americans from the horrifying memory, the rupture in American myth, called Vietnam.

Notes

1. The classic articulation of this myth may be found in Frederick Jackson Turner's 1893 lecture 'The significance of the frontier in American history'. For a comprehensive analysis of Turner's lecture, and of the significance of the frontier myth for American memory in the twentieth century, see Slotkin (1992).
2. Stone (1974), p. 57.
3. Schroeder (1992), p. 34.
4. For an extended discussion of *Dispatches* as journalism, see Hellmann (1981), pp. 126–38.
5. Herr (1977), pp. 141–3. All of my quotations from this text will be found in these cited pages.
6. Lemon (1995), p. 126.
7. Franklin (1992), p. 168.
8. Gibson (1994), p. 12.
9. Klein (1990), p. 32.
10. White (1991), p. 212.

Bibliography

Franklin, H. Bruce (1992), *M.I.A. or Mythmaking in America*, New Brunswick, NJ: Rutgers University Press.

Gibson, James William (1994), *Warrior Dreams: Paramilitary Culture in Post-Vietnam America*, New York: Hill and Wang.

Hellmann, John (1981), *Fables of Fact: The New Journalism as New Fiction*, Urbana: University of Illinois Press.

Herr, Michael (1977), *Dispatches,* New York: Knopf.

Klein, Michael (1990), 'Historical memory, film and the Vietnam era', in L. Dittmar and G. Michaud (eds), *From Hanoi to Hollywood:*

The Vietnam War in American Film, New Brunswick, NJ: Rutgers University Press, pp. 19–40.

Lemon, Richard (1995), 'The last showdown', *Entertainment Weekly*, 25 August–1 September, p. 126.

Schroeder, Eric James (1992), *Vietnam, We've All Been There: Interviews with American Writers*, Westport, Conn.: Praeger.

Slotkin, Richard (1992), *Gunfighter Nation: The Myth of the Frontier in Twentieth-Century America*, New York: Atheneum.

Stone, Robert (1974), *Dog Soldiers* (reprinted New York: Ballantine, 1975).

White, Susan (1991), 'Male bonding, Hollywood orientalism and the repression of the feminine in Kubrick's *Full Metal Jacket*', in M. Anderegg (ed.), *Inventing Vietnam: The War in Film and Television*, Philadelphia: Temple University Press, pp. 204–30.

Part VI

Popular Memory

12

Past Wars and Present Conflicts: From the Second World War to the Gulf

Martin Shaw

In the fifty years since 1945, the real-life relationships of people in Western society to war have been transformed: in important senses we live in a 'post-military society'.[1] The transformation has had three major aspects. Geopolitically, war has been abolished among the major Western powers and, more recently and problematically, between the West and some of the other world powers such as Russia and China. Institutionally, there has been a major shift away from conscription: the result today is that no man under the age of fifty in Britain (which initiated this trend) has experience of compulsory military service. Last but not least, there have been cultural shifts, which are the focus of this chapter.

It has been argued that the participatory mass militarism of citizen warfare has been replaced by a culture of the weapon ('armament culture', as Robin Luckham has described it[2]) or a 'spectator sport', popular militarism which is no more than one element in a consumer culture.[3] Wars take place at a safe distance from the people of the West, who view them on television as 'high-tech' spectacles. Mann takes this case to the extreme when he concludes that in the way they become media events, wars like the Falklands or Grenada 'are not qualitatively different from the Olympic Games'.[4]

If there has been such a transformation of militarism in Western societies, it cannot be assumed that all national societies and cultures experience it in the same way. This is because if militarism is in considerable part a matter of culture, it will be mediated by traditions and myths, which are themselves the products of historic experience, and thus depend on memory. We can hypothesize that tradition, myths, memory and propaganda to do with past wars will be extremely important in our relationships to current conflicts.

It is important to define these concepts. 'Tradition' refers to the collective construction of values and practices, arising from past experience, with which certain social activities in the present are approached. 'Myth' refers to specific stories and beliefs about the past which are commonly constructed and play a part in a culture. 'Memory' refers to images, beliefs and feelings which arise primarily from individual experience, although they are often constructed and reconstructed in terms of tradition and myth. 'Propaganda' refers to images and statements which are utilized to persuade people to take a particular view and usually to support a particular policy: tradition, myth and memory are often exploited in this way.

In our times, national traditions hardened and reinforced by both myths and memories of the Second World War are playing central roles both in the eruption of bitter new civil wars and in the ways in which people in the West perceive them. At the centre of the current conflicts in former Yugoslavia, for example, are national traditions which cultivate fiercely opposed myths of 1939–45.

It is heroic struggle in the context of defeat and victimization that forms the stuff of myths of war. Defeat and victimization are, of course, a large part of what war is about for individual combatants and their families, even in the most successful of campaigns. When they are the collective experience of peoples and nations, they are especially potent, and in the Second World War, only the North Americans largely escaped the horrors of occupation and mass slaughter of civilians, although these were unevenly visited elsewhere. The British had a unique experience, avoiding the fate of invasion which was suffered by most European and Asian peoples, but facing a very real threat and a reality of bombardment from the air which the North Americans were spared. It is this combination, linked to forms of mass participation and sharing in victory, which account for the specific form of British myths of war.[5] The British share of victory in 1945 is supremely important in setting the tone for the experience of militarism in British culture. It built on a century or more of similar successes, not only in the First World War, but before that in South Africa, the Crimea and even the Napoleonic Wars, not to mention countless colonial conflicts – we have to go back to the American War of Independence to find a major British defeat.

It would therefore be unsurprising if British attitudes to war were not rather more positive than those of other nations. In the period since 1945, moreover, while American confidence has been greatly deflated by Vietnam, the British have had nothing worse than the Suez débâcle, largely expunged from the national record by the remarkable success of the Falklands War. If we examine militarism in British culture, we find a pervasive 'nostalgia militarism', a cosy celebration of wartime gardening and the shared heroism of the Blitz, neatly summed up in the studied ambiguities of the redesigned Imperial War Museum.[6]

Mention of the Falklands brings us to the role of propaganda in the construction of myth and tradition. Memories are not just there, nor do they simply evolve: they are consciously stimulated and appropriated by political forces. In the former Yugoslavia, for example, memories of all the awful things that happened in the Second World War had been suppressed, repressed or at least endured for over forty years after 1945, in order to enable people of all nationalities to live together and a federal state to function. It was only when it suited politicians in the various republics to revive nationalist traditions and myths that memories of 1939–45 moved back to the centre of Yugoslav life.

During the Falklands War Margaret Thatcher clearly tried, in a way in which no other British leader has done since 1945, to revive a wartime nationalism and beliefs about British heroism, to put as she phrased it 'the Great back into Great Britain'. She played effectively on the British national myth of war – centred on the belief in the need to stand firm militarily against aggressive dictators – a myth which has served not only for the Cold War but at Suez and, more recently as I shall discuss shortly, in the Gulf. In Thatcher's appropriation of the Second World War memories there was, however, a particularly limited version of wartime experience, since she wished to claim the patriotism while jettisoning the sharing of equality under threat.[7]

This discussion is designed to underline the case that memory cannot be understood as free-standing. Memories of the Second World War are the products both of the ways individuals appropriated their experiences at the time, and of the ways in which these initial memories have shaped and been shaped by their subsequent experience. Memories are also the products of national traditions and myths and both sustain and are sustained by these wider forces, shaping collective versions of memory.[8] These traditions and myths, in turn, are constantly renewed in political and ideological contexts, as political leaders seek to turn them to their own advantage and as interpreters, notably in mass media of communication, seek to project new versions for our consumption. This chapter, like other academic studies, can also be understood as just such an attempt, although I hope less narrowly motivated than many.

Memories of the Second World War in the Gulf Conflict

The rest of this chapter examines the roles of memories of past wars in responses to current conflicts. I base my discussion on several different kinds of research which I carried out concerning the Gulf War of 1991. It is important to emphasize that none of this research was designed primarily to uncover or understand evidence of memories of past wars as such. On the contrary, its aim was to understand attitudes in the present, but a major hypothesis of the project was that past experiences of war would be a powerful factor in forming current responses. I wanted to find out both the extent to which this could be said to be true and also something about how it worked – for example, the extent to which responses were based on deeply felt memories of the violence and hurt of war, or on more ideologically constructed memories of sets of political circumstances. For memory, of course, comes in many forms, and an important question is why different people remember similar general sets of historical events, such as the Second World War, in very different ways.

Although the Gulf War was under preparation for five months, my own research was planned mainly in the last ten days before American jets attacked Baghdad on 17 January 1991. In devising schemes of research at the last minute, with limited resources, I faced a dilemma between extensive and intensive research strategies. I could find out a lot about how a few people were responding to the war, or correspondingly less about the responses of larger numbers. In the event I did both, by carrying out (together with my colleague Dr Roy Carr-Hill) two postal surveys based on random samples of a local population, and by later utilizing diaries of the war collected by the Mass-Observation Archive at Sussex University. This work was carried out in conjunction with a study of newspaper coverage of the war in the British Library at Colindale.

In the surveys, the questions we could ask relating to the influences of past experiences, in the context of many other factors, were inevitably limited. Our data are based on correlating answers to factual questions about war-participation with general attitude questions on the war. This gives us nothing directly on memory, but it does give us statistically significant information about relationships in which memories are undoubtedly involved.[9] In particular, it suggested that there was a particular set of attitudes to the Gulf War more likely to be held among men who had served in the armed forces in the Second World War than by other groups in the population. Such men were, like other people who had had some direct or indirect involvement with war or the military, more likely to approve of the war than people who had no such involvement.[10] They were less likely to agree that television coverage 'glorified the war too much' or was 'too patriotic'. They were less likely also, however, to acknowledge that they felt 'excited' or even 'fascinated' by the war – these responses were almost exclusively those of a minority of younger men (not women), too young to have direct experience of the Second World War.

Men with Second World War service, in our surveys, were not likely to favour using nuclear weapons against Iraq – this was a view particularly concentrated among a minority of *Sun* readers. They were, marginally, even more strongly concerned than other groups in the population about the fate of British service personnel, and less concerned about the fate of Iraqi soldiers. When asked about their personal responses to the war, they were less likely to express anxiety (this was overwhelmingly a female response) and more likely to agree that they 'felt good about British and allied successes'.

Perhaps most indicative of a 'Second World War' mindset in reactions to the Gulf War was the response to our question, 'What do you think of Saddam Hussein?' While most people agreed that he was 'a dangerous man', older people, both male and female, were more likely than younger people to agree that he was 'like Hitler', and less likely to agree that he was 'mad' (which was very much a young person's response). Older people were also more likely than younger to endorse the anti-appeasement view that 'we have to stand up to dictators' as a reason for justifying the war.

The influences of a Second World War mindset at this level may not, however, equate with the effect of memory as much as with that of manipulation. In particular it seems to testify to the effect of popular newspapers in diffusing images of current conflict which mobilized myths about the past, and played on the memories of older people. The memories on which they were playing were, moreover, memories of wartime propaganda, as much as wartime memories of other kinds.

The importance of this point is underlined by the fact that the differences in attitudes between people of the Second World War generation, especially men, and younger people were relatively small, especially when compared with the differences between the readers of different newspapers in our sample.[11] At the level of political attitudes, therefore, the significance of past experience of war seems modest in contemporary Britain.

There may, however, be other levels at which it counts more. If Mann's idea of 'spectator sport militarism' is right, how do we account for the widespread anxiety which the onset of the Gulf War occasioned? Despite the relatively small numbers of British personnel involved and the technical advantages which minimized the risks to them, no fewer than one in eight respondents in our sample claimed to be 'worried about family or friends in the Gulf'.[12] Almost one-third – especially women, older people and readers of quality papers – acknowledged that they were 'anxious about the violence of the war in general'. Others reported that family members had been adversely affected by the war. 'Anxiety' responses were far more commonly reported than those of 'feeling good' or 'excited' or 'fascinated', or not being personally affected by the war. This survey evidence, moreover, is corroborated by evidence of panic at the onset of war – the large number of calls to the Samaritans, the widespread fear of conscription among young people – and of the depression of consumer spending during the war.

Why, we might ask, were people anxious about a war far away, which was portrayed on television with images widely perceived as more akin to video games than the horrors of previous wars? Virtually no images of anyone dead, dying or even wounded appeared on screen or in most of the newspapers for almost four weeks after the war started, until the bombing of the Amiriyah shelter in Baghdad on 13 February 1991. Even this incident was explained away with a large measure of success.[13] This apart, death stalked the television screens and the pages of most newspapers only fleetingly, and chiefly after the bombing of fleeing Iraqis at Mutlah Ridge, when the war was almost over.

Some of our survey respondents added comments which suggest where the fear and anxiety about war was coming from. 'I am not a war-monger,' wrote one woman, 'having been blitzed out during the last war. I dread to think of my grandchildren and what they are going to have to live through in the future.' Or from another older woman, 'I have been on the receiving end of bombs from the air, and I would not wish it on anyone.' It seems plausible to suggest that personal memories like these, although likely to be held only by a minority of the population who were affected in this way, are an important source of anxiety about war in general and resistance to war-enthusiasm (although this is not to deny that many, perhaps most, people with such memories are likely to give political endorsement to what is presented as a justified war). These individual memories no doubt combine with knowledge about the horrors, dangers, hardships and coercion of war, imparted in families as well as by mass media and education, to form a popular perception of war partially at odds with, although doubtless also partly compatible with, the more heroic and patriotic myths of past conflicts.[14] Without such a substratum of popular knowledge, how could one explain the fact that my students immediately believed that the onset of war could lead to their being conscripted, despite the fact that no general, politician, media commentator or strategist had mentioned the possibility, and that any of these would immediately have disabused them of their anxiety had they been asked?[15]

In order to investigate such issues further we undoubtedly needed more qualitative evidence than a survey can provide. I have been fortunate in being able to examine the 'diaries' which the Mass-Observation Archive asked their national panel of respondents to keep during the Gulf crisis.[16] The panel is more female, middle-class and middle- or even old-aged than the British population at large. The responses to the Gulf 'directive', of just over half the panel, certainly reflected if they did not exacerbate these biases, and the writings – which are mostly not diaries as such – are a rich source of evidence on how recollections of the Second World War informed the responses of older people to the Gulf conflict.[17]

Here I point up some of the most significant features of the Mass-Observation evidence. Chief among these must undoubtedly be the differences between men's and women's responses. Those who confine themselves to studying political attitudes to war sometimes argue that the differences between the sexes are small. We found in our surveys that when we look instead at feelings about war, the gap is much wider.[18] When we look in detail at how people expressed on paper, in their own words, their interest in and approach to the Gulf War, we find the most striking differences between men and women, especially in the Second World War generation.

Women's responses often reflect the personal recollection of the horror of war which we have already illustrated. At its strongest, memory is harnessed to a very firm rejection of war, as in this comment by a retired medical secretary in her sixties: 'I suppose there are many who did not see the results of the blitz on London and South East England. I saw a mentally and physically handicapped boy left in his wheelchair with his mother dying in the ground beside him, that's war. War in the Gulf – NEVER, NEVER, NEVER.' The same woman, writing a month before the outbreak of war, has a vivid picture of the way in which it will turn out: 'The poor souls who fought in the sand will be left with their legs shot off, maybe half a face missing. War in the Gulf – NO, NO, NO.'[19] Another woman, comparing air-raid sirens remembered from the Second World War, makes the imaginative leap from her own to the Iraqis' experience: 'It must have been terrible living in Baghdad with air raids every night, something the children will never forget.'[20]

At the other extreme, some of the older women's fears of war are for a return of the mundane hardships associated with life on the home front. A social worker reports her 71-year-old mother as being 'convinced that the Gulf War would bring rationing like they had in the Second World War. She advised me to buy up metal items like saucepans.' The daughter, who reports that when she first heard the news of the Iraqi invasion she 'felt very anxious and frightened', also reports her own worries of a mundane kind – about petrol shortages, plans to close down local maternity wards to deal with Gulf casualties and the appeals for blood donors.[21]

Different ways in which concern about war is expressed reflect the contrasting experiences of women according to their age at the time of the Second World War. A woman in her fifties, for example, who articulates a common female denial of expertise on the politics of war, makes a strong statement of a child's perspective on war: 'This is not a subject that I am equipped to comment upon but I have lived as a child through World War II and I would not with that experience on other children.'[22] It is actually quite rare to find a woman respondent who does not express some concern about the threatening side of war. Doubtless the panellists, having volunteered to write about their feelings, are likely to include a higher proportion of more critically minded people than would be found in the general population. Nevertheless, these sentiments are not found in the same way among the male panellists, and the patriotic woman whose main point is that 'I object strongly to various councils who are preventing people from displaying the Union flag. I'd like to see it flying from every flagpole. There's a lack of patriotism which I would like to see back again'[23] is actually quite exceptional. Perhaps the best general impression of the contradictory feelings of many women who had experienced the Second World War is given in the diary entries of a retired secretary in her seventies:

(16/11/90) Having lived through two world wars, I cannot believe I could see another.
(16/1/91) It is Dead Line. Memories of World War II are still flooding back.
(17/1/91) Awoke to find war had started. My head felt in a whirl and I started to tremble.
(19/1/91) I met many of my friends of my own age group (late 70s) this afternoon. All were saying how they are reliving the days of World War II.
(3/2/91) The older ones who remember war . . . are apprehensive and regretful that we should have arrived at this state of affairs, yet they are fiercely patriotic. [A nurse told her of an 11-year-old girl who said 'I'm glad we are at war', and when asked why replied, 'I missed the other two!'] 'I wonder how long she will feel like that?'
(27/2/91) I have also observed there is a generation gap, it is the grandparents and their grandchildren who are most apprehensive. The middle generation are confident of victory.
(1/3/91) I still think war is so futile but with dictators such as Saddam Hussein it was necessary. He is a megalomaniac, as Hitler was.[24]

The equation of Saddam with Hitler is volunteered by very many of the older women, just as it is by the older men: it is rare that we find any exceptions to this view. One was the woman who spotted a different likeness – a physical one of Saddam with Stalin, which she demonstrated with photographs.[25] A less common response was that of the woman who wrote, 'I get sickened by some of the cant and hyperbole too – Saddam Hussein is certainly aggressive, but a "Hitler?" – no!'[26]

Older women are less likely to express the feeling shown by quite a number of younger women, who admit to being confused or even simply uninterested in world events, as in this not untypical comment:

I've two main responses – one is boredom and the other is worry. I know I should be interested in world affairs, but the Gulf has no direct connection with me, or my family. The news – or is it the speculation – is so unremitting that one gets saturated by the coverage and switches off . . . As yet the crisis is too remote, in place not time.[27]

This sort of complaint is rarer among men, almost all of whom aspire to some political or strategic knowledge. Even one unusual writer – who confesses, early on in the conflict, that 'I have a mental blockage with this subject – I just shut it out, so that I cannot remember the names of various politicians, generals, etc.' – later finds the common male appetite for this sort of information.[28] Men, younger as well as older, tend to think strategically, politically, logistically and back to previous wars, as in this reflection of a man in his forties, too young to have actually experienced it himself:

> We can deliver a boy with a broken leg or an upset tummy to a UK hospital within, say, 12 hours of him arriving at the Gulf airhead for the flight home – probably comparable with the time from Etaples to Charing Cross in 1914–18! ... With all that going on, we probably don't think too much about the whys and wherefores: a lot of time is taken up with studying intelligence reports and operational data; little time is devoted to explanation.

However 'what stands out', he says, is that Saddam Hussein is like Hitler, 'if you substitute Kurds for Jews . . . Kuwait for Poland and so on'.[29]

Older men manifest this greater aptitude for things political and military within the context of their own experience of war, often very different from the women's, but which is also relived as they write about the Gulf. A surprising number of respondents were actually in the Middle East or North Africa, suggesting that panellists with this background may have been stimulated to write by the Gulf events. The comments which are thrown up range from these rather desultory and mildly racist remarks: 'My only personal experience of the Middle East was during the war, in Egypt and the Western Desert . . ... As far as we were concerned they were all wogs (wily oriental gentlemen) but to be fair I didn't have much to do with them as the army led its own life in vast base camps'[30] to these altogether sharper and more vivid statements (by a retired civil servant in his sixties), which contrast the apparent ease of the Gulf War victory with the horrors of his own war more than four decades previously:

> (8/11/90) My only experience of the Middle East is WWII back and forth across that desert like a yo-yo, hot clammy days and freezing nights . . .
> (28/2/91) The Gulf War has ended, lost lives, revenge wanted on Hussein, Yanks basking in the glory they could never achieve in Vietnam . . . How could they lose, the odds of 30-to-1 against. Did they face Tobruck, Benghazi, did they hell, 6 weeks was all it took, no Rommel to outwit them . . . But plenty of books telling how it was, what I did, what I saw, then the armchair general giving versions on TV at £75 a throw, we should have done this, we should have done that, Monty was missed.[31]

This point about the difference between the Gulf and the Second World War is reinforced by a teacher, ex-RAF:

I lived through the phony war in uniform, I can only call this the screwy war. Here we had troops ringing up their Mum from the front – asking for sweets and comics – spilling the beans about all sorts of security matters . . . I wondered at times who was fighting on our side little boys – and girls . . . We heard of stress – even battle fatigue was mentioned – before a shot was fired. Oh dear! What a do . . . I might have written home – I did from Burma – but not for sweets and comics . . ..[32]

Whereas many women relive the fear of being bombed and sympathize with civilians on the receiving end in Iraq, men tend to imagine what it must be like to face the Gulf War as combatant: 'Imagine,' writes one, 'as I read in the Daily Mirror, of being vapourized by 3000 degrees Centigrade of a shell passing through a tank and out the other side.'[33]

It is only those who were in the Middle East whose memories are stimulated. Personal experience and political logic are related in many men's minds, as these comments by an ex-sailor illustrate:

Believe me, I am no jingoist. I was born in 1926, and saw the last war, and was in the RN for the last 18 months of it. The nearest thing I had to a hero was Mahatma Gandhi, in my schooldays . . . Short of letting this monster devour our fellow-men, the military build-up is inevitable . . . Saddam Hussein is another Hitler . . . in some ways he is worse.

After the shelter bombing, the same man writes that 'From a personal point of view I'm outraged that civilians might have been placed in harm's way and I blame the Iraqi government and leadership for that.' He agrees with Dennis Healey – who has his respect as a 'beachmaster' in the Second World War – quoted as saying 'If you engage in a very large bombing campaign a lot of civilians are bound to be killed.'[34] Other men make similar points, with a greater implicit acceptance of the inevitability of the horrors of war than among women.[35]

For younger generations, the Second World War is still a pivotal experience which has been passed on to them in many ways, but it is reinforced by their own memories of wars experienced only via the television screen and newspaper column, as in this comment of a man in his forties:

I was born during WWII, of now-abused memory, and that war has always been a paradigm to me of the need, when history offers no other way out, to fight and destroy anti-human forces. As a relatively young adult I watched the heroism of the Vietnamese people in their resistance to invasion. No one had the right to ask them to die down under the American onslaught. Pacifism has never made any sense to me, if only because (as Orwell says) it means in practice allowing other people to do the fighting, and dying, on your behalf. But there is no cause in the Gulf comparable to the defeat of fascism or the winning of national liberation.[36]

These comments suggest that, even as the individual lived memories of the Second World War die away with the generations which experienced it, the records of these memories remain, helping to sustain the myths with which, indeed, the memories themselves are so powerfully intertwined. Even a post-military society is still a society in which memories of war are both aroused and mobilized, in the cultural struggle which has replaced 'the front' in current conflicts. The success of the tabloids' evocation of Hitler in their presentation of Saddam Hussein should remind us how potent are these myths of war, and to what uses those who propagandize them will put the fruits of memory.

Notes

1. Shaw (1991).
2. Luckham (1984).
3. Mann (1987).
4. Ibid.
5. Shaw (1988).
6. Shaw (1991), pp. 126–9.
7. Shaw (1987).
8. Since memory is, in its most basic meaning, a quality of individual human beings, I am reluctant to use terms such as 'national memory' which imply a common memory among whole populations, when such a common memory does not exist as *memory* (although it may as myth). Hence the term 'collective *versions* of memory' seems appropriate to suggest the active construction of memories *for* people which tends to be involved.
9. For fuller information on how the surveys were carried out and on the findings see Shaw and Carr-Hill (1991b) and Shaw (1996). Both surveys were based on random samples of about 1,300 with response rates of over 40 per cent, very high for postal surveys, especially considering that the registers used were fifteen months old.
10. Shaw and Carr-Hill (1991b), pp. 30–1, divide the population into 'warriors' and 'non-warriors' (in the ratio 39:61 in the sample). The most significant difference was that only 10 per cent of the former, but over 20 per cent of the latter, opposed the war.
11. Shaw and Carr-Hill (1991a).

12. It is of course probable that this is a slight overestimate since people who had these sort of anxieties may have been more liable to respond to our survey than those who did not.

13. Data from our second survey suggest that the vast majority of the population either accepted that the shelter was a legitimate military target (the official line), or even believed that Saddam Hussein had deliberately placed civilians in it to obtain the propaganda benefit which their deaths would achieve (the line of many tabloid papers), Fewer than a quarter thought that it was a mistake, as suggested by British TV reporters on the spot.

14. That a widespread awareness of the horror of war is brought by television viewers to their viewing of newsreels is also suggested by Morrison's report of responses to uncut footage of the Amiriya shelter bombing, compared with that actually broadcast (Morrison (1992), p. 33).

15. I have not come across any published references to the possibility of reintroducing conscription during the Gulf War, though it was interesting that during discussion of the original version of this chapter at the Portsmouth conference, members of the audience insisted that they had seen such references. The only documentary evidence I know of was the publication by the Militant organization of posters proclaiming 'No Conscription', a speedy opportunistic response to the fears of young people by a group well-informed enough to have known that there was virtually no likelihood of conscription's reintroduction.

16. The request (known in Mass-Observation as a 'directive') was sent out quite early in the crisis, in October 1990, so that responses cover the build-up to war as well as the war itself. The material can be consulted in the Archive which is based at the Library of the University of Sussex.

17. The Mass-Observation panel for the Gulf directive was made up of 1,100 people, of whom 591 (54 per cent) replied. As the following table shows, the breakdowns by sex of this panel, of the respondents, and of a wider group of M-O panellists, were almost identical.

	Ever taking part in M-O panel	Gulf directive: panel	Gulf directive respondents
Men	700 (30.5%)	341 (31%)	181 (30.6%)
Women	1596 (69.5%)	759 (69%)	410 (69.4%)
Total	2296	1100	591

I read and analysed the files of 149 respondents (92 women, 57 men), i.e. just over 25 per cent of the total.

18. Crewe (1985), discussed in Shaw and Carr-Hill (1991b), p. 24.

19. Mass-Observation Archive (hereafter MOA): Directive Respondent (hereafter DR) 666.
20. MOA DR 1424.
21. MOA DR 826.
22. MOA DR 68.
23. MOA DR 1559.
24. MOA DR 36.
25. MOA DR 2053.
26. MOA DR 2258.
27. MOA DR 1673.
28. MOA DR 828.
29. MOA DR 1810.
30. MOA DR 2134.
31. MOA DR 2185.
32. MOA DR 2506.
33. MOA DR 38.
34. MOA DR 276.
35. This acceptance of the inevitability of the horrors of war does not, however, imply that men make light of them, as John Major found to his cost when his proposed 1994 'celebration' (rather than commemoration) of the fiftieth anniversary of D-Day aroused outrage amongst veterans, many of whom remembered the large numbers of their comrades who had fallen in the Normandy landings.
36. MOA DR 1671.

Bibliography

Crewe, Ivor (1985), 'Two and a half cheers for the Atlantic alliance', in Gregory Fynn and Hans Rattinger (eds), *Public Opinion and Atlantic Defence*, London: Croom Helm.

Luckham, Robin (1984), 'Of arms and culture', *Current Research on Peace and Violence*, vol. 7, no. 1, pp. 1–64.

Mann, Michael (1987), 'The roots and contradictions of modern militarism', *New Left Review*, vol. 162, pp. 35–6.

Mass-Observation Archive, University of Sussex (1990–1), Directive on the Gulf crisis.

Morrison, David (1992), *Television and the Gulf War*, London: John Libbey.

Shaw, Martin (1987) 'The rise and fall of the military-democratic state: Britain 1940–85', in Colin Creighton and Martin Shaw (eds), *The Sociology of War and Peace*, London: Macmillan, pp. 143–58.

Shaw, Martin (1988), *Dialectics of War: An Essay on the Social Theory of War and Peace*, London: Pluto.

Shaw, Martin (1991), *Post-Military Society: militarism, demilitarization and war at the end of the twentieth century*, Cambridge: Polity.

Shaw, Martin (1996), *Distant Violence: Media and Civil Society in Global Crises*, London: Pinter.

Shaw, Martin and Carr-Hill, Roy (1991a), 'Mass media and attitudes to the Gulf War in Britain', *The Electronic Journal of Communications/ La Revue Electronique de Communications* (Montreal), vol. 4, no. 1.

Shaw, Martin and Carr-Hill, Roy (1991b), *Public Opinion, Media and Violence: Attitudes to the Gulf War in a Local Population*, Hull: Department of Sociology & Social Anthropology.

Taylor, Philip M. (1992), *War and Media*, Manchester: Manchester University Press.

Acknowledgements

I wish to express my gratitude to Roy Carr-Hill, who collaborated on the survey research referred to in this chapter; to the Joseph Rowntree Charitable Trust and the University of Hull which funded that research; and to Dorothy Sheridan and Joy Eldridge of the Mass-Observation Archive, University of Sussex, for their generous assistance.

-13-

Remembering Desert Storm: Popular Culture and the Gulf War

Jeffrey Walsh

The recent D-Day commemorations, sombre, restrained and elegiac, gave appropriate public recognition to the events of 1944. Despite the crass attempts of the public relations firm employed by John Major's government to trivialize the bitter and prolonged Battle of Normandy by turning its fiftieth anniversary into a celebration comprising street parties and jitterbug contests, the public's will prevailed: the ceremonies were solemn and dignified. Watching the various low-key acts of remembrance an attentive viewer would surely find it hard not to be moved. Running through the media coverage three themes were represented: admiration for the complexity and logistic brilliance of the amphibious landings; mourning for the heavy loss of life that followed; and barely disguised pride in Britain's central role in the decisive Overlord battles. It hardly seemed to matter if memory simplified, that Dunkirk and the British Army's former defeats were rarely mentioned, that Russia's contribution to the war effort was largely ignored or that military blunders in the Normandy operations themselves, for example in the fighting around Caen, were generally overlooked. The events that took place in Portsmouth and in Normandy during June 1994 became an important public ritual, giving expression to a national consciousness usually repressed. What the D-Day ceremonies articulated was a moment of collective memory: they symbolized a lost sense of coherent nationhood. If the ending of the Second World War is taken to signal the End of Empire, then D-Day, redolent with images of heroism and redemptive action, was its apotheosis.

Television pictures of frail British veterans in their seventies and eighties emphasized what *The Times* in its memoir of 6 June 1994 called 'their valour, deeds and sacrifices'.[1] Such rhetoric is unfashionable yet communicates historical truth, especially if we extrapolate from it a projection taking in the war as a whole. A single fact will perhaps confirm its validity. In contemporary cinema the American experience of loss in Vietnam is represented through such *Angst*-ridden narratives as *Platoon*, yet the 58,000 military deaths suffered by the United States in its ten-year Asian war are almost exactly paralleled by the military personnel lost by Scotland during the 1939–45 conflict.

Even allowing for the mistiness of memory and the unreliable sentiment of patriotism, the recent Normandy commemorations were impressive, and the reason for this lies in their historical roots. Their reference point, the campaign for the liberation of France in 1944, demonstrated archetypally how a genuine international coalition could defeat a repugnant political system founded upon genocide. The Second World War showed the British in a favourable light, acting in time of crisis as a resolute and united people possessed of a powerful sense of national purpose and identity. Metaphors borrowed from these years, of daring, of extraordinary triumph in the face of adversity, were often recalled during the Falklands War of 1982 and in the Gulf conflict of 1991; the latter war was frequently described as an international crusade against a Hitler-like dictator, Saddam Hussein.

Despite the jingoism evident in tabloid newspapers during the conflict, the Gulf War of 1991 was not an exclusively British patriotic war in the sense that the Falklands was; no sovereign United Kingdom territory was invaded in the Persian Gulf as in the South Atlantic a decade earlier, and no legitimate case could be made that the Gulf War represented a national crusade to defend specifically 'British' values or peoples. The Falklands War, echoing 1939–45, could in many ways be presented as a Defence of Empire expedition. The conflict in 1982 was more emotionally coherent than the United Nations-sponsored Gulf War a decade later. Memories of the Falklands are boys' own stuff: of dramatic flag-waving at the fleet's departure, of burning ships, of Simon Weston's heroism, of yomping, of Colonel 'H' Jones's valour at Goose Green and of the triumphant liberation of Port Stanley. This copybook adventure, in the finest tradition of Rudyard Kipling, may be interpreted from a Thatcherite perspective as a fulfilment of 'imperial' mission, reversing the United Kingdom's long decline stretching back to Suez. The confidence of the British military, as shown for example in their contemporary pivotal involvement in United Nations' peacekeeping forces, dates from the Falklands success.

Desert Storm transcended the Falklands logistically, and was the biggest campaign the British military had fought since 1945, easily surpassing the Korean War in men and machines. Although massive by United Kingdom standards, British involvement in the Gulf War was minimal when compared with American troop deployment: forces from the United Kingdom comprised only 4 per cent numerically of coalition personnel, and were fewer than the women serving in the United States' contingent. Britain's ties with the Middle East were, of course, long-standing, and both Iraq and Kuwait were significant territories within the old imperial

domain. After the decline of the Ottoman Empire Britain set up a protect-
orate over Kuwait in 1899, and administered Iraq until 1932. Such firm
historical bonds became highly visible when, at the end of the Gulf War,
John Major reinforced the United Kingdom's ties with the region by
visiting Kuwait only five days after the end of the ground offensive.
Ironically the British military also has historic links with Iraq: for example,
when Andy McNab was captured (as described in his *Bravo Two Zero*
(1993), the story of a covert SAS operation during Desert Storm), he
discovered that the elite commandos who captured him proudly displayed
red lanyards that they were awarded by Montgomery 'to commemorate a
victory from the Second World War'. [2]

Britain's role in the Gulf crisis was more political and symbolic than
militarily significant. From Margaret Thatcher's initial lobbying of President Bush in August 1990, which is credited with stiffening his resolve,
extending to the support offered in policing the no-fly zones up to the
present, Britain's attitude has been elegantly hawkish. (The Falklands
factor is apparently still at work in 1996 in bolstering British morale in
Bosnia under the Nato flag.)

The journalist Martin Walker of the *Guardian*, alluding to the 'special
relationship' between Britain and America, has written of the Gulf conflict
as an ending, a defining moment signifying the close of an era: he refers
to the war as 'the last act of the Anglo-American imperium'.[3] The image
works retrospectively to explain the Persian Gulf intervention as the
endgame of Reaganite and Thatcherite foreign policy during the 1980s
which affirmed the doctrine of assertive force in the Falklands, Grenada,
Libya and Panama. Memories of D-Day are relevant here. Reagan, his
successor Bush and Margaret Thatcher were all of an age to remember
the crusade against fascism, and they each displayed an ideological consciousness of what we may call 'the good war' as a paradigm for action
when forging their reputations as strident Cold War warriors. The collapse
of the Soviet Empire in the late 1980s apparently vindicated their tough
stance.

This tendency to look backwards to the twin evils of Nazism and
Communism, culminating in the eventual defeat of both systems, was
crucial in the framing of George Bush's State of the Union Address on 29
January 1991 when he envisioned his famous New World Order: 'What
is at stake is more than one small country: it is a big idea: a new world
order – where diverse nations are drawn together in common cause, to
achieve the universal aspirations of mankind: peace and security,
freedom and the rule of law.' Bush's rhetoric perceives the Gulf crisis as
a watershed, offering a unique opportunity to create a benign future for
the post-Communist world. Many of the public myths enlisted to narrate
the Gulf War were initially founded upon this characteristically American

metaphor of universal aspiration. (Bush's personal war experience as a fighter pilot also lent moral authority to his comments upon military matters, an authority conspicuously lacking when President Clinton, as Commander-in-Chief, reviewed his D-Day veterans in summer 1994.)

The British poet, Tony Harrison, in responding to the Gulf War, came to exactly the opposite conclusion to George Bush in his long narrative poem, *The Gaze of the Gorgon* (1992).[4] Whereas Bush interprets the forthcoming war in his New World Order speech as leading to a shining new dawn, Harrison, similarly following the logic of history, sees the Gulf conflict as integral to a bloody sequence of earlier wars. He imagines the 1991 campaign as a war which turns men to stone in the desert, thus revealing its nature as the twentieth century's most barbarous and technically advanced war. Harrison's volume is saturated with historical vision, making reference to the Blitz, VE-Day, and active memories of the Second World War as well as the Gulf. His poems which are directly concerned with Desert Shield and Desert Storm, especially 'A Cold Coming' and 'Initial Illumination', are meditative discourses which evoke abhorrence of war's inhumanities.

The American imagination of war, unlike Harrison's boyhood revisiting of the war in Europe, turns back inevitably to Vietnam, and to the ludicrous myth that the United States fought their Asian war with far too much restraint. The public statements of George Bush resonate with this axiomatic belief, which explains, too, the military strategy underlying Desert Storm. Memories of the traumatic Indochina war, which is falsely understood by many American politicians to be a conflict which the United States fought with one arm tied behind its back, spawned the doctrine of 'extreme lethality', the use of unlimited firepower to erase past failure and thus avoid the damaging incrementalism of Vietnam. The shadow of Vietnam haunts the Gulf, and psychologically at least Desert Storm was born out of the memory of Indochina and the compulsion to exorcize the so-called 'Vietnam Syndrome'. This idea underpins a short poem by the Vietnam veteran, W. D. Ehrhart, the best American poet to have written on the Gulf conflict. Ehrhart, an ex-marine sergeant, anti-war activist and Vietnam veteran, entitles his piece, 'Why the Kurds Are Dying in the Mountains'.[5]

> Twenty Years was long enough.
> We were tired of being abused.
> We said: it's time to win one
> for the Gipper, for John Winthrop,
> General Jacob Smith, the twilight's
> last gleaming, and that gleaming
> black wall of fallen heroes.

Think of all that shame,
those 58,000 dead in vain
because we did not have the stomach
for a fight.
Never again.
Never.

The *Sunday Times* newspaper suggested in January 1991 that 86 per cent of the British population firmly supported the Gulf War once it had begun, an approval rating that remained remarkably constant until the end of hostilities. Television, as did virtually all newspapers, endorsed the war effort, and was equally influential in shaping pro-war opinion. As Jean Baudrillard, the French postmodernist philosopher, has argued, television created a simulacrum of war, the screen itself becoming a copy of military action and acting as a strategic site to bombard the reader with images.[6] A feature of television coverage was the recurrent recourse to panels of experts who discussed the war coolly and intellectually in a manner that packaged the conflict into easily digestible sound bites. Although Channel 4 and the radio programme *Today* frequently gave air time to dissenting voices, mainstream broadcasting tended to marginalize anti-war opinion. As the *Guardian*, the only consistently anti-war quality paper, frequently reminded its readers, the war was contested *within* the United Kingdom; there was considerable opposition to it throughout the whole of Britain, in Parliament, in the universities, within the Church and more overtly in traditional pacifist groups such as CND. This criticism was not represented widely in the 'television war', although critics were allowed occasional air space, such as Professor Paul Rogers from the Peace Studies department of Bradford University, who was sometimes employed as an in-house expert.

The war which was represented in the most popular media programmes seemed sometimes to be governed by public relations; for instance, it was often described as a 'just war' in a moral and philosophical sense, and was commonly praised by retired military bigwigs for being strategically superior to previous 'campaigns'. Perhaps the abiding television memory of Desert Storm, though, is live pictures of Tomahawk cruise missiles turning left and right down Baghdad streets before hitting their military targets with unerring precision. For a younger generation nurtured on Atari and Nintendo games, the Gulf War often seemed like an amusement-arcade contest where blips substituted for human deaths. The screen, during the short time video hits on targets were being shown, was transformed briefly into an imitation 'kill box', where real death and mayhem became a surrogate for game-playing. This kind of spurious activity, expressive of a modern technophile sensibility, had a socializing function of an unpleasant kind. In public discourse about the Gulf battles the metaphor of the game occupied a prominent place in narratives of precision-guided warfare. The concept of 'virtual reality' is also relevant here whereby computer graphics created a sanitized space where no human cries were heard. The hand-to-hand fighting of the Normandy campaign or the bloody bayonet engagements that took place on Mount Tumbledown in the Falklands seemed light years away from this new computer-aided combat which appeared to be more like a Sega fighting game of Doom where death was utterly remote and wounding infinitely distant. Popular culture thus worked wonders in turning war's primeval and blood-letting side into a kind of software leisure ritual involving surreal weapons and bloodless casualties.

Although such poets as Harrison and Ehrhart offered powerful imaginative critiques of the war, their work was read by only a minority readership, and the dominant narratives of the war were communicated through mass television and high-circulation newspapers. A study of television coverage of the period or of tabloid newspapers will confirm that Desert Shield, Desert Storm and Desert Sabre were consensually presented as 'civilized' operations, military campaigns that were by and large models of limited, humanely conducted warfare. Such a hegemonic viewpoint, though, did not have things all its own way; textual analysis of a range of alternative artefacts, images, cultural forms and icons demonstrates how this predominant thesis of a sanitized, clean, surgical war was concurrently subverted and shown to be inadequate. Indeed, such a unitary interpretation of Desert Storm by way of an apparently coherent commentary can be shown to be flawed, incoherent and deeply contradictory. Popular fiction, film and other cultural genres such as pop music can often surprise their audience by exposing ideological disunity, by deconstructing what appears 'obvious' and 'self-evident'. Pierre Macherey, the French critical theorist, has hypothesized that literary works in particular when closely analysed reveal fissures, lacunae and 'breaks' in the text which demonstrate ideological inconsistency. Such an approach is useful in understanding the public impact of the Gulf War in contemporary culture, and in outlining a methodology that seeks to uncover concealed historical truth. This chapter will argue that the Gulf War was not as straightforward or unproblematical as the influential media premise suggests, and that the style, narrative forms and public language most commonly deployed as Gulf War stories and 'war speak' are anything but consistent, uncomplicated and easily comprehensible.

Above all, the language most commonly spoken by commentators and military experts has its pitfalls. Probably the most famous phrase used to describe bombing raids was the expression 'collateral damage', which means 'damage exceeding the predicted level' and exemplifies the kind of suppression, renaming and evasion that took place. To speak of 'degrade' when what is meant is 'to pulverize' or 'massacre' is an effective linguistic trick; MSBs do not sound as sinister as multiple scatter bombs used on runways; and phrases such as 'deconfliction' are impenetrable. Brian Appleyard has theorized that this kind of jargon is consonant with military propaganda; it is a rhetoric of cleanliness, efficiency and high-tech hardware, a speech practice far removed from the blood and dirt of Vietnam or the amputations suffered at Omaha Beach.[7] Such proactive locutions are similarly found in the film *Top Gun*, a hymn to Reaganite revisionism. Tony Scott's film anticipates the Gulf War through its narrative of boy racers in the sky in control of state-of-the-art planes, who speak a techno-jargon of one-syllable words.

Top Gun presents no problems to the cultural analyst, as its strident macho politics are foregrounded in the film's narrative. It is also relatively easy to identify the nostalgia of tabloids such as the *Sun* which wallowed in old myths at the time the war was being fought: references were frequently made to the Desert Rats, the Dambusters, the Battle of Britain, 'our finest hour', and the Blitz; Saddam was usually likened to Hitler, and his secret police to the Gestapo, images used to warn against appeasement. Such straightforward jingoism and the recycling of myths of a glorious past, however inappropriate, are transparently obvious to readers. However, other more 'official' versions of the war's progress, including Defence Ministry statements and military information packs, gave more cause for concern. For instance, there was an abundance of press releases, still photographs, fact sheets, video-graphics and animated diagrams about Apache jet-powered helicopters, Stealth bombers, Harm missiles and Warthog tank-busting planes, but there were no battlefield photographs or television pictures showing such advanced technology causing any close-up human deaths. No pictures of dead bodies were shown as in Vietnam. The obscene, utterly offensive celebration of the number of bombs dropped and sorties flown, which exceeded in their intensity and frequency those of any previous war, was not matched by estimated statistics of enemy casualties or civilian deaths. Indeed the greatest mystery about the Gulf War relates to how many Iraqis actually died from allied attacks and how many were seriously wounded.

At the time of the war such quality broadsheets as the *Independent*, the *Guardian* and the *Sunday Times* estimated the number of Iraqi military deaths at about 100,000 to 150,000, a figure that was confirmed in March 1991 by a US military spokesman. However, respected historians such as Lawrence Freedman and Efraim Karsh now put the figure only at about 30,000.[8] An American academic, John Hiedenrich, who based his research upon Pentagon figures of confirmed deaths and other relevant data, suggests that the figure could be as low as 1,500, an estimate reported by Chris Bellamy in the *Independent* in March 1993.[9] Clearly it was in the interest of both Saddam Hussein and also the allied commanders to conceal Iraqi casualties, and the truth will never be known. In any case where are the figures covering civilian deaths from bombing, from starvation after the war, from insurrection and civil war? The war had massive repercussions later on the civilian population.

The whiff of a cover-up lingers in memories of the war. Such massive discrepancies in estimates of casualties create intense unease and suspicion, especially when weighed alongside dissident voices which introduce evidence that runs counter to prevalent contemporary assessments of the war. Ramsey Clarke, for example, argues in his book, *The Fire This Time: U.S. War Crimes in the Gulf* (1994), that the United States perpetrated heinous atrocities in the conflict, and that the coalition exceeded its remit permitted by the United Nations by systematically destroying Iraq's infrastructure.[10] He also accuses the RAF of breaking the Geneva Convention on warfare by killing an estimated 200 civilians in two separate attacks, in February 1991, on bridges near the town of Falluja.

While British television did report sceptically about some tragic events such as the coalition raid on the Al Amiriyah shelter which killed 300 women and children, and therefore helped to create a public debate over the legitimacy of the attack, it is often the lesser-known reports by witnessing journalists that cause most disquiet. In what is perhaps the most impressive and restrained chronicle of the Gulf War by a front-line reporter, entitled 'Martyrs' Day', Michael Kelly, a US newspaper correspondent, describes incidents of an apparently peripheral kind. In one passage for instance, he records a conversation with two GIs on the coastal road to Basra when he noticed an overpowering stink. He was informed that the bad smell emanated from 'Dead Iraqis. Them's graveyards either side of that water. Couple hundred fresh bodies in there. That's where we been burying 'em. Smell gets into the water.'[11] In this apparently offhand anecdote there is confirmation of the suspicion that in modern warfare military commanders recognize the urgent need that enemy bodies must not be seen lest the sight of them fosters public disaffection. This strategic imperative may have underpinned the decision to back off after the massacre of retreating Iraqis on the Mutlah Ridge despite Schwarzkopf's reported desire to pursue enemy troops and finish them off decisively. Several excellent British reporters bore witness to this callous 'turkey shoot' of fleeing troops and other personnel.

The theme of human fragmentation is addressed in two of the most powerful works of popular culture to address the Gulf War, Sophie Ristelhueber's book of photographs, *Aftermath: Kuwait 1991* (some of which appeared later in the *Guardian* and *Independent on Sunday*) and

Werner Herzog's film *Lessons of Darkness*, broadcast on BBC television.[12] Ristelhueber's photographs concentrate upon the detritus of war, its dismembered material, upon abandoned tanks, ruined fortifications and vehicle tracks in the sand. Her fractional images seem to convey an essential truth about the conduct of modern war, that the photojournalist can only visit the scene of carnage *after* the battles have long subsided; the military censor, alert to the passion that a telling photograph can inflame, forbids old-style reporting as it happens from the battlefield. Donald McCullin's newsphotos from Vietnam would no longer be possible. Only the aloof, 'shots from a distance' mode, after the events, is now permissible.

Werner Herzog's film symbolizes the war in a broadly comparable manner, although reminding us again and again that it was fought for oil; his camera shots of burning oil wells filmed from the air in Kuwait lend the film an apocalyptic, hellish vision. Like Ristelhueber's photographs, abstract and vestigial images serve to imply human insignificance in time of war. The pitted and pock-marked desert, requiem-like, mocks such grandiloquent ideas as 'a new world order': sands, scarred and suppurating, where vehicles and huge machines are decomposing and sinking, figure as a template for human suffering. The traces of human habitation are scrutinized metonymically and forensically.

Both of these visual form of representation, Ristelhueber's photographs and Hertzog's film, are gravely resonant and sombre, yet the Gulf War offered plenty of material for those who believe in the cock-up theory of history. Cartoonists such as Doonesbury, Heath, Garland and Steve Bell ridiculed the self-importance and stupidity of politicians and generals, and two feminist comic artists, Cath Tate and Carole Bennett,[13] satirized macho, militaristic values in their anti-war comic, *Ceasefire*. Most interesting and outrageously funny of such burlesque attacks on the so-called surgical and state-of-the-art war is the film *Hot Shots, Part Deux*, a witty parody of *Rambo*, which transports the saturnine Vietnam vet to the Persian Gulf and mercilessly lampoons a Reagan-like US President.

It is a cliché that life sometimes imitates art, and the slapstick of the laugh-a-minute film, *Hot Shots, Part Deux* is not too far removed from the gaffes and blunders that were associated with the actual conduct of the war. Three computer hackers, for instance, scrambled data in the computer which gave Norman Schwarzkopf vital weather intelligence in advance of the air attack on Iraq.[14] The hackers, calling themselves 8LGM, after a Manchester-based pop group called the Eight Legged Groove Machine, almost fatally jeopardized the international effort against Saddam, putting thousands of servicemen's lives at risk. Another reluctant anti-hero was Wing Commander David Farquar who went into a car showroom and had his laptop computer with full details of the ground campaign stolen. Schwarzkopf is reported to have been on the verge of cancelling the plans.

Ken Livingstone, the radical Labour MP, caused a furore after the war when he suggested that British intelligence agents in Baghdad were duped into unwittingly causing the Al Amiriyah shelter bombing.[15]He claimed that false information was passed on to the Americans that the shelter was a military complex. Livingstone further alleges that the *faux pas* led to a trade-off: if the Americans remained quiet over this scandalous British intelligence failure the UK authorities would not embarrass the US military over the friendly-fire incident when nine British soldiers were accidentally hit by a US missile.

Intelligence failures seem to have been endemic during the period leading up to the war and during hostilities. For example, according to an official war report presented to the US Congress, American military intelligence was hilariously wrong in its assessment of battlefield damage. It claimed to have destroyed a number of vessels equal to three times the size of the entire Iraqi navy. Military surveillance also reported that four times the number of launchers actually possessed by Iraq were disabled.[16] Even the deadly accuracy of 'smart bombs' proved a red herring. During the war only 7 per cent of weapons were precision-guided, and of the other 93 per cent of 'dumb' bombs, less than 50 per cent hit their targets. One novel excuse offered by the US military for its failure to realize earlier than it did that Iraq was developing a nuclear capacity was that intelligence units deployed three times the number of men looking for non-existent MIAs in Vietnam than they did on checking out Saddam's war machine.

For popular culture as a whole the Gulf War was a bit like the Falklands conflict: it was over far too quickly. In fact it was also much more one-sided that the Falklands campaign, and Desert Storm did not offer too many stirring deeds of heroism for later incorporation into mythical, gung-ho plots. Only *Bravo Two Zero*, top of the UK best-seller lists for over six months, and potentially a BBC film, supplied a factual narrative of superhuman courage and endurance. This story of a heroic long march in enemy territory, of three deaths of courageous SAS warriors, and of deadly weapons and faces blacked out is a fable of British Rambos.

Their actual exploits had much in common with popular stereotypes of elite masculinity. There was already in the cinema a tradition that anticipated the formulaic representations since drawn upon to portray combat in the Persian Gulf; as Edward Said has justly argued, 'during the past decade nearly every film about American Commandos pits a hulking Rambo or technically whizz-like Delta Force against Arab/Muslim terrorist desperadoes'.[17]

This line of narrative shaped much of the popular fiction written about the war. Perhaps because the politics of oil and underlying issues were confusing and unglamorous, best-selling books have tended to avoid ethical inquiry and focused instead upon criminal adventure, hostage-taking, terrorism and assassination. Generically such fiction traces out the well-tried pattern of action thrillers: it is well-researched, providing a plausible context, motives and background, and is organized around fast-moving plots which involve conspiracy, crime, financial corruption, pursuit, escape, death, shoot-outs, violence and suspense.

Despite such apparently repetitive structure and form, popular fiction is worthy of serious consideration. Popular fiction, such as Frederick Forsyth's *The Fist of God*, Jack Higgins's *Eye of the Storm*, Jeffrey Archer's *Honour among Thieves* and David Mason's *Shadow over Babylon*, demonstrates a remarkably astute understanding of postmodern 'displaced' warfare where almost all of the world's peoples are producers or consumers of terrorism and espionage.[18] In the contemporary world of sinister gadgetry a smaller country can terrorize a major one if its supplies of Semtex are large enough and it has urban guerrillas capable of detonating it. A ready example of this occurred in 1993 through the bombing of the World Trade Center in New York City, followed by the discovery of a plot in June to blow up the United Nations building. Assassination attempts are also rampant though hard to verify, as, for instance, in April 1993 when eleven Iraqis and three Kuwaitis were arrested on suspicion of trying to kill ex-President George Bush. Throughout such narratives of terror Saddam Hussein is regularly featured as a demonized figure.[19] In June 1994 it was reported that he had executed three senior military commanders because they dared to question the competence of Saddam's son, Uday. Equally as exciting in the popular press are accounts of shadowy assassination attempts against Saddam, such as the Israeli plan that misfired in 1993. Thriller writers by virtue of their trade are uniquely attuned to this pervasive culture of secrecy and violence because they recognize in their fictions that warring countries in the late twentieth century wage a disguised version of war not on the battlefield but in the car park or alley way where explosives are planted or gunmen hide.

Jack Higgins's slick, professional thriller *Eye of the Storm* (which sold over 140,000 copies in 1993) interprets the Gulf conflict in this metonymic way. Its plot centres on the abortive attack on John Major and his war cabinet on 7 February 1991, in Downing Street, which is represented in the novel as the work of an ex-IRA terrorist called Dillon, operating on behalf of Saddam Hussein. The attack, which fails through lack of adequate preparation, is carried out by mortars fired from a parked van, using exactly the same technique as that employed in the attacks upon Heathrow Airport on 10 and 11 March 1994. Higgins's novel characteristically (he wrote a book called *Exocet* about the Falklands war) offers what T. S. Eliot in a famous phase called an 'objective correlative' for the murkier side of the Gulf War, involving dirty tricks, double agents and linked terrorist networks.

The Middle East, perhaps verifying Edward Said's arguments in *Orientalism* about its exotic appeal to the imperialist occidental nations, has been clichéd as a breeding ground for terrorism. Murray Sayle, for instance, has suggested that in the Gulf region there are only two ground rules that continue to govern foreign affairs: '(1) no honest, open policy is possible; (2) there's lots of money to be made in the shadows'. [20] The Scott Inquiry, now the subject of a docudrama, exemplifies Sayle's paradigm in a UK context.[21] An investigation of arms sales to Iraq by British companies, it centred upon the purchase in 1987 by Iraqi agents of a moribund Coventry engineering firm, Matrix Churchill. The US government also has its skeletons in the cupboard, and a National Security Directive proposed lucrative financial incentives for Iraq, after its war with Iran. US exchanges of arms for oil, to keep Iraq on side, grew from 80,000 barrels a day in 1987 to 1.1 million just before Iraq invaded Kuwait. Alan Friedman, in a fascinating study, reveals in *Spider's Web* (1994) a fascinating pattern of corruption and intrigue linking President Bush and Prime Minister Margaret Thatcher to Saddam Hussein.[22]

The whole Gulf episode, a war which emerged from complex politics going back to the shady dealings of the 1950s when Mossadeg, the moderate nationalist Persian leader, was overthrown by British and US agents, has the rich imaginative potential for a library of thrillers. Allegations of dirty tricks are regularly reported in the press. In June 1993 David James, a British businessman, told investigators that he had found parts for the supergun to Iraq at his factory in the West Midlands. He told this, he alleged, to an M16 agent codenamed 'Two'. *Today* newspaper, feeding off the excitement generated, described how 'the thriller-like plot was revealed to Lord Justice Scott's inquiry'.

This aspect of the Gulf War, its tenebrous and corrupt side, is the basis for Frederick Forsyth's *The Fist of God*, and supplied the plot for the first British-directed film of events leading up to Desert Storm. The 4-million-dollar film, called *The Doomsday Gun*, is directed by Robert Young, and includes the actors Alan Arkin, James Fox and Michael Kitchen. Uncannily paralleling the Scott Inquiry, the film dramatizes (as does Forsyth) the life and death of Dr Gerald Bull, the scientist, who designed the supergun and was assassinated in Brussels. It reconstructs Saddam's Project Babylon, two superguns intended to fire over 1,000 miles, enabling them to reach Teheran, Tel Aviv and Cairo. A journalist has written that cinema is today's fastest and most influential history teacher, and *The Doomsday Gun*, together with other works such as *Honour among Thieves* and *Shadow over Babylon*, is an interesting example of the genre of 'faction', fiction pretending to be fact. The Gulf War rumbles on, its repercussions felt in movies and best-selling adventure stories as a kind of cultural coda.

In conclusion, the connection between the Gulf War and popular cultural artefacts is a problematical and shifting one. As in the case of the Vietnam War before it, the process of remembering has itself become a deeply political and ideological conflict. Cultural battles for the meanings of the war will continue to be fought on the cinema screen and within the narratives of mass-market fiction. Films, novels and other such texts are not simply reflective of aspects of Desert Shield and Desert Storm; their relationship to historical events, to cause and effect, is much more ambiguous. Popular culture is a primary vehicle of remembering because it influences collective memory through taking sides in the economic and intellectual struggles underlying war.

Almost any cultural genre will verify this premise, as John Storey has shown in his study of popular music and the Gulf War.[23] Storey demonstrates how large numbers of the population, and especially young people, opposed the war. He describes how Billy Bragg sang to 70,000 war demonstrators in Trafalgar Square, how Sean Lennon, Lenny Kravitz, Dave Stewart, Peter Gabriel, KLF and the Ruthless Rap Assassins all condemned the war and resisted the BBC's 'caution list' censoring 'sensitive' songs and records. In this case study active ideological confrontation may be perceived in the BBC's fatuous attempts to support the war effort by banning such supposedly belligerent songs as 'Boom Bang a Bang', and in the way DJs, artists and music critics ridiculed the corporation and defied it.

Every war is subject to reinterpretation after its end, and the Gulf War will be further revised in cultural and academic discourse as time elapses. The historian of culture will then have a varied range of texts and forms to analyse. Simplest of such expressions is the straightforward jingoistic memoir, such as John Peters and John Nicholl's book *Tornado Down*, which presents the conflict in simple humanist terms as a didactic narrative with moral lessons to be drawn from individual conduct.[24] Such a 'reading' of the war, which emphasizes military discipline, ignores larger economic and political issues. A more valuable response to the war is the pacifist one which connects Desert Storm to other 'failed' imperialist wars such as Vietnam or Britain's Suez campaign. This traditional consciousness of war is found in much of the most memorable literary work treating the events of 1990–1, such as Sam Shepard's *States of Shock* (1991) or Trevor Griffiths's *The Gulf Between Us* (1991), two plays which bitterly opposed the war. Poetry, too, is resonant with a similar countercultural agenda that connects back with a Vietnam anti-war movement: poets portray the war imaginatively as a failure of the human spirit: in such poetic resistance old Beat poets such as Ferlinghetti and Ginsberg are conjoined discursively with war resisters such as W. D. Ehrhart whose verse communicates the aura of Quakerism. An impressive anthology edited by H. Palmer Hall juxtaposes Ehrhart's work with that of other poets who wrote about the Gulf War.[25]

For a historian there is much polemical writing, taking in established dissident intellectuals such as John Pilger in *Distant Voices* (1993) and Edward Said in *Culture and Imperialism* (1993), as well as Noam Chomsky in the United States. Most interesting perhaps of all the material in the Gulf archive is the work of newspaper journalists who bear witness to the suffering and wanton destruction of war, yet whose work is riven by contradiction. An attentive reading of Brian MacArthur's fine collection of pieces by different correspondents, *Despatches from the Gulf*,[26] testifies to this sense of intellectual struggle and moral uncertainty. The activity of war is thus portrayed as both conflagration and confusion.

The Gulf War will continue to supply popular culture with plentiful resources for documentary, myth and narrative. On the fifth anniversary of Desert Storm in 1996 the processes of revision were starkly demonstrated through two diametrically opposed television programmes, the BBC's four-part documentary *The Gulf War*,[27] written and produced by Eamon Matthews, Channel 4's *Riding the Storm: How to Tell Lies and Win Wars*, written and directed by Maggie O'Kane who was present in the region during the conflict.[28] What is most apparent in comparing these two documentaries is the sharp ideological difference between them. Maggie O'Kane's account of the war, as its title suggests, was a polemical essay accusing the Americans and their coalition allies of indefensible military tactics disguised by propaganda. Her position is similar to that taken by the US poet Naomi Wallace in her 1994 play, *In the Heart of America*, which links the events of 1990–1 with the atrocities of Vietnam.[29] *Riding the Storm* similarly argued that coalition weapons such as napalm, fuel-air explosives and shells tipped with depleted uranium were barbarous, and that military operations involving carpet bombing, the ploughing of Iraqi soldiers, the strafing of infrastructural targets, etc. were also morally repugnant and unnecessary.

O'Kane's polemic has the virtues of indignation and clarity when it criticizes the allies for oil pollution, for covering up chemical attacks on soldiers and for radioactive damage caused to civilians, etc., yet the programme suffered from its brevity and its overt partiality. The BBC's more heavyweight and extensive four-parter was, of course, equally as partisan as Channel 4's adversarial critique, although less apparently so. Its strengths lay in its copious use of the main political and military figures who were the decision-makers at the time. Except for President Bush, all of the principal players were called upon to offer their version of events, including Tariq Aziz, the Iraqi foreign minister and Wafic al Samarrai, formerly Saddam's chief of intelligence, who has now defected.

By and large the BBC series reinforced the official US and UK governments' positions that the war was broadly justified to safeguard two-fifths of the world's oil supplies, a point ignored by O'Kane. What was most interesting in Eamonn Matthews's programme were the more controversial and revealing opinions of senior politicians and commanders. Margaret Thatcher, for example, criticized the allies for not finishing off Saddam; Norman Schwarzkopf admitted that the US military mistakenly believed Saddam would be overthrown; Colin Powell showed himself to be extremely cautious and in favour of extending sanctions; General Sir Peter de la Billière blamed the British Ministry of Defence for persisting with low-flying tactics which caused the deaths of RAF Tornado pilots; Wafic al Sammarai revealed that by allowing the Iraqi military to use helicopters after the ceasefire, the coalition generals enabled Saddam to put down the revolt of the Shias and Kurds.

Matthews's series was also fascinating because it included camera footage not shown before. This ranged from cockpit videos of planes and tanks, through to footage of Kurds fleeing and Shias being massacred. Drawing upon such disturbing images, the BBC documentary portrayed the war as a tragic though justified conflict. Its point of view was Anglo-American, which allowed little mention of the contribution of other coalition troops, and the series tended to excuse such massacres as the Al Amirayah bombing as human errors made in the fog of war. (The programme partly exonerated the allies for the deaths of women and children in the shelter by accepting the evidence of Saddam's disaffected former head of security, Sammarai, that it was used by Saddam's intelligence staff. The series also differs from O'Kane's estimate of 300 deaths in the bombing of Al Amirayah, reporting instead that 204 died.) Whereas O'Kane's approach is personal and tendentious, Matthews's interpretation of the war is rhetorically elevated.

The repercussions will inevitably roll on, new narratives supplanting old ones, as in the case of Chris Ryan's rewriting of *Bravo Two Zero*. Ryan's account of this legendary SAS mission, *The One That Got Away*, is different from Andy McNab's, and a film version of it directed by the radical director, Paul Greengrass, suggests that his former companion's account of the long march is flawed, jingoistic and racist.[30] Old comrades thus fight each other.

Such disagreements and cultural battles are increasingly to be expected as the memories of 1990–1 fade, and rival tales and myths compete for an audience. The historical Gulf War, like Vietnam before it, will be constituted by future discourses: in popular culture feature films such as *The Finest Hour* have already begun to appear, presenting a revisionist account of the conflict through patriotic stereotype and formulaic convention.[31] The Gulf War is rapidly being transformed into a cultural commodity to become yet another product on the shelves of pop history.

Notes

1. This commemorative supplement, an authoritative recreation of D-Day events, is entitled 'D-Day, 6 June 1944, 6 June 1994'.
2. McNab (1993), p. 173.
3. Walker (1993a).
4. Harrison (1992), p. 57.
5. Ehrhart (1993), p. 12.
6. See Norris (1991) for a discussion of Baudrillard's arguments.
7. Appleyard (1991).
8. Freedman and Karsh (1993), pp. 408–9.
9. Adding to the suspicion that there is an element of 'orchestration' in revising downwards statistics of Iraqi dead, the *Sunday Times* reported in March 1991 that it had announced before Desert Storm began a likely figure of 30,000 enemy dead. See 'Victory in the Gulf', *Sunday Times*, 3 March 1991, p. xiv. This may be compared with the further reduction in estimates mentioned in Chris Bellamy's article in the *Independent* of 11 March 1993, p. 1.
10. Clarke (1994), pp. 75–83.
11. Kelly (1993), pp. 234–5.
12. Ristelhueber (1993). See also Hertzog (1992).
13. Huxley (1995), pp. 171–88.
14. Stern (1993).
15. 'Britain's "Friendly Fire" deal, by MP Ken', *Manchester Evening News*, 4 December 1992, p. 17.
16. Walker (1993b).
17. Said (1991).
18. Forsyth (1992); Higgins (1992); Archer (1993); Mason (1994).
19. See, for example, Urban (1993), or Colvin (1993).
20. Sayle (1994).
21. See Nightingale (1994a) for a review of Richard Norton Taylor and John McGrath's docu-drama, *Half the Picture*, Tricycle.
22. Friedman (1993).
23. Storey (1995).
24. Peters and Nichol (1992).

25. Peters (1992) includes a selection of poetry opposing the Gulf War.
26. MacArthur (1991).
27. *The Gulf War*, written and produced by Eamonn Matthews, BBC1, 7, 9, 14, 16 January 1996.
28. *Riding the Storm: How to Tell Lies and Win Wars*, written and directed by Maggie O'Kane, Channel 4, 3 January 1996.
29. Wallace (1994). Wallace has written an experimental, anti-war play underpinned by feminist ideas. It was performed at the Bush Theatre, London, during August 1994. For a review see Nightingale (1994b).
30. *The One That Got Away*, directed by Paul Greengrass, ITV, 26 February 1996.
31. *The Finest Hour*, directed by Shimon Dotan, USA, 1996.

Bibliography

Appleyard, Brian (1991), 'Shell-shocked by war's words', *Sunday Times*, 'War in the Gulf', 27 January, p. 16.

Archer, Jeffrey (1993), *Honour among Thieves*, London: HarperCollins.

Clarke, Ramsey (1994), *The Fire this Time, US War Crimes in the Gulf*, New York: Thunder's Mouth Press.

Colvin, Marie (1993), 'How the Iraqis tried to kill Saddam', *Sunday Times*, 18 April, p. 19.

Ehrhart, W. D. (1993), *The Distance We Travel*, Easthampton, Massachusetts: Adastra Press.

Forsyth, Frederick (1992), *The Fist of God*, London: Transworld.

Freedman, Lawrence and Karsh, Efraim (1993), *The Gulf Conflict, 1990–1*, London: Faber and Faber.

Friedman, Alan (1993), *Spider's Web, Bush, Saddam, Thatcher and the Decade of Deceit*, London: Faber and Faber.

Harrison, Tony (1992), *The Gaze of the Gorgon*, Newcastle upon Tyne: Bloodaxe Books.

Higgins, Jack (1992), *Eye of the Storm*, London: Signet.

Huxley, David (1995), '*Ceasefire*: an anti-war comic for women', in Jeffrey Walsh (ed.), *The Gulf War Did Not Happen, Politics, Culture and Warfare Post Vietnam*, Aldershot: Arena, pp. 171–88.

Kelly, Michael (1993), *Martyrs' Day: Chronicle of a Small War*, New York: Random House.

MacArthur, Brian (ed.) (1991), *Despatches from the Gulf War*, London: Bloomsbury.

McNab, Andy (1993), *Bravo Two Zero: The True Story of an SAS Patrol behind the Lines in Iraq*, London: The Bantam Press.

Mason, David (1994), *Shadow over Babylon*, London: Bloomsbury, repr. Signet.

Nightingale, Benedict (1994a), 'Murky men at arms', *The Times*, 17 June, p. 39.

Nightingale, Benedict (1994b), 'War crimes and punishment', *Arts Section, The Times*, 8 August, p. 27.

Norris, Christopher (1991), *Uncritical Theory: Postmodernism, Intellectuals and War in the Gulf*, London: Lawrence & Wishart.

Peters, John and Nichol, John (1992), *Tornado Down*, London: Michael Joseph.

Peters, Nancy (ed.) (1992), *War after War: City Lights Review*, San Francisco: Number Five.

Said, Edward (1991), 'Empire of sand', *Weekend Guardian*, 12–13 January, p. 5.

Sayle, Murray (1994), 'Crude awakening', *Night and Day: Mail on Sunday Review*, 16 January, pp. 6–15.

Stern, Chester (1993), 'Hackers' threat to Gulf War triumph', *Mail on Sunday*, 21 March, p. 15.

Storey, John (1995), 'The politics of pop and the Gulf War', in Jeffrey Walsh (ed.), *The Gulf War Did Not Happen, Politics, Culture and Warfare Post Vietnam*, Aldershot: Arena, pp. 101–18.

Urban, Mark (1993), 'The secret war against him', *Daily Telegraph*, 8 January, p. 17.

Walker, Martin (1993a), 'America is coming home,' *Guardian*, 25 May, p. 20.

Walker, Martin (1993b), 'Gulf War's lessons for Clinton', *Guardian*, 17 August, p. 6.

Walsh, Jeffrey (ed.) (1995), *The Gulf War Did Not Happen, Politics, Culture and Warfare Post Vietnam*, Aldershot: Arena.

–14–

Religion, Politics and Remembrance: A Free Church Community and its Great War Dead

Barry M. Doyle

On the morning of 19 April 1917, following a two-hour bombardment, the 4th Battalion of the Norfolk Regiment began its assault on the Turkish positions outside the Palestinian city of Gaza. Watching from the Brigade HQ, Captain M. B. Buxton observed that 'it was a magnificent sight to see them going in extended order as if on a field day',[1] but it was soon apparent that this was no field day as the Turks unleashed 'a perfect hell of artillery and machine gun fire' into the oncoming troops.[2] The attack was a complete failure and, in one of the worst days of the war for the city of Norwich, almost half the 4th Battalion's strength were reported killed, wounded or missing. Six officers, including Captain S. D. Page and Major W. H. 'Harry' Jewson, lost their lives in the battle,[3] with Jewson becoming the focus for a peculiarly Liberal and dissenting 'lost generation'.

The untimely deaths of thousands of young men of rank and promise during the Great War has led to the production of a rich literature devoted to the idea of the 'lost generation'.[4] Yet within this body of work little reference has been made to the experience of the nonconformist middle class,[5] a strange omission given the perceived impact of the war on the power and influence of the free churches and the deleterious effect on the faith and membership of the various denominations.[6] Participation in war was, in fact, a rather unusual situation for nonconformists to find themselves in. Baptists, in particular, had been divided over the Boer War,[7] and throughout the Edwardian period leading members of the denomination such as Sir George White had striven to achieve arms reduction and a conciliation system through, for example, support for the negotiations at The Hague.[8] Yet when the war with Germany broke out, most middle-class Baptists supported their government's decision to fight, with many playing a significant part in the conflict both at home and abroad.[9]

Despite the obvious importance of this involvement, surprisingly little has been written about the particular way free churchmen adapted to the physical loss of significant members of their community, or the political use they made of their 'lost generation'. This chapter will investigate the ways in which nonconformist Liberals in Norwich employed the memory of Major Harry Jewson, the most significant member of their community to die in the Great War, to help them understand their involvement in the conflict. In particular, it will focus on the various constituencies that laid claim to his memory – his parents, his extended family, the free churches, the city of Norwich, Liberalism, the Boys' Brigade – and the ways in which each utilized his death to construct an appropriate memory for their situation. In the process, it will emphasize the way in which most remembrances eschewed militarism – concentrating instead on Jewson's character, his past achievements and the loss suffered by his passing – and the manner in which his death was employed to reaffirm the existence of God, justify the participation of the dissenting middle class in the type of military conflict they had campaigned against throughout the Edwardian era, and to reassert Liberal values of voluntarism and the fight for freedom, in the face of growing 'Prussianism'. Finally, it will show how the use of his memory changed as Liberals, seeking a return to the values of the pre-war era, emphasized his consensual characteristics in opposition to the increasing class conflict of the early 1920s. Its conclusions will draw attention to the long-term failure of the dissenting middle class to maintain control over the production and use of war memory, and the part this loss of power played in the ultimate collapse of their culture in the years running up to the Second World War.

The Life and Death of Harry Jewson

Born in Norwich in 1875, Harry Jewson was a junior partner in the family firm of timber merchants and a 'fine figure of a man . . . [who] . . . spared neither money nor himself in whatever he took in hand'.[10] Liberal in politics and Baptist in religion, the first generation of Jewsons were 'a shining example of that combination of business ability and philanthropy and piety found in the old Nonconformist families of Norwich'.[11] Harry's father, George, was the eldest of eight brothers, four of whom lived in Norwich and played a prominent part in the social, political and religious life of the city. George, a leading Liberal, was an alderman from 1895 until his death in 1922; his brother Richard was the city's Lord Mayor in 1918; Frank, the youngest brother, also sat on the city council for nearly twenty years, whilst John, although he took no part in politics, was secretary of Norwich's nationally renowned St Mary's Baptist Church.[12] Harry shared this family commitment to public service, and his association with a variety of religious, social and political causes made him a prominent figure in the city's new generation of radical dissent.

Jewson could best be described as a muscular Christian socialist who adopted most of the novel trends in turn-of-the-century nonconformity. Although he does not seem to have been a member of the family church of St Mary's, he was a practical evangelist with a strong interest in the social problems of youth. He taught in a Baptist Sunday school in the rapidly expanding working-class suburbs of north Norwich, where he became involved in the Boys' Brigade (B.B.), and particularly the 5th Norwich group. Thanks to Jewson's hard work and dedication, by 1913 the membership stood at 120 and the Company occupied its own eighteen-room premises at Bull Close Road – 'acknowledged to be amongst the finest in the country'[13] – and destined to be the site of a number of the memorials to Jewson which followed his death.

Jewson soon became involved in the B.B. nationally, giving papers like 'The Attitude of B.B. Officers to Social Problems Relating to Boy Life' which merged his interests in youth and social problems. In the course of one such paper he is quoted as saying: 'It is not enough to give physical drill, moral and religious instruction, as they come and go. They must be followed, their social circumstances studied, and, if need be, changed, so as to make them the ally, not the enemy, of the best training the movement can give.'[14] It was this approach which led one obituarist to claim 'there is no doubt that he aroused the social conscience of Officers to an extent to which it had never been aroused before'.[15] In recognition of his ability and dedication he was appointed president of the Norwich Battalion, with Sydney Durrant Page, a Congregationalist businessman and close personal friend, as vice-president.[16]

His support for 'the progressive movement on both its social and religious sides'[17] led him into the Liberal Christian League, and subsequently into local politics as secretary to a non-party committee investigating the level of Poor Law outdoor-relief in Norwich.[18] In 1912 the committee published a report entitled *The Destitute of Norwich and how they Live*,[19] which showed that the Guardians' relief was woefully inadequate. Although the Poor Law Board refused to act on these findings, the campaign earned Jewson considerable respect within the radical and dissenting worlds. It also revealed the extent to which he was moving away from a traditional Liberal political position. Although the committee was non-party – receiving the support of a few Liberals and Conservatives – its closest contacts were with members of the Independent Labour Party (including Jewson's sister Dorothea) who provided logistical support and access to the Board of Guardians.[20] Although there is no evidence that he was a member of the Labour Party at this time, he does seem to have been moving in that direction. Thus by mid-1914 Harry Jewson was playing an important role in the religious and political life of the city, but it is apparent that he was beginning to cut free of the family commitment to both Liberalism and Baptism in favour of more radical alternatives.

When war was declared he renewed his commission with the 4th Battalion of the Norfolk Regiment, the Norwich-based territorial battalion from which he had resigned the previous year.[21] He served with distinction in the Dardanelles, where he was left 'for a considerable time . . . in command of a sadly depleted Battalion',[22] but his luck finally ran out at Gaza when he and Page perished, along with hundreds of others, in the abortive assault on the Turkish defences. The flood of obituaries, letters, memorial services, portrait unveilings and other commemorations which followed his passing gave dissenters the opportunity to ruminate on the loss sustained by his family, their community and Norwich as a whole, and the political and religious significance of the untimely death of one of the city's most gifted younger men.

Reactions of Family, Friends and Community

First and foremost in this process of mourning was the very personal loss sustained by Jewson's parents. A few days after the news of his death had reached Norwich the Primitive Methodist minister, the Reverend Albert Lowe – a colleague of Jewson from the B.B. and the Poor Relief campaign of 1912 – addressed a memorial service for Jewson and Page. Lowe concluded his peroration with thoughts of the family, always the backbone of the Free Churches:

> It is difficult to find words in which to express our sorrow for the loss which has overtaken the families of our ennobled friends. It is in the sacred circle of the home that their loss will be most unutterably felt. Our greatly sorrowing friends have their consolations. They have the consolation of the lives their loved ones lived; the high regard they won in the community that is proud to name them among her foremost sons; the brave, brave deaths they died.[23]

But these were insufficient consolations for George and Mary Jewson. George was a staunch Baptist, an exemplary Liberal and a Victorian patriarch. Nothing in his background had prepared him for the premature violent death of his eldest son fighting for the British army. When George died in March 1922 the *Eastern Daily Press* observed that:

> In a very real sense, his death may be counted amongst our war casualties; for it was the loss of his son, Major Harry Jewson . . . which struck so much of the zest of life out of him; and although he faced the loss with the quiet courage which so many parents were called upon to exercise when our younger men were marching to their death in that grim time, he never recovered from the blow.[24]

Jewson's mother was similarly affected, the *Eastern Daily Press* noting at her death in 1933 that 'since the death of her eldest son, the late Major W. H. Jewson, at Gaza, for reasons of health she has lived a life of retirement, finding solace in her garden and letter writing'.[25]

Although his death was not exceptional – over 3,000 Norwich men were killed in the war[26] – the nonconformist community and the local press continually emphasized the significance of Harry Jewson. In part this reflected the close-knit nature of the city's Free Church elite, for it is only in the context of the Jewsons' predominant position within Norwich, and in particular Harry's status as the standard-bearer of the next generation of nonconformist social leaders, that we can understand the effect of his death on the city's dissenting community.

For dissenters the family was not simply the conjugal unit, but extended outwards to incorporate a complex web of intermarriage and beyond that to the church itself, where the lines between the family and the wider chapel membership were often blurred. The Jewsons were at the centre of just such a kinship network, linking many of Norwich's leading nonconformist families.[27] Through marriages which brought together Baptists, Congregationalists and evangelical Anglicans, their close connections included the Jarrolds, who owned the city's leading printing works, the Howletts, who ran one of the country's biggest shoe firms, and the Boardmans, who were successful architects. In turn these families linked the Jewsons with the Colmans, of mustard fame, Sir George White, MP, and the Cozens-Hardys. These families were Norwich's economic leaders – the largest employers and top professionals – as well as its social and political leaders. Excluding the Jewsons, three of the families produced a Liberal MP between 1880 and 1910 and five families had at least one member who held high civic office in the Liberal interest in the Edwardian period. In the years following Harry's death, his uncle Richard Jewson was Lord Mayor (1918), his uncle W. T. F. Jarrold was Sheriff (1920), his sister Dorothea became Labour MP for Norwich in 1923, and his cousin Percy Jewson was Lord Mayor in 1935 and Liberal National MP for Great Yarmouth from 1941 to 1945.[28] Furthermore, this network dominated not only the business, political and religious world of Norwich, but also the press, for both the Colmans and the Cozens-Hardys held significant interests in the *Eastern Daily Press*, the city's main newspaper.

It was this environment which allowed Albert Lowe to encapsulate the sense of loss felt by nonconformist Norwich, by asserting that:

In their passing our common life has suffered a great impoverishment. The gloom which fell upon the community with the coming of the sad news of their death, a gloom, I venture to say, greater than the loss of a battle . . . is a tribute more eloquent than the most eloquent speech could frame, to the worth and work of our late fellow citizens.[29]

That these deaths could be seen as more significant than the loss of a battle bears testament to the close and closed nature of the urban gathered churches, where marriage and theology combined to give all chapel goers a sense of belonging to one big family.

But Jewson also warranted mourning for what he had achieved, and what he might have achieved had he lived. Most if not all of the obituaries and memorials emphasized his participation in Norwich's social, religious and political life and the loss the city had sustained by his death. The *Eastern Daily Press* stated that: 'He was a man of singular capacity, gifted with a strong sense of the need for social amelioration . . . There is little question that if he had lived he would have taken a considerable place in the public life of Norwich.'[30] Similar testaments to his worth were made by Lowe, Jewson's uncles W. T. F. Jarrold and Richard Jewson, and as late as 1922 in the obituary of his father, which referred to him as 'one of the most promising of all our younger men who fell in the war'.[31]

Furthermore, praise for Jewson crossed both religious and political lines. The Conservative Lord Mayor, George Moore Chamberlain, made a special statement at the police court where, on behalf of the Norwich magistrates, he expressed 'deep sympathy with Mr. George Jewson on the death of his son, who had been killed in action. They desired to send to Mr. and Mrs. Jewson an expression of sympathy in their bereavement.'[32] The non-sectarian approach was taken further in a lengthy letter to the editor of the *Eastern Daily Press* from the Reverend F. W. Bennett Symons, the Anglican vicar of the city-centre parish of St Saviour, who wrote:

> May I bear my testimony to the zeal and enthusiasm for the welfare of the boys of Norwich, of the two young men, Major Jewson and Captain Page . . . Their loss is a great blow to the city . . . In offering sympathy to their families and in thanking you for your testimony to the faith and labours of these two soldiers of the Cross, I trust their example and sacrifice will be remembered, and their moral and spiritual influence will be animated by their consecration and devotion to the highest duties of life . . .[33]

Although Jewson was clearly a prominent civic figure whose death was a blow to the whole of Norwich – Anglican and nonconformist – it was definitely the dissenters who felt his loss most acutely. In consequence of his central position within this Free Church, radical world, very little militaristic rhetoric accompanied his idolization. Admittedly the *Boys' Brigade Gazette*, in an effort to create a Free Church *Boys' Own* hero, gave Jewson the classic hero's end. Utilizing the device of a 'brother Officer' they related that 'he was hit early in the advance, but continued to head his Company until mortally wounded by a bullet through the heart. "Come on, we will fight to the death", were the last words addressed to his men.'[34]

This image may have been appropriate to the requirements of the Boys' Brigade hierarchy,[35] but it was not, by and large, what middle-class dissenters wanted. For them, a rather more realistic account of events was provided by Jewson's servant, Private Atkins, in a letter to George Jewson which seems to have been published in the local press.[36] Atkins related that:

> I also was present at his end, and was the only one. He received four bullet wounds. The first one in the foot, which we managed to get out fairly well, and bound the foot up, but he insisted on going on. We got about another 8 hundred yards and the Major got the second across the back which compelled him to lie down. We had been lying about an hour continually being sniped at, when he received the third which went through the fleshy part of the right side of the chest, but that did not make any difference to the Major, he was still in good spirits. Soon after I received mine in the back which rendered my lower limbs almost useless. We lay there about two more hours, and circumstances made it impossible to stay any longer, and the Major managed to get up and go back . . . He had gone about 500 yards, when I saw him stagger and fall. When I reached him I found he had got his fourth wound, in the chest, and was past all human aid. He did not recognize me at first. After about 10 minutes he spoke. His words were 'Give my love to my people' he never spoke no more . . .[37]

Although obviously somewhat stylized, this version of events, showing the ordinary mortal man rather than the comic-book hero, was an image better suited to the sensibilities of the nonconformist middle classes. It was more comforting for them to believe that he died thinking of his 'people', among whom they could all number themselves, rather than urging his men to fight to the death.

Despite this aversion to militarism, they did not entirely ignore the fact that Jewson died in battle and, by employing the metaphor of the 'soldier of the Cross', they were able to justify his death as part of a religious crusade. As Clyde Binfield has pointed out, there was nothing new in a language of conflict for nonconformists whose 'hymns were all of war'.[38] But, though they supported their government in 1914, many had been distressed at the thought of hostilities with Protestant Germany.[39] However, the circumstances of Jewson's death, falling in what the Reverend Lowe described as 'the advance against the Turk with a view to ridding the Holy Land of his corrupting presence',[40] added a moral aspect to the sacrifice and presented that part of the conflict as a just war. Even the Liberal theologians at the *Christian Commonwealth*[41] latched onto the significance of the Palestinian conflict, noting that Jewson 'like one of the Crusaders of old' met his end 'in the Holy Land . . . fighting the greatest and most unscrupulous tyrant the world has ever seen'.[42] It seems likely that Jewson came to symbolize the Liberal 'lost generation' partly because of his very Christian death – fighting the infidel in Palestine, not through an ambiguous conflict with fellow Protestants in Flanders.

The Creation – and Re-creation – of an Image

Because conventional militarism had no place in the Free Church community of Norwich, they dealt with Jewson's death by constant reference to the values which they had held dear prior to the war – faith, social service, love, duty and voluntarism – and in the process created a distinctly Liberal and dissenting hero. Fulsome praise was heaped upon his selfless character. Albert Lowe painted a picture of a man deeply imbued with the spirit of discipline and Christian duty in whom he saw burning 'almost more brightly than in any man I have known, the spirit of justice and compassion'.[43] In language steeped in the homoerotic imagery which Paul Fussell has shown to have played such an important part in the male mourning process,[44] the *Christian Commonwealth* expressed shock and disbelief at the death of so noble a creature.

> 'Killed' – it is so unnatural, so cruel, so senseless, so almost impossible. You recall that manly figure, that bright, clear face – now with a merry light in the eye, now with a slightly sad and far-away look – you remember the firm grasp of the hand and the always kindly voice; and, try as you will, you simply cannot believe that it is all at an end.[45]

whilst an 'intimate friend', quoted in the same journal, wrote that:

> To me, Harry was ever a wonderful man, with his great purpose of mind, his courage, his complete simplicity of manner, his abhorrence of injustice, his wonderful breadth and depth of sympathy, and his extraordinary unselfishness . . . We remember his great efforts towards the uplifting of suffering humanity; the struggle against poverty and the oppressor had always his practical sympathy.[46]

Similar praise was found elsewhere. At the *Boys' Brigade Gazette*, the personal obituary was merged with homily to create an appropriate role model for the lads to emulate. The author, highlighting the effort Jewson put into the B.B. movement, noted 'His absolute unselfishness, unfailing tact, wide social outlook, and broadmindedness',[47] whilst the heroic nature of his service was developed in the description of his military career, in which 'He faced the enemy in' a 'calm and cool manner' before falling at the head of his troops, leaving the writer to conclude that 'it is such lives as his that give us inspiration and strength to "carry on"'.[48]

Furthermore, on more than one occasion his impeccable character drew comparison with Christ. Catherine Moriarty has highlighted this tendency in war memorials, suggesting that 'the parallel of His sacrifice with that of the soldier killed during the First World War was a particularly poignant analogy: it met an urgently felt need to place the losses in a historical continuum of needful sacrifice'.[49] For Free Churchmen this comparison seems to have been less troublesome and more freely utilized than may have been the case with the Anglicans, leading Lowe to assert that Jewson and Page had sought to 'walk in the footsteps of the Man Christ Jesus'.[50] In similar vein, the 'intimate friend' writing in the *Christian Commonwealth* suggested that 'no man was ever so fortunate in having such a Christ-like character in a friend as I found in him'.[51] Although Christ's sacrifice is not explicitly referred to, it is certainly implicit in both analogies.

Yet the fact that war, even a just war in Palestine, had led to the premature death of such a 'Christ-like' character did raise uncomfortable questions of faith for Free Churchmen. Dissenters, especially Baptists, had been in the vanguard of opposition to militarism in the Edwardian period,[52] so how could they justify the slaughter of their sons and still remain good Christians? Tackling these fears head on, the obituarist in the *Christian Commonwealth* reasserted the existence of a 'divine plan' in which disasters, wars and 'the sudden cutting off of young lives full of promise and potency' were 'working out something far more glorious than anything we can conceive, but in which we shall all share'.[53] This justification was vital for dissenters attempting to come to terms with their war dead, for without this 'Divine plan' not only the war, but the very existence of God would have to be brought into question. Evidence from post-war church membership suggests that most Norwich Baptists were not sufficiently shaken in their faith to abandon the denomination,[54] although it is possible that the conflict encouraged Dorothea and Christopher Jewson (Harry's brother and sister) and their cousin Violet to move towards the pacifist religion of Quakerism.

The events of 1914–18 had also put Liberal principles to the test, and thus the sacrifices made by Jewson and his friend Page were utilized to justify how and why Liberals had fought the war. At various memorial presentations, leading dissenters broadened the memory of Harry Jewson to satisfy political needs. Thus at the unveiling of a portrait of Sydney Page in September 1918, the Lord Mayor Richard Jewson (Harry's uncle) used his speech to give meaning to Free Church involvement in the conflict. 'The keynote of the life of Sydney Page was to be found in the words "Voluntary Service" for in all the spheres of his life he was willing and ready to give the best service to whatever he undertook. Finally with his face to the foe, he died voluntarily for his country.'[55] In November 1918 the opportunity arose for Richard Jewson to speak of his nephew when he unveiled a portrait of Harry at the Boys' Brigade rooms in Bull Close Road. According to the *Eastern Daily Press*:

> The Lord Mayor spoke of Major Jewson as one of the purest, strongest, and most unselfish men he had ever known, one of whom he could hardly trust himself to speak, for they had lived together in the closest comradeship, union and sympathy. He had spent lavishly his time, his strength, and his money to make the boys of the 5th Company better in health, physique, and tone. It accorded fully with his character that in the end he should be numbered with those who had laid down their lives in order that men, women, and children might be happier and freer in future from tyranny and wrong.[56]

Through such reiterations of Liberal principle the dissenting middle class coped with the profound loss they had suffered by the deaths of these two men. The aims of the war and the means of fighting it might have been hijacked by a Conservative-dominated coalition, 'Prussianism' may have triumphed,[57] but by emphasizing the voluntary service of Jewson and Page in the pursuit of freedom from tyranny, Liberals could, and did, renew their convictions.

By the early 1920s, however, the political imperative in the repro-duction of Jewson's image was beginning to change. The war had brought issues of class into the centre of politics, leading to greater industrial militancy, a breakdown in relations between employers and employees, and a diminution of cross-class sociability.[58] In December 1921, again at the home of the 5th Norwich B.B. in Bull Close Road, W. T. F. Jarrold – Liberal Sheriff in 1920 and Harry's maternal uncle – presented a Challenge Cup to the boys in memory of his nephew. In the course of his speech he observed, in the customary fashion, that Jewson, 'was modest, retiring, and thorough in all he undertook, and above all a true follower of Jesus Christ'.[59] But Jarrold, although a Liberal into the 1930s, was strongly anti-union,[60] and he also took this opportunity to make some coded political points. Referring to the need for continued cross-class relations he noted that 'the secret of success of the 5th Norwich Company was that its officers gave themselves wholly to their duties', whilst in a passage which reflected the changing aims of Liberalism, he went on to warn the assembled boys that 'they were living in different times; the aftermath of the great world war. The accumulated wealth of the country was wasted and destroyed; not only money, but the lives of some of their finest men were sacrificed. What they wanted today was real comradeship, goodwill, co-operation, and hard work.'[61]

Thus in the altered circumstances of the early 1920s, Jewson's memory was employed to symbolize those Christian, Liberal virtues, such as cooperation and hard work, which men like Jarrold wished to recover for a world palpably more secular and divided by class than before the war.

But he was fighting a losing battle, for the experience of 1914–18 had made profound changes to the social and political fabric of Norwich, and in particular to the culture and values of the Free Church community.

Conclusion

The dissenting middle class, unlike the traditional Anglican elite, were not used to physical sacrifice as an aspect of public service (the Conservative Lord Mayor, George Moore Chamberlain, had forty-four members of his family serving in the forces, five of whom, including one of his sons, had died by 1918[62]). As a result dissenters were completely unprepared for the irreparable losses of 1914–18. In coping with the trauma this caused they avoided militaristic images and instead utilized Jewson's passing to justify their participation in the war and rebuild their shattered faith in God and Liberalism. They were aided in this task by the manner of their hero's end – fighting the infidel in the Holy Land rather than in the senseless futility of the Western Front – and by the Christ-like character of the man himself. In life Harry Jewson had proved himself to be the complete Christian gentleman, a worthy 'soldier of the Cross', and a credit to the Free Church community from which he sprang. In death he was to serve as the perfect figurehead for a nonconformist 'lost generation'.

But pre-war Liberals like the Jewsons and Jarrolds were only partially successful in their aim of utilizing Harry's memory to renew the closed culture of the Edwardian era in which their values and style of politics had been dominant.[63] Although the experience of war shook the faith of this older generation in the gathered churches and the Liberal Party, most of them continued to serve both until their deaths. However, for the younger men and women who had experienced the fighting, the effects were more enduring. New commitments were made to organizations such as the territorials, the Quakers, the Labour Party and even the Conservatives, whilst the 'lost generation', in the hands of men like the Unitarian R. H. Mottram, were employed, not to bolster traditional Liberalism, but to build opposition to any future war.[64] As this new generation replaced their fathers in the civic and religious life of the city, the full impact of the war on the closed world of the Liberal dissenting middle class became apparent. The Free Churches and the Liberal party moved into a period of rapid decline, as the political and religious culture they had developed in the Edwardian period was replaced by the secular, class-based politics of the mid-twentieth century.[65]

The memory of Harry Jewson was utilized by many people in the years following his death for a variety of social, political and religious ends. The Boys' Brigade saw in his death the opportunity to create a heroic figure for the lads to emulate; the Liberal Christians of the *Christian*

Commonwealth saw a chance to reiterate the divine plan; whilst the people of Norwich mourned the death of one of their most promising young men. Yet because of the size and social importance of his family, control over the reproduction of Jewson's memory passed from his deeply grieving parents to his extended family, and particularly his uncles. Despite the fact that he seems to have severed all formal links with both Liberalism and Baptism before 1914, they recreated him as a potent symbol of the Liberal Free Church world of Edwardian Norwich. By the early 1920s he had come to embody the lost cross-class sociability of that era and to personify the generation of leaders which the war had taken from the city.

Notes

I am grateful to the School of History and International Relations, University of St Andrews, for financial assistance towards the completion of this work.

1. Petre (1924), p. 145.
2. Ibid., p. 144.
3. Ibid., p. 147.
4. For a general assessment of the literature and debate, see Winter (1986), pp. 65–99. For an attempt to put a figure on the 'lost generation', see Winter (1977).
5. The main exception is Clyde Binfield, in particular Binfield (1977), pp. 232–48; Binfield (1983).
6. See, for example, Stevenson (1984), pp. 356–7; Koss (1975), pp. 125–44; Wilson (1968), pp. 25–8.
7. Koss (1975), pp. 32–7; Jewson (1957), p. 140.
8. Morris (1971); Jewson (1957), pp. 142–3.
9. Clements (1975–6).
10. Anon. (1917a), p. 118.
11. *Norwich Mercury*, 21 September 1918.
12. See the cuttings relating to various members of the Jewson family in the newscuttings collection of the Norwich Local Studies Library (hereafter NLSL newscuttings).
13. Anon. (1960), p. 118.
14. The Boys' Brigade, Norwich Battalion (1917) (hereafter *In Memory*), p. 14.
15. Anon. (1917a), p. 118.

16. *Eastern Daily Press*, 25 April 1917; *In Memory*, p. 13.
17. Anon. (1917b).
18. Whiteley (1968).
19. Committee of Investigators (1912).
20. *Norwich Mercury*, 25 May 1912 and 22 March 1913; Whiteley (1968), p. 32.
21. Anon. (1917b).
22. *In Memory*, p. 11.
23. Ibid., p. 17. For the family as the backbone of the Free Churches see Jewson (1957), p. 143.
24. *Eastern Daily Press,* 24 March 1922.
25. *Eastern Daily Press*, 7 April 1933.
26. Kent (1988), p. 72.
27. For the full extent of these connections see Doyle (1995a); Doyle (1995b).
28. NSL newscuttings on Jarrolds, Jewsons, Howletts, Colmans, Boardmans and Cozens-Hardys; Bebbington (1981); Bebbington (1986); Palgrave-Moore (1978).
29. *In Memory,* p. 12.
30. *Eastern Daily Press*, 25 April 1917.
31. *In Memory*, pp. 11–12; *Eastern Daily Press*, 8 November 1918; 3 December 1921; 24 March 1922.
32. Although Chamberlain mentioned the loss of two other officers, Captain Page and Captain W. V. Morgan, it was Jewson who was singled out for special praise. *Eastern Daily Press*, 25 April 1917.
33. *Eastern Daily Press*, 26 April 1917.
34. Anon. (1917a), p. 119.
35. For militarism within the pre-war Boys' Brigade, see Sprighall (1977); Bailey (1983).
36. There is a typed copy of the letter entitled 'Copy of letter to Alderman Jewson from No. 1848, Pte. C. C. Atkins, 1/4th Norfolk Regiment, Officer's servant of Major Harry Jewson, Nasrish Hosp. CAIRO. B.E.F.' in Jewson, NLSL newscuttings. It seems likely that this letter was published in the press, although I have been unable to confirm this.
37. Ibid.
38. Binfield (1977), p. 233.
39. Ibid., p. 234; Clements (1975–6), esp. pp. 81–4.
40. *In Memory*, p. 11.
41. The journal described itself as 'The Organ of the Progressive Movement in Religion and Social Ethics', *Christian Commonwealth*, 2 May 1917.
42. Ibid., p. 379.

43. *In Memory,* p. 12.
44. Fussell (1975).
45. Anon. (1917b).
46. Ibid.
47. Anon. (1917a), p. 118.
48. Ibid., pp. 118–19.
49. Moriarty (1991).
50. *In Memory*, p. 12.
51. Anon. (1917b).
52. Clements (1975–6), pp. 79–80.
53. Anon. (1917b).
54. Anon. (1929).
55. *Norwich Mercury*, 21 September 1918.
56. *Eastern Daily Press*, 8 November 1918.
57. Turner (1992).
58. Adams (1990).
59. *Eastern Daily Press*, 3 December 1921.
60. Holmes (1906).
61. *Eastern Daily Press*, 3 December 1921.
62. *Eastern Daily Press*, 17 February 1918.
63. For dissenting Liberalism in Edwardian Norwich, see Doyle (1994).
64. Mottram (1924); Mottram (1957), pp. 167–8.
65. Doyle (1995).

Bibliography

Newspapers and Journals

Eastern Daily Press, 25 April 1917; 26 April 1917; 2 May 1917; 17 February 1918; 8 November 1918; 3 December 1921; 24 March 1922; 7 April 1933.
Norwich Mercury, 25 May 1912; 22 March 1913; 21 September 1918.
Cuttings relating to various members of the Jewson family in the news-cuttings collection of the Norwich Local Studies Library.

Books and Articles

Adams, T. (1990), 'Labour and the First World War: economy, politics and the erosion of local peculiarity?', *Journal of Regional and Local Studies*, vol. 10, no. 1, pp. 23–47.
Anon. (1917a), 'W. H. Jewson', *Boys' Brigade Gazette*, June 1917, pp. 118–19.

Anon. (1917b), 'Killed in action', *Christian Commonwealth*, 2 May 1917, p. 379.

Anon. (1929), 'Annual report of the Norfolk Baptist Association, 1929', *St Mary's Church Magazine*, Norwich: St Mary's Church, p. 20.

Anon. (1960), *1910/1960: Fifty Years of Baptist Witness. The Story of Silver Road*, Norwich: Silver Road Baptist Church, unpaginated.

Bailey, V. (1983), 'Bibles and dummy rifles: the Boys' Brigade', *History Today*, vol. 33, no. 10, pp. 5–9.

Bebbington, D. W. (1981), 'Baptist M.P.s in the nineteenth century', *Baptist Quarterly*, vol. 29, no. 1, pp. 3–24.

Bebbington, D. W. (1986), 'Baptist M.P.s in the twentieth century', *Baptist Quarterly*, vol. 31, no. 6, pp. 252–87.

Binfield, C. (1977), *So Down to Prayers: Studies in English Nonconformity 1780–1920*, London: J. M. Dent.

Binfield, C. (1983), 'Et Virtutem et Musas: Mill Hill School and the Great War', in W. J. Shiels (ed.), *The Church and War: Studies in Church History 20*, Oxford: Blackwell, pp. 351–82.

The Boys' Brigade, Norwich Battalion (1917), *In Memory of Major W. H. Jewson . . . and Captain S. D. Page*, Norwich: Boys' Brigade.

Clements, K. W. (1975–6), 'Baptists and the outbreak of the First World War', *Baptist Quarterly*, vol. 26, pp. 74–92.

Committee of Investigators (1912), *The Destitute of Norwich and How They Live: A Report on the Administration of Out-Relief with an Introduction by B. Seebohm Rowntree*, London: Jarrolds.

Doyle, B. M. (1994), 'Business, Liberalism and dissent in Norwich, 1900–1930', *Baptist Quarterly*, vol. 35, no. 5, pp. 243–50.

Doyle, B. M. (1995a), 'Gender, class and congregational culture in early twentieth-century Norwich', *United Reformed Church History Society Journal*, vol. 5, no. 6, pp. 317–35.

Doyle, B. M. (1995b), 'Urban liberalism and the "Lost Generation": politics and middle-class culture in Norwich, 1900–1935', *Historical Journal*, vol. 38, no. 3, pp. 617–34.

Fussell, P. (1975), *The Great War in Modern Memory*, Oxford: Oxford University Press, pp. 270–309.

Holmes, W. (1906), 'The wages and conditions of the workers of Norwich: the Empire Press', *Norwich Elector*, May.

Jewson, C. B. (1957), *The Baptists in Norfolk*, London: Carey Kingsgate.

Kent, P. (1988), 'Norwich: 1914–18', in G. Gliddon (ed.), *Norfolk and Suffolk in the Great War*, Norwich: Gliddon Books.

Koss, S. (1975), *Nonconformity in Modern British Politics*, London: Batsford

Moriarty, C. (1991), 'Christian iconography and First World War memorials', *Imperial War Museum Review*, vol. 6, p. 71.

Morris, A. J. A. (1971), 'The English Radicals' campaign for disarmament and the Hague Conference of 1907', *Journal of Modern History*, vol. 43, pp. 367–93.

Mottram, R. H. (1924), *The Spanish Farm*, London: Penguin 1936 edition.

Mottram, R. H. (1957), *Another Window Seat or Life Observed 1919–1953*, London: Hutchinson.

Palgrave-Moore, P. (1978), *The Mayors and Lord Mayors of Norwich, 1836–1974*, Norwich: Elvery Dowers.

Petre, F. Loraine (1924), *History of the Norfolk Regiment*, vol. II: 4th August 1914–31st December 1918, Norwich: Jarrolds.

Sprighall, J. (1977), *Youth, Empire, and Society*, London: Croom Helm.

Stevenson, J. (1984), *British Society 1914–45*, London: Penguin.

Turner, J. (1992), *British Politics and the Great War: Coalition and Conflict 1915–1918*, New Haven and London: Yale University Press.

Whiteley, J. (1968), 'Social investigation and the Poor Law in Norwich, 1906–1914', unpublished MA thesis, University of East Anglia.

Wilson, T. (1968), *The Downfall of the Liberal Party*, London: Fontana.

Winter, J. M. (1977), 'Britain's "lost generation" of the First World War', *Population Studies*, vol. 31, no. 3, pp. 449–66.

Winter, J. M. (1986), *The Great War and the British People*, London: Macmillan.

15

Memories of the Second World War and National Identity in Germany

Gerd Knischewski and *Ulla Spittler*

This chapter will focus on the relationship between memories of the Second World War and the creation of a national identity in post-1945 West Germany. It will argue, firstly, that in Germany, commemoration of the Second World War in relation to the construction of a national identity cannot be separated from the debate about National Socialism (NS). Secondly, it will argue that the development in Germany after 1945 of a national identity comparable with that of Great Britain or France was difficult if not impossible. Within the context of the Cold War, however, the political conflict with East Germany (the GDR) became an important part of the West German national identity. Thirdly, it will be argued that the way in which the Second World War is remembered has passed through several phases, in which different political interests have in turn gained the upper hand. Our final conclusion is that official war commemoration in Germany cannot have a unifying character but is always polarizing.

Perspectives on the Second World War

War memory and commemoration are problematic notions in Germany: the Second World War cannot be perceived as an isolated phenomenon. In the German collective memory, it finds an extension on the time-scale in both directions: backwards to the start of the NS regime in 1933 and forwards to the division of Germany during the Cold War.

There are, therefore, essentially two ways in which the Second World War is commemorated. In the first of these, the war is perceived and categorized as part of the NS crimes against humanity. Within such a framework, official commemoration can concentrate on either the victims of persecution (such as the Jews, mentally handicapped, homosexuals, gypsies, 'inferior races' as defined by the Nazis, the political Left, etc.) or on the various opposition groups and forms of resistance. In this perspective, the guilty can clearly be identified, and indirect political imperatives for the future can be drawn. It is obvious that in this context the Germans are viewed as culprits. The question of who was responsible for NS crimes cannot be separated from that of what caused National Socialism to be successful in the first place, and how popular consent was achieved.

In opposition to this view, the second interpretation focuses on the military defeat of Germany at the end of the war. In this context German losses and victims are the focus (and can be mourned for): these include German soldiers who were killed in battle as well as victims among the German civilian population, in particular those killed by Allied bombers, but also the victims of the 'vengeance campaign' initiated by the advancing Red Army. This is also the context in which the loss of the *Heimat* east of the rivers Oder and Neisse, and of German lives through expulsion and flight, are emphasized. The final aspect of this second view on the war and its consequences is the division of Germany into two separate political entities and the loss of a single German statehood. This second perspective implies a change in direction insofar as it tends to see Germans primarily as victims, and it blurs a crucial dimension of war memory, namely that of Germans as perpetrators within the NS regime. Although on the level of the individual this second perspective has proved to offer more options for identity and commemoration, on a political level it seems that only the first perspective allows an acceptance and a coming to terms with the implications of the NS regime.

In West Germany there have been four distinct phases in the way in which the Second World War is remembered. Each of these will now be examined in turn.

Phase I: No Positive National Identity after 1945 and Repression of the NS Past

The moral incrimination through the knowledge of NS atrocities committed before and during the war made a renaissance of German national pride almost impossible. There were, however, additional factors which hindered the development of a traditional positive national identity. Under the conservative German chancellor Konrad Adenauer (1949–63), the Federal Republic of Germany was firmly integrated into the Western alliance systems (the European Economic Community (EEC), the West European Union (WEU), the North Atlantic Treaty Organisation (NATO). The initial lack of state sovereignty turned the Germans into dedicated Europeans overnight, and thus Europe served as a substitute for national identity.

At the same time, the Cold War and Germany's division into two separate states led the Federal Republic of Germany (FRG) in West Germany to claim for itself an all-German national identity, within which the German Democratic Republic (GDR) in East Germany was considered a state without democratic legitimation. This claim to an all-German identity allocated the FRG the status of being a provisional arrangement, a mere stopgap until reunification was achieved. This special post-war situation led to an obvious break with tradition where national symbols were used only very cautiously. As a substitute for a national identity in traditional terms, West Germans started to take pride in, and identify with, their economic success.

Within this context, the interpretation of the NS regime became an important ideological battleground between the FRG and the GDR. The GDR saw itself as the morally superior German state. It asserted the legitimacy of its statehood as stemming from being the only really anti-fascist German state. According to GDR Marxism-Leninism, fascism constitutes the ultimate stage of capitalism, with the organized working class as its main target. Therefore, the GDR refused to take on any historical responsibility as successor of the *Deutsches Reich*. Accordingly, financial compensations to NS victims, for instance to Israel, were not paid. In the context of official commemoration of the recent past, anti-fascism gained the status of an official state doctrine, the main emphasis of which was on the capitalist enemy and the resistance of its socialist counterpart. Taking part in official commemoration rituals for the political victims of the NS regime was an integrated part of GDR society. The anniversary of the capitulation of the German troops (8 May 1945) was celebrated under the name of 'the day of the liberation from fascism', and became one of many national remembrance days in the GDR.[1]

However, this artificially stimulated anti-fascism had some important flaws. Firstly, as an ideology imposed from above, it was perceived by many only as a tiresome duty to which lip-service had to be paid. More seriously, the mass support the NS regime had enjoyed was blotted out, and the focus was on the working class as the principal NS victim rather than the Jews. Thus the collective memory of the East Germans was relieved from personal guilt or confrontation with any personal involvement with, or support of, the NS regime.

Meanwhile, in West Germany legal attempts to deal with the legacy of the NS past were sluggish in this period and soon came to a halt. Thus the collective memory of the West Germans was also soon exonerated from reproaches and accusations of guilt. In the West German political debate this is described as 'suppression of the past', as opposed to 'coming to terms with the past'. The psychologists Mitscherlich have alluded to this failure as an 'inability to mourn'.[2]

Official commemoration in West Germany during this phase comprised the following: in 1954 another national holiday (apart from 1 May) was introduced. This was 17 June, which was named the 'Day of German

Unity'. In the previous year, there had been an uprising in the GDR which had culminated in demands for more democracy and later unity. Although never an official national holiday, the anniversary of the erection of the Berlin Wall (13 August 1961) soon gained some prominence in the commemoration rituals of the political establishment. Thus in the public conscience, the ideological confrontation with the GDR had apparently replaced the moral confrontation of the German past.

There were, however, two remembrance days which made a direct connection to National Socialism and war: the *Volkstrauertag*, literally the 'people's day of mourning', i.e. the equivalent of the British Remembrance Day, and 20 July. The *Volkstrauertag*, which is held on the second Sunday before the first Sunday in Advent, commemorates in a parliamentary ceremony and in church services the victims of the two World Wars, including the victims of the Holocaust and other victims of National Socialism, but also the victims of the GDR regime. The organizer of the parliamentary event has always been the *Volksbund Deutscher Kriegsgräberfürsorge* (VDK), a private but state-supported war-graves commission which was founded in 1919 with the aim of 'supporting German war-graves . . . in accordance with the public feeling'.[3] Thus the *Volkstrauertag* can hardly be interpreted as a remembrance day exclusively dedicated to the Second World War. The date itself and the organizer VDK are too clearly in the tradition of the Weimar Republic to make the *Volkstrauertag* an anti-fascist commemoration day.

Although the VDK could have been accused of glorifying the deaths of soldiers in its First World War cemeteries, it was allowed to resume its activities in the Western occupation zones in 1947. The VDK proved to be an organization which had problems with coming to terms with the German past, i.e. accepting the German responsibility for the war and NS atrocities. Guilt and responsibility were shifted onto the '*Führer*' in order to leave the institutions of soldiership and armed forces morally intact and thus guarantee their further existence. This mingling of perpetrators with victims even led to the VDK burying SS soldiers alongside foreign forced labourers who had been shot by the SS. 'Death has erased all differences' was the title of an (almost programmatic) article in the central organ of the VDK in 1963.[4]

In the 1950s, West German society was dominated by utilitarian thinking rather than mourning and commemoration. Places in which NS atrocities had been committed were either used for different purposes, e.g. as clinics for the mentally ill or as accommodation for refugees, or they were even razed to the ground, as was the case in Dachau.[5] It was not the political elite but former inmates and victim organizations who brought about the erection of commemorative stones and memorials, and only in the 1960s were public funds made available for the preservation of memorials. However, there was a prevailing tendency to disguise or cover up any direct connections to National Socialism: 'To the dead of war and tyranny' was probably the most widely used phrase on memorial signs. The abbreviation KZ (*Konzentrationslager*, i.e. concentration camp) was frowned upon during these years.[6]

The second remembrance day, 20 July, can be regarded as the West German answer to the 'anti-fascist resistance of the working class' in the GDR. On 20 July 1944, a group of Wehrmacht officers had attempted unsuccessfully to assassinate Hitler. Since 1951, official commemoration ceremonies were held, chiefly at Berlin.[7] The Plötzensee prison in West Berlin, where most of the conspirators involved in this plot, together with many others, had been executed, was turned into a memorial.

Phase II: Intensified Attempts to Come to Terms with the Past

The 1960s and 1970s saw significant changes in West Germany's perception of its national identity with regard to both the NS past and the relationship with the GDR. At the heart of this reassessment was the student movement *Außerparlamentarische Opposition* (APO) (the name means literally 'extra-parliamentary opposition') which had the long-term effect of a cultural revolution. In the FRG, the conflict took a generational form with the young reproaching the older generation for their Nazi past. As early as 1959, the *Sozialistischer Deutscher Studentenbund* (SDS) (the socialist German students' organization) organized an exhibition entitled *Ungesühnte Nazi-Justiz* ('unatoned Nazi Justice').[8] In the eyes of the student movement, the Auschwitz trials which took place from 1963 to 1965 and the surrounding media coverage forced the older generation to face up to the past. Through such public pressure the legal limitation period for NS crimes was extended from twenty to thirty years. In 1979, it was abolished altogether.

To what extent the memory of National Socialism influenced government politics from 1969 on (even if only for a short period of time) can be demonstrated by the example of Willy Brandt, the first Social Democratic chancellor of the FRG, and also a well-known anti-fascist and former resistance fighter. While visiting Warsaw in 1970 to conduct negotiations with Poland about a non-aggression treaty and the recognition of the Oder–Neisse line as the Polish western border, Brandt visited the memorial for the victims of the Warsaw ghetto uprising. In a deeply symbolic gesture he knelt down. With this gesture of humility, Brandt admitted German guilt. Neither before nor since has there been a gesture which better signified the stance the political Left in the FRG has taken towards responsibility for National Socialism and its war. As was to be expected, this gesture was heavily criticized by the Right.

In 1979 and again in the 1980s, West German television broadcast the US series 'Holocaust'. The German public was emotionally stirred up and deeply divided. About one-third of the letters to the broadcasting company were negative: some commented on the atrocities committed by other nations; others demanded that the whole affair should be regarded as finished; some were expressions of anti-semitism in its purest form.[9] However, this broadcast certainly contributed to the impetus that research into local NS history received at this time. 'Everywhere in the Federal Republic "history workshops" emerged with the purpose of establishing the local NS history. Schools were tracking down labour camps and following the fates of Jewish citizens.'[10] There was also a marked change in research paradigms at universities. Left, and even Marxist, categories gained some weight in the analysis of, and debate about, fascism.

In 1980, the first official attempt was made (by the *Bundeszentrale für Politische Bildung*) to draw up a list of all NS memorials in the FRG. Since then, however, local initiatives have erected a great number of new memorials. In 1993, Faulenbach and Stadlmaier commented that 'for the last twenty years, the range and variety of work surrounding memorials has been very impressive indeed'.[11]

On a political level, the new *Ost- und Deutschlandpolitik* (West German detente policy towards eastern European states and the GDR) in the wake of the change of government in 1969 resulted in the signing of the Basic Treaty between the FRG and the GDR in 1972. This treaty marked the starting point of a process which was to narrow down the national identity of the West Germans to the FRG. The FRG was on its way to becoming a state-nation (*Staatsnation*), and its citizens were essentially performing an act of self-recognition.

While hostility to the political system of the GDR continued, the objective of reunification had been postponed in temporal as well as geographical terms. It was now expected to be achieved only within the framework of an all-European peace order. On a legal level, the Social Democratic Party in particular became more and more prepared in the 1980s to recognize the existence of the concept of GDR citizenship in exchange for those citizens obtaining more liberal travel concessions.[12]

In the context of this 'policy of rapprochement', it was suggested by the political Left that 17 June should be abolished as a national holiday in favour of 23 May, the day on which the Basic Law, i.e. the FRG constitution, had been passed. This was a further step in the direction of self-recognition. An indicator for the depth of this process of self-recognition is the term 'constitutional patriotism' which had been suggested by the social scientist Dolf Sternberger.[13] This theory promoted an identification with a people's democratic constitution rather than with symbols, ethnic origins or a positive historical tradition. 'The Germany of "constitutional patriotism" is evidently reduced to the FRG.'[14]

However, the notion of an all-German nation was revived in the early 1980s by sections of the peace movement who envisaged neutrality for the two German states. In view of a lost security for the whole of Germany, *Angst* became a unifying force. As a late consequence of the Second World War, strong anti-militaristic attitudes were, and still are, widespread in the German public; these attitudes again became apparent during the Gulf crisis in 1990–1.

Phase III: The Conservative Backlash of the 1980s

For the conservatives, on the other hand, the concept of national identity remained an important category within their attempts to counteract the 'spiritual and moral crisis' (Helmut Kohl) they felt had taken hold in the FRG. They re-established the notion of an all-German national identity. The FRG and the GDR were again referred to as a unity, namely 'our German fatherland' (Kohl). The West German conception of history was to be freed from its 'negative fixation' on the years from 1933 to 1945. In this context, critics from the Left speak of attempts to 'relativize', 'historize' or 'revise' NS history. In this same context, efforts were undertaken to emphasize and institutionalize national symbols more strongly than before. This process had started in the late 1970s, but was enforced when the conservatives took over government in 1982. Since unification in 1990, it has gained new impetus.

It seems obvious that long before unification there was a visible contest for 'cultural hegemony' in West German society, and this has led to a politicization of national identity, especially with regard to history (in particular NS history), and national symbols. This ideological debate between Right and Left will now be illustrated with some selected examples.

The 1980s saw a change of national climate. Chancellor Kohl instigated a kind of language policy which aimed at establishing an all-German identity. He spoke of 'our compatriots in the GDR', of 'our German fatherland', and he made the fine distinction of 'two states in Germany' (as opposed to 'two German states') which suggests a bigger unifying entity, i.e. the *Deutsches Reich*. These are phrases which had not been used by the preceding (Social Democratic) chancellors. It is also in this context that Kohl's address to a Silesian expellees' organization in 1985 should be viewed. Although Kohl's speech in itself was not in tune with the revisionist potential German expellees' organizations still have (for which he was harshly criticized by his hosts), his presence at the conference indirectly put the question of former eastern German territories, borders and identities dating back to the time before the war, back on the political agenda.

Kohl's attempts to establish an all-German identity by a use of language which included the GDR in the nation were supported by a conservative enhancement of traditional national symbols such as the flag and the national anthem. For his annual TV address to the German public on New Year's Eve, since 1983 Kohl has included a big German flag as a dominant part of the background decoration. Flags and national anthem also seemed to enjoy omnipresence in the process which finally led to German unification. Thus on 9 November 1989, the day the Berlin Wall came down, members of the FRG parliament in Bonn began singing the national anthem spontaneously in a parliamentary session.

Over and above that, Kohl has made some symbolic attempts at re-defining national identity even with reference to the two World Wars. In 1984, he met the French president François Mitterrand in Verdun to commemorate the dead of the First World War. Standing in front of a memorial, Kohl and Mitterrand held hands in a symbolic gesture. The significance of this gesture lies in its double meaning as a symbol of reconciliation and as a demonstration of the equality in French–German relations. In this sense, the symbolic commemoration refers to the present rather than the past. The controversial visit of Kohl and President Reagan to Bitburg in 1985 had a similar dimension. The occasion was the fortieth anniversary of the end of the Second World War on 8 May 1985. The meeting was arranged at Bitburg, a German military cemetery. Again, former enemies were to demonstrate reconciliation and their willingness to be partners. But the idea was discredited and heavily criticized when it emerged that in this cemetery not only 'normal' German soldiers but also members of the *Waffen-SS* had been buried. The intended symbolic gesture of reconciliation in commemoration in order to emphasize the importance of the present was destroyed by the re-emergence of the past. Nevertheless, the meeting took place. After public protests in the FRG as well as in the United States, the programme was extended to include a visit to the former concentration camp in Bergen-Belsen.

So far, this meeting has been the most far-reaching official attempt to relativize the NS past in a sense of 'let bygones be bygones', here directly relating to the Second World War. What is new in this conservative way of commemorating is that, unlike the 1950s and 1960s, when every memory of National Socialism was suppressed, 'they now remember in order to forget'.[15] 'Bitburg was meant to close the books on Germany's guilt, and to foster an unburdened national past.'[16] It seems obvious that only through relativizing National Socialism, including the war, can an unburdened national identity in its traditional form be achieved.

The responses of supporters and enemies of such an approach were correspondingly frank. The conservative Alfred Dregger, then leader of the parliamentary group of the Christian Democratic Union (CDU), insisted that 'Germany has to become normal again . . .. The Germans must step out of Hitler's shadow.'[17] The necessity of a continuous coming to terms with the Nazi past, and the ways in which this had been previously dealt with by the Left, were increasingly questioned not only by conservative politicians but also by parts of the conservative media and intellectuals.[18]

The neo-conservatism of the 1980s realized that a normal national consciousness based on history needed public organization of memory. Kohl himself announced the initiative for two national history museums: a 'German History Museum' in West Berlin, and a 'House of the History of the FRG' in Bonn. Both projects have been accompanied by party-political and specialist controversies.[19]

However, probably the most famous discussion and controversy about the classification and assessment of the time of National Socialism, and especially the war, is the so-called historians' debate of the late 1980s. E. Nolte initiated the debate with the revisionist theses that Hitler accomplished an 'Asian deed' as a reaction to a threat posed by Stalin, and thus National Socialism loses its singularity in history when compared to Stalinism.[20] The consequences of this view for the consolidation of a traditional national identity could not be more positive: the Germans lose their negative status in comparison with other nations; furthermore, National Socialism and the war did not have their roots in, and were not consequences of, a specifically German development, but were a mere reaction to an external, Asian threat. This smoothes the way for a positive, history-based national identity. The twelve years of National Socialism can be neglected in this wider perspective, or are at least not necessarily crucial for German national identity.

In the next step, the well-respected historian A. Hillgruber made an attempt at relativizing the role of the German army – something which nobody had 'dared' to do before. He explicitly identified with the 'heroic struggle' of the Wehrmacht during its retreat on the Eastern Front, and claimed that it was only this heroic struggle which enabled millions of Germans to escape in time from the Red Army. Although in the same essay he also dealt with the systematic extinction of the European Jews by the Nazis, he did so in a very sober, detached style.[21]

This approach has been strongly criticized by the West German Left in the media and at universities, which emphasizes the singularity and the German origin of National Socialism, and therefore German responsibility for it. The main representative of the Left in the historians' debate was Jürgen Habermas, who again suggested constitutional patriotism (*Verfassungspatriotismus*) as the focal point for German national identity.[22] In the view of the West German Left, German national identity should be derived from the nation's obligation to support anti-fascism. National Socialism including the war thus serves as a negative backcloth for the development of a political self-understanding of the FRG which is based on its constitutional law. In the eyes of the Left, Germany has a special obligation to draw conclusions from the time of National Socialism and the war and to put these into practice in everyday politics. The following two policies are current examples of this way of thinking: firstly, Germany must retain its liberal asylum law, as only a liberal asylum law in other countries would have been able to help German exiles during the time of National Socialism. Secondly, Germany must not allow a militarization of its foreign policy, as this might mark the starting point of a revival of old German power politics.

For this school of thought, anti-fascist and anti-militarist commemoration and constant reminders of the victims of National Socialism and its war (as well as the naming of those responsible and guilty) is imperative, and a necessary prerequisite for national identity. In this perspective, war memory is a kind of ideological 'zero-sum-game'. What is gained by the Right in terms of reconciliation and forgiving is lost by the Left in terms of maintaining historical guilt and the limitation of German political power.

Even in the conservative party, the neo-conservative revisionist attempts to conquer the concept of national identity did not remain unchallenged. A good example of a more liberal approach to commemoration was delivered by the then president of the FRG, Richard von Weizsäcker, on 8 May 1985, i.e. the date Kohl visited Bitburg. In his speech, Weizsäcker not only insisted that the majority of Germans had known about NS crimes, but he also emphasized that in his view the date had been a day of liberation for Germany.[23] He was harshly criticized for this by members of his own party, but even more so by members of the Bavarian Christian Social Union (CSU). An example of how official commemoration can go disastrously wrong in Germany occurred in 1988, when the then president of the federal parliament, Philipp Jenninger, gave a speech in commemoration of the fiftieth anniversary of the first big pogrom against the Jewish population in Germany on 9 November 1938. His speech included, as a stylistic device, some rhetorical questions such as 'Didn't the Jews deserve their fate?', and 'Didn't Hitler give the German people back their pride?'[24] Although he obviously answered these questions in the negative, some members of parliament from the opposition benches were outraged and left the scene. Eventually, Jenninger had to resign over the issue. This example demonstrates that in Germany even ritualized public commemoration demands a special degree of sensitivity, dignity and intellectual maturity from those performing it in order to be accepted and perceived as adequate.

Phase IV: After Unification

The unification of the two German states has not ended the debate about NS history and German national identity. However, there is fear that the agonizing argument about the assessment of the NS past will be replaced by the assessment of the GDR (i.e. socialist) past, a process which has already started. If this happens, National Socialism will cease to be the focal point of the German conception of recent history, and the way will be open for the acquisition of the whole of German history.

The argument about the national memorial in Berlin is only one among many possible examples. The discussion proves the truth of Garbe's statement about war memorials: 'While in countries which became victims of the Nazis they have a unifying character, in Germany they have the opposite effect, stimulating the questioning of national identity.'[25] Plans for a national memorial date back to the 1980s when it was still intended to erect it in Bonn. Even then, there was no consensus among the political parties. In a parliamentary debate in 1986, the opposition Green Party challenged plans for a central, i.e. national, memorial, favouring government support for local and regional initiatives instead. Furthermore, they believed that 'in Germany, commemoration of the dead must distinguish between victims and perpetrators. Even death must not be allowed to erase guilt from memory.'[26] In the same debate, representatives of the conservative parties claimed that 'we owe thanks to our dead and their bereaved families' and: 'the memorial must unify, it must not separate our people'.[27] The leader of the CDU parliamentary group, Alfred Dregger, felt that 'one must not separate the dead of our people into just and unjust. Besides, every single one of these dead has already stood before his Supreme Judge.'[28] Herbert Czaja, an official of one of the expellees' organizations, supported this view: 'With this memorial, we will also commemorate the more than 2 million German refugees who lost their lives due to flight and expulsion.'[29]

Like the Greens, the speakers of the opposition Social Democratic Party had reservations about a national memorial: 'We cannot agree to a confinement to German victims of tyranny and German dead of the war . . . On the right wing, there is a tendency to relativize the burden of NS unlawfulness by a big national gesture in order to re-instate "normal" national commemoration.'[30] They also reiterated the views of the groups representing resistance fighters and those persecuted by National Socialists, who insisted that victims and perpetrators must not be commemorated in the same place and at the same time. In the eyes of the SPD, the consent of these groups to a national memorial was absolutely vital. Failure to reconcile these conflicting views meant that the project was not realized during the 1980s.

However, after unification, Kohl decided to establish a national memorial in the *Neue Wache* in Berlin. On 14 November 1993, the *Volkstrauertag*, the ceremonial opening of the 'Central Memorial of the Federal Republic of Germany for the Victims of War and Tyranny' in Berlin was held.

The *Neue Wache* is a classicistic building, designed by the architect Schinkel, and erected in 1817–18. It is a national monument of victory, erected after the triumphant wars of liberation against the Napoleonic army. In the gable triangle of the building, a goddess of victory leading ancient warriors is depicted. Initially, there were statues of the Prussian generals Scharnhorst and Bülow to the right and left of the *Neue Wache*. In 1930–1, the government of the day commissioned H. Tessenow to redesign the interior for a memorial in honour of the dead of the First World War. The curator of monuments, G. Dolff-Bonekämper, described this interior as a 'war memorial which ascribed almost religious dimensions to the voluntary self-sacrifice of soldiers'.[31] In 1933, under the Nazis, this became the *Reichsehrenmal* (national memorial of the Reich) where 'hero remembrance days' were stage-managed. After 1945, the interior was gradually altered by the GDR government. In 1960, an inscription was installed which read 'To the victims of fascism and militarism'. In the late 1960s, the granite block installed by Tessenow, which had been damaged by bombs during the Second World War, was replaced by an eternal flame in a square glass block.

It could be argued that Kohl's decision in favour of this place can also be viewed in the tradition of the previous German East–West conflict. If the GDR could redefine and use the memorial for its purposes, the new FRG could not be denied the right to do the same. The takeover and rearrangement of the GDR memorial is certainly a triumph for the FRG, and a humiliation for all who identified with the style of commemoration in the GDR.

The centrepiece of the new arrangement of the *Neue Wache* is a sculpture by Käthe Kollwitz (1867–1945), an artist who was committed to the labour movement and for that reason was expelled by the Nazis from the Prussian Academy (whose first female member she had been) in 1933. The sculpture, a *pietà* she created in memory of her son (who had died as a wartime volunteer in Flanders in 1914), is a powerful and very moving outcry against war. However, it can be argued that it is still closely attached to the context of its origin, and is primarily a war memorial. This view is confirmed by the fact that after 1945, depictions of the *pietà* and the crucified Christ became the dominant forms of memorials on German war cemeteries which were looked after by the VDK.[32] The effects of National Socialism and its war, on the other hand, can only very partially be comprehended and represented as the grief of mothers who lost their sons in battle. Women and children lost their lives, too, as victims of the

National Socialist racial extinction and euthanasia policy (and if all 'victims' were to be commemorated at the same time, similar objections could be raised with regard to the German civilian victims of Allied bomb attacks). The *pietà* is attached to, and remains in, the imagination of the First World War, and cannot depict the qualitative change which is marked by the National Socialist racial war (if this is at all possible in representational art). Possibly even more serious is the objection that the *pietà* is basically a Christian symbol of grief and hope, which implicitly excludes the biggest group of victims, i.e. the Jews, by means of symbolism and artistic object and style.[33]

There were also arguments about the inscription on the memorial, and only very shortly before the official opening was a compromise found. Two plaques installed next to the entrance of the building were intended to pacify the debate. The main inscription follows the customary phrase which mingles victims with perpetrators: 'To the victims of war and tyranny'. It names those to be commemorated: Jews, Sinti and Roma (gypsies), homosexuals, victims of euthanasia, members of the resistance; but also includes expellees and 'victims of the totalitarian dictatorship after 1945', which again alludes to the GDR. The suggestion made by the historian R. Koselleck, 'Killed in battle, murdered, gassed, missing, perished', was rejected.[34]

The opening of the national memorial marks a big step in the neo-conservative attempt to reinstate a positive German history, and thus a traditional national identity. This memorial will contribute to a further relativization of NS history, and, being the focal point of state representation of war memory, will shape future official commemoration in Germany.

Notes

1. Faulenbach and Stadlmaier (1993), p. 15.
2. Mitscherlich and Mitscherlich (1967).
3. From the VDK's 1919 statute, quoted in Kuberek (1990), p. 76.
4. Wittig (1990), p. 93.
5. Eichmann (1986).
6. Ibid.
7. Schiller (1993), p. 37.
8. Röhrich (1988), p. 78.
9. Ibid., p. 139.

10. Eichmann (1986), p. 3.
11. Faulenbach and Stadlmaier (1993), p. 13.
12. Hacker (1992), pp. 197–219.
13. Sternberger (1979).
14. Korte (1988), p. 49.
15. Geyer and Hansen (1994), p. 176.
16. Hartmann (1994), p. 10.
17. Quoted in Röhrich (1988), p. 161.
18. Dudek (1992), pp. 49–52.
19. Maier (1992), pp. 152–95.
20. Nolte (1987), pp. 45–7.
21. Hillgruber (1986).
22. Habermas (1987), p. 75.
23. Weizsäcker (1985).
24. Quoted in Bergdoll (1988).
25. Quoted in Hessing (1993).
26. Ströbele (1986).
27. Schneider (1986).
28. Dregger (1986).
29. Czaja (1986).
30. Ehmke (1986).
31. Quoted in Riedle (1993).
32. Kuberek (1990), p. 85.
33. Koselleck (1993).
34. Ibid.

Bibliography

Bergdoll, U. (1988), 'Jenningers Rede führt zum Eklat im Bundestag', *Süddeutsche Zeitung*, 11 November.

Czaja, H. (1986), 'Auch der Heimatvertriebenen gedenken', *Das Parlament* 20–1, p. 21.

Dregger, A. (1986), 'Nicht in Opfer und Täter einteilen', *Das Parlament* 20–1, p. 21.

Dudek, P. (1992), 'Vergangenheitsbewältigung. Zur Problematik eines umstrittenen Begriffs', *Aus Politik und Zeitgeschichte* 1–2, pp. 44–52.

Ehmke, H. (1986), 'Gemeinsamkeit ist nötig', *Das Parlament* 20–1, p. 21.

Eichmann, B. (1986), 'Denkmäler: Grabsteine für Denkprozesse? Wie wir es versäumten, mit NS-Geschichte umzugehen', *Das Parlament* 20–1, p. 3.

Faulenbach, B. and Stadlmaier, M. (1993), 'Zur Geschichte und Gegenwart der Gedenkstätten in Deutschland', in Ideen Redaktion (eds), *Wer sich des Vergangenen nicht erinnert*, Göttingen, pp. 11–21.

Geyer, M. and Hansen, M. (1994), 'German-Jewish memory and national consciousness', in G.H. Hartmann (ed.), *Holocaust Remembrance*, Oxford, pp. 175–91.

Habermas, J. (1987), 'Eine Art Schadensabwicklung', in *"Historikerstreit". Die Dokumentation der Kontroverse um die Einzigartigkeit der nationalsozialistischen Judenvernichtung*, München, pp. 62–77.

Hacker, J. (1992), *Deutsche Irrtümer. Schönfärber und Helfershelfer der SED-Diktatur im Westen*, Berlin, Frankfurt/Main.

Hartmann, G. H. (1994), 'Introduction', in G.H. Hartmann, *Holocaust Remembrance*, Oxford, pp. 1–23.

Hessing, J. (1993), review of H. Loewy (ed.) (1992), *Holocaust. Die Grenzen des Verstehens*, in *Frankfurter Allgemeine Zeitung*, 3 July.

Hillgruber, A. (1986), *Zweierlei Untergang. Die Zerschlagung des deutschen Reiches und das Ende des europäischen Judentums*, Berlin.

Korte, K. R. (1988), 'Deutschlandbilder. Akzentverlagerungen der deutschen Frage seit den siebziger Jahren', *Aus Politik und Zeitgeschichte* 3, pp. 45–53.

Koselleck, R. (1993), 'Geschichte und Gedenken', *Lippische Landeszeitung*, 99.

Kuberek, M. (1990), 'Die Kriegsgräberstätten des Volksbundes Deutsche Kriegsgräberfürsorge', in M. Hütt, H.-J. Kunst, F. Matzner, I. Pabst (eds), *Unglücklich das Land, das Helden nötig hat. Leiden und Sterben in den Kriegsdenkmälern des Ersten und Zweiten Weltkrieges*, Marburg, pp. 75–91.

Maier, C. S. (1992), *Die Gegenwart der Vergangenheit. Geschichte und die nationale Identität der Deutschen*, Frankfurt/Main.

Mitscherlich, A. and Mitscherlich, M. (1967), *Die Unfähigkeit zu trauern*, München.

Nolte, E. (1987), 'Vergangenheit, die nicht vergehen will', in *"Historikerstreit". Die Dokumentation der Kontroverse um die Einzigartigkeit der nationalsozialistischen Judenvernichtung*, München, pp. 39–48.

Riedle, G. (1993), 'Die Gedenkzentrale', *Die Woche* 44, p. 33.

Röhrich, W. (1988), *Die Demokratie der Westdeutschen*, München.

Schiller, D. (1993), 'Politische Gedenktage in Deutschland. Zum Verhältnis von öffentlicher Erinnerung und politischer Kultur', *Aus Politik und Zeitgeschichte* 25, pp. 32–9.

Schneider, O. (1986), 'Kein Kriegerdenkmal', *Das Parlament* 20–1, p. 21.

Sternberger, D. (1979), 'Verfassungspatriotismus', *Frankfurter Allgemeine Zeitung*, 23 May.

Ströbele, H. C. (1986), 'Wir lehnen dieses Denkmal ab', *Das Parlament* 20–1, p. 21.

Weizsäcker, R. v. (1985), *Zum 40. Jahrestag der Beendigung des Krieges in Europa und der nationalsozialistischen Gewaltherrschaft. Ansprache am 8. Mai 1985 in der Gedenkstunde im Plenarsaal des Deutschen Bundestages*, Bonn.

Wittig, M. (1990), 'Der Tod hat alle Unterschiede ausgelöscht', in M. Hütt *et al.* (eds), *Unglücklich das Land das Helden nötig hat,* Marburg, pp. 91–9.

All quotations from German sources are translated by the authors.

16

War and Memory in the New World Order

Phil Melling

If the memory of war narrows a nation's sense of self, the prospect of war invariably creates a fixation with history. As a political instrument, war confirms an officially sponsored view of the past; it provides us with a reason to reflect on history, to confirm an event which has proved indispensable in the process of nation-building. For this reason martial mythology always justifies its maker and denigrates its opponent, promoting the idea of the 'right cause'. As early as the fifth century, St Augustine defined the moral detour made by the supporters of 'just' wars when he wrote in *De Civitate Dei*:

> he to whom authority is delegated, and who is but the sword in the hand of him who uses it, is not himself responsible for the death he deals. And, accordingly, they who have waged war in obedience to the divine command, or in conformity with His laws have represented in their persons the public justice or the wisdom of government, and in this capacity have put to death wicked men; such persons have by no means violated the commandment 'Thou shalt not kill'.[1]

The sense of God's command or just law inevitably accompanies exceptionalist mythologies on a national scale. 'National myths', says Loren Baritz, 'become important to the rest of the world when they are coupled to . . . power sufficient to impose one nation's will on another.'[2] Such myths usually promote the concept of a 'chosen nation' and evolve into political myths whenever they are used for war propaganda. From the times of biblical Israel and the Roman Empire to twentieth-century Germany, Japan or Iran, the wars fought by 'chosen' nations were sanctioned by exceptionalist myths. American national myth, incorporating the notions of the 'city on a hill' and 'chosenness' was, Baritz argues, also 'at the center of thought of the men who brought [America] into the Vietnam war'. The myth used by the American policy-makers rested on a deep strata of myth-narrative that used the archetypal images of redemption and errand. The spiritual focus of an errand stemmed from a belief that America had been granted divine sanction for its role as world policeman and the guardian of freedom and democracy, a responsibility which frequently involved the practice of war.[3]

Karen Rasmussen and Sharon D. Downey assert that throughout their history Americans have seen wars as cleansing struggles in pursuit of holy victory; these wars have been justified as errands in the wilderness, a 'sacred purifying, culturally regenerative quest for victory against a sinister foe'.[4] For example, in his State of the Union Address of 29 January 1992 President Bush congratulated the United States on its willingness to seek out and expose the enemies of civilization, whether it be 'imperial Communism' or Ba'athist nationalism. The task, said Bush, had been a divine duty unequivocally accepted by a country which had proved itself to be, by the end of Operation Desert Storm, 'the undisputed leader of the age'. America had confronted her adversaries, each of whom had identified themselves as the master practitioners of hostage-taking. From Korea to Vietnam American soldiers had disappeared in pursuit of freedom. The liberation of Kuwait and the return of the 'last American hostages' to the United States had retrieved the memory of those lost in battle and had 'vindicated' the 'policies' that underwrote the act of sacrifice. With Hussein routed and the Cold War won, the United States had proved itself the dominant power in an age when 'changes' had occurred of 'almost biblical proportions'. Only the steadfastness of the nation's moral vision to defend freedom and democracy throughout the world – in Vietnam, Grenada, Libya and Kuwait – had secured the eventual peace and upheld the 'idea of America' as the last best hope for mankind, the ultimate expression of human aspiration.[5]

Certain types of war are so intense that we find ourselves unable to stand aside in our memory 'from the passion of identity politics'.[6] Many of those who live under the shadow of the Holocaust, argues Amos Elon, have turned the memory of genocide into a tool of advocacy, an excuse for 'vengeance or vindictiveness'.[7] In Israel, suggests Elon, the Holocaust has become a symbol of exceptionalism, a thing of incomparable horror, an experience that confers, in a post-war tradition of Zionist historiography, an aura of uniqueness on a chosen race. For those historians thrust into the role of 'political actor', Hitler's genocide of the Jews has been transformed into a 'bleak, hard' legitimizing myth for the state of Israel and a primary reason for Israel's aggression against the Palestinians. Hence:

> At a time in Israel when much of the national ethos and much of the political idiom were being formed, the images that were cast upon the dark mirrors of the mind were those of a veritable hell. The early Zionists had intended Israel

to be a safe haven for persecuted Jews, yet Israel had come into existence too late to save the dead millions. To this day there is a latent hysteria in Israeli life that springs directly from this source. It explains the paranoiac sense of isolation that has been a main characteristic of the Israeli temper since 1948. It accounts for the towering suspicions, the obsessive urge for self-reliance, the fear – which sometimes collapses into contempt – of outsiders, especially of Arabs and lately of Palestinians. Standing behind each Arab or Palestinian, Israelis tend to see SS men determined to push them once again into gas chambers and crematoria.[8]

In Israel, generations of Jews, claims Elon, have been brought up to believe that they have been 'singled out to die not because of their religion, or their politics, but because they were there, they existed'. This message, says Elon, has had 'far-reaching, political, cultural and religious consequences', one of which has been the inability to separate an event in history from national myth and the ritual of politics. A profound 'intransigence', a belief that the whole world is against the state of Israel, has left an 'imprint' on Israeli historiography which, during the first two decades of Israeli independence, 'was handicapped by reasons derived from mainstream Zionist ideology'. The result was a series of ideological and apologetic works aimed at proving the historic need for a Jewish state. As a result, says Elon, most of the serious works by Jewish writers on Nazism were written by non-Israelis and – perhaps because they did not fully conform with current formulas – only a handful of those were translated into Hebrew, nearly always belatedly. In post-war Israel 'the writing of history intensified the trauma of the past, it did not relieve it. It took more than a generation to produce Israeli historians able to detach the history of the Holocaust from their own biographies.'[9]

Elon warns us of the dangers involved in allowing memory to be used as a political instrument that legitimizes state myth and nationalist propaganda. This happened during the government of Menachim Begin when laws were passed which made it a criminal offence to deny the existence of the Holocaust. Should Israel continue to reference itself through the events of the Holocaust – a familiar convention in Israeli schools – then memory, says Elon, will continue to be exploited as a political instrument and the master narratives of persecution and victimism will fan the flames of hatred for the Palestinians. In other words, if Israelis continue to believe in the principle that 'the same right of self-determination' they claim for themselves should be denied the Palestinians, then the assassination of men like Yitzak Rabin, who opposed that principle, will remain a fact of Israeli life. To challenge the role of memory is not to destroy or defile but to invigorate. When memory is beyond reproach it is deadened and emptied of all responsibility, deprived of the sustenance of legitimate enquiry. A victimized people like the Jews in Israel can endanger themselves and others by structuring their lives as a memorial to a past which threatened to destroy them in the ghettos and gas chambers. Because of this, Elon argues that less, rather than more, attention should be paid to the Holocaust by Israel. He offers a warning from Yehuda Elkana, himself a survivor of Auschwitz: 'The deepest political and social factor that motivates much of Israeli society in its relation with the Palestinians is a profound existential "Angst" fed by a particular interpretation of the lessons of the Holocaust and the readiness to believe that the whole world is against us, that we are the eternal victim.'[10] In Israel, Elkana was criticized for his beliefs, as he was for asserting that while 'history and collective memory are an inseparable part of any culture', the 'past is not and must not be allowed to become the dominant element' that determines 'the future of society and the destiny of a people'. For those whose 'traumatic memory' is either 'innocently or deliberately mobilized for political purposes', says Elon, 'a little forgetfulness might finally be in order'.[11]

In the 1990s there is little evidence of an honourable amnesia among those nations for whom war remains a primary component of national identity. Today the age-old process through which war continues to structure our imagination remains relatively undisturbed. The changes of 1989 have not marked, as Francis Fukuyama claimed they would, the ending of history – and, by implication, the ending of war. On the contrary, the demise of the Cold War has signalled a 'return to history', a reawakening of those memories and anxieties and conflicts 'we thought were closed for good'. In 1990, as the New World Order began to take shape, it became apparent to the writer Malcolm Bradbury that effective political control of world events had diminished rather than increased. Bradbury identified what has now become a common hypothesis among *fin-de-siècle* historians: namely, that loss of governance in superpower structures would heighten political and social uncertainty. 'The ends of millennia', said Bradbury, 'are notorious for the rise of apocalyptic fear, and though our Einstein's monsters change, from nuclear threat to ozone depletion and global warming, the consciousness of uncertainty is with us again.'[12] Freed from the ideological constraints of the last 'fifty years', the veil of 'historical interpretation' which has 'imprisoned' the 'imagination and intelligence' has been lifted. The political process through which we are passing is one of 'rising uncertainties', for we live 'in a world that will not stay still'. Not surprisingly, we remain anxious. The borders of our very existence are unstable. 'If we have been losing our parochialism, becoming more European and more global, we find that we do not know where the edges of the larger globe will be. This tempts new philosophies, it encourages new fundamentalisms.'[13]

From the perspective of the mid-1990s it seems clear that the Hegelian trajectories observed by commentators like Francis Fukuyama in the late 1980s have amounted to very little. Failure on the part of the New World Order to deliver the stability and growth that was promised to Central and Eastern Europe at the end of the Cold War has not encouraged political or economic optimism but a new military pathology, a regression into violence, a love affair with war. In the 1990s the opportunities for ethnic ideologues like Franjo Tudjman and Slobodan Milosevic have flourished in a Europe that is haunted by the ghosts of fascism and authoritarianism. The image of a dynamic and tyrannical parent has a definite attraction for a world which has 'exchanged', says Richard Gott, 'the desperate certainty of the ancien regime for the dangerous complexity of a highly uncertain future'. The prospect of living in a world of undefended frontiers has given way to a 'dubious embrace of artificially created natural loyalties' and the tensions and prejudices of what Gott refers to as 'clerical fascism'.[14] In parts of Central and Eastern Europe a new iron curtain has threatened to come down as divisions between societies re-emerged. As maps were redrawn and borders reformed the rattle and clank of a new fundamentalism reawakened the 'ghosts of particularism' – what Ian Traynor calls 'the old securities'.[15]

According to Eric Hobsbawm, fundamentalist ideologies do for the disadvantaged what poppies do for heroin addiction. 'They provide that missing ingredient of a "glorious" past to a present that doesn't have much to show for itself.'[16] In the 1990s, the trajectories of history, East and West, converge at a point where the politics of invention begin to take over as a refuge for the 'disappointed' and the old political movements that channelled idealism and expectation into military activity recover some of the ground that had been lost since the Second World War.[17] In a series of articles tracing the rise of neo-fascism, Umberto Eco located the 'ghosts of particularism' in a new and invigorated 'cult of tradition' that has sprung up as a source of hope for ethnic and nationalist communities in the 1990s. The earthly representatives of these 'ghosts' are the charismatic leaders and conservative populists of the New World Order, the celebrants of an 'ideology' of 'heroism' which sets its face firmly against the rationalism of the Enlightenment and regards the secular and rational morality of the Age of Reason as 'the beginning of modern depravity'. The proponents of the cult of mythic memory, says Eco, tend to subscribe to a religion of Ur-Fascism, a syncretic blending of magic, myth, romantic memory, supernatural revelation and pre-millennial occultism. For societies which 'feel deprived of a clear social identity', says Eco, Ur-Fascism tells them 'that their only privilege is the most common one, to be born in the same country'. The reference of nationalism transforms the enemy into a symbol of central importance since the enemy is the one who 'can provide an identity to the nation'. In pursuing an enemy the nation can feel 'besieged' and its paranoia can be clearly articulated through 'an appeal to xenophobia'. Irrationalism or Ur-Fascism relies on a 'cult of action', a programme which vilifies the role of analysis and reflection and the treacherous modernism of a liberal intelligentsia. If 'thinking is a form of emasculation', and if action is 'beautiful', the purpose of life is the engagement with 'struggle'. For believers in Ur-Fascism, 'pacifism' is tantamount to trafficking with the enemy and life a matter of 'permanent warfare', the conclusion of which is a craving for heroism through violent death.[18]

In Russia the need to placate conservative nationalists encouraged Boris Yeltsin in 1994 to believe that he could find 'an effective substitute for elusive success in economic and social reforms' by committing himself to a neo-imperialist adventure in the breakaway republic of Chechenia.[19] At a time when right-wing nationalists like Vladimir Zhirinovsky were seeking to reinstate a new Cold War, the conflict with General Dudayev offered Yeltsin a number of 'glittering political prizes', including an opportunity to restore Russia's prestige after the failure of the Cold War. Yeltsin wanted to look tough in Chechenia after a string of failures in domestic and foreign policy, some of which had appeared to dim his chances of re-election in 1996. A love affair with 'great power dramatics' was Yeltsin's way of deflecting attention from a domestic economic crisis and of substituting a costume drama in the Caucasus for the politics of economic reform at home. This 'drift towards authoritarianism' was Yeltsin's attempt to stem nationalist resentment among those who felt that he had sold Russia's soul and wealth to the West and capitalism.[20] Yeltsin's decision to allow the Russian army to retrace its steps as a nineteenth century 'imperial army' in the Caucasus, says Martin Woollacott, was motivated by a desire to assert his authority when 'the uncertainty over whose hand is on Russia's many rudders' was at a new height.[21] Lifting the Soviet yoke in this way, says Stanley Aronowitz, 'revealed the plain truth that under the rock of suppression seethed yearnings that cloaked strong authoritarian currents'.[22]

In politically intransigent societies – such as Serbia and Croatia, whose liberation the breakup of the old Soviet Union was instrumental in creating – ethnic ideologues and Balkan warlords have grasped any opportunity to exploit the 'cult of tradition' in the rush to defend their borders from real or imagined aggressors. In a series of articles on the Serbian military commander, General Ratko Mladic, Robert Block presents us with a picture of a bloodstained warlord who relies heavily for his support on the 'veil of legends' which surrounds Serbia's military history; in particular, the memory of St Vitus Day in 1389, the national day of the Bosnian Serb army, when the 'heroism of Serbian knights . . . stopped the powerful Arabic sea which threatened to drown Europe'. Mladic sees himself, says

Block, 'as a solitary knight on the ramparts of European civilization', trying to repel an invading horde of Bosnian Muslims and expansionist Croats who are 'acting under the instructions of their powerful masters in Tehran and Bonn'. For him, past and present are part of 'a seamless continuum' in which the Serbs 'are still fighting to turn an Islamic tide away from Europe'.[23]

Although Mladic is referred to by the Bosnian Serbs as 'a God', a 'saviour' and 'the greatest man in the world', the truth is that his fundamentalist faith appeals by virtue of its theatricality to a people who feel, as Eric Hobsbawm puts it, 'disappointed in their past, probably largely disappointed with their present, and uncertain about their future'. Where a vacuum is left by the collapse of the old state apparatus the situation is dangerous, says Hobsbawm, for 'people will look for someone to blame for their failures and insecurities'. The movements which are 'most likely to benefit from this mood' are not those which seek to promote a consensus or a multicultural agenda but those which are 'inspired by xenophobic nationalism' and 'blame' the corrupting influence of 'strangers' on the nation's cultural heritage and the violation of its borders.[24]

The process is deeply authoritarian, reminding us of Richard Slotkin's suggestion that 'a shattered mythology [in this case Communism] preserves elements of the cultural past' and that a 'new mythology will inevitably find connection with the old'.[25] In *Balkan Express* Slavenka Drakulic discusses the appeal of Franjo Tudjman's ethnic nationalism during a time of war (the early 1990s) and the rooting-out of alien memories and cultural histories in order to legitimize Croatian nationalism. The speed with which Tito's multi-ethnic client federation was dismantled, says Drakulic, left the people of the former Yugoslavia disoriented. A mood of uncertainty accompanied this extraordinarily rapid and exhilarating transformation of history. People were elated at the downfall of Communism but their minds remained unreconstructed. This left them vulnerable to fundamentalist texts:

> They simply had no chance to become mature political beings, real citizens ready to participate, to build a democratic society. When people in Croatia held the first free multiparty elections in 1990, as in most of the rest of East Europe they voted primarily against the communists. Despite that, the new governments were all too ready to proclaim themselves the sole bearers of democracy, as if it were a fruit or a gift there for the taking. If there is any reason at all behind the historical animosities dividing the Yugoslav nations, it is that this society never had a proper chance to become a society not of oppressed peoples, but of citizens, of self-aware individuals with developed democratic institutions within which to work out differences, conflicts and changes instead of by war. Continuing to live with the same kind of totalitarian governments, ideology and yet untransformed minds, it seems the people were

unable to shoulder the responsibility for what was coming – or to stop it. War therefore came upon us like some sort of natural calamity, like the plague or a flood, inevitable, our destiny.[26]

What Tudjman promised the people of Croatia was self-transformation through rigorous action (what Slotkin describes, in another context, as 'regeneration through violence'). The ideals of revitalization and purification were implemented in mythic and military theatres in cathartic acts of ethnic cleansing, against real or imagined enemies of the state. Tudjman not only went to war with his neighbours; he erased the memory of failure in the Second World War (and the Nazi collaboration of the Ustashe regime led by Ante Pavelic) by reviving and remythologizing the folklore of nationalism. What the Croats aspired to – cultural independence and political autonomy – Tudjman invented through programmes of cultural and military renewal. Following the victory of his Croation Democratic Union in April 1990, Tudjman brought back the older heraldic flags and the red-and-white chequered shield, the *Sâhovnica*, and installed a new urban programme with major changes to street and place names. Rigour, discipline and authoritarianism were the key components in Tudjman's vision of a redesigned Croatia. 'The new historical justice' of the state, says Drakulic, was totalitarian and premised on the need for a singular vision of history, 'a total abstraction' in which there was no middle position. It was a construct which not only reinvented the immediate past but also returned the people to a vision of the state as controller of 'a new bolshevism'. It provided a thesis of 'national homogenization' which went beyond anything that Tito had previously insisted upon.[27]

After Croatia declared independence in 1990, Tudjman's preoccupation with cultural purity as the basis of the new nationalism led him, says Misha Glenny, to 'install the infrastructure of a fascist state'.[28] Tudjman romanticized the memory of fascism by 'hanging the red and white chequered shield, the *Sâhovnica*, the core of Croatian heraldry' – the flag of the wartime, pro-fascist Ustashes, under whose regime large numbers of Serbs had been exterminated – 'from every building'. The desire to cleanse Croatian culture and rid it of Serbian/Slavic impurities became an obsession with Tudjman. In an attempt to exploit nationalist sentiment, Tudjman tried 'to create the nation in the image of an ancient ethnic community', a community whose mind 'was inclined to abstraction' and symbolic ritual. In the medieval period the colours of the *Sâhovnica*, says Jacques Le Goff, were 'considered beautiful' because they were 'a mixture of red and white, excellent colours which symbolised purity and charity'. Just as in medieval times 'a handsome man [had] a red skin', so the blood of the Croatian people could be observed in the 'taste for blood', as represented in the flowing colours of the *Sâhovnica*.[29]

For those who correlate the emblems of tradition with national purity, the use of symbolic icons, shields, titles, flags, nomenclatures, arcane grammars, allegorical codes, heraldic devices, mythic inscriptions and alphabets is an integral part of national identity. Thus after his election Franjo Tudjman pronounced literary Croat the only language of administration and dismissed the Serbs' Cyrillic script. 'The move was as senseless as it was provocative', says Misha Glenny, since only a tiny percentage of Serbs used Cyrillic, and most spoke Croatian and wrote in Latin script.[30] Changes of name, especially of buildings and streets, were equally common in the reconstruction of Croatia's identity. The practice was rigorously authoritarian yet consciously ceremonial, as if the meaning of history was easily changed by new vocabularies, names and scripts.

In European cities, says Slavenka Drakulic, historical events and personalities are reflected in street signs which 'bear the names of military victories, revolutionary martyrs'. In Communist regimes street names were changed 'to belittle or deny the past'.[31] In post-Communist Croatia, this practice continued among militant nationalists willing to redefine or 'falsify' the past when the memory of history proved uncomfortable. In Tudjman's Croatia new authoritarian styles continued to mimic the old ideological practice of 'defaming history and truth'. In Zagreb, says Drakulic, the removal of monuments and the changes of street names dedicated to the victims of fascism clearly illustrated the government's willingness to celebrate the memory of collaboration and to transform the country into an inherently fascist state committed to racist policies against people who were not Croats. 'Many thousands of Jews, Serbs, Gypsies and Communists died in the Jasenovac concentration camp run by the Ustashe regime led by Ante Pavelic', says Drakulic. 'Today it is simply a falsification of history to ignore that regime's fascism and emphasise only its independence.' The policy of re-evaluation was little short of an active distortion enforced by a 'ruling ideology'. Tudjman remythologized the past and in 'a violent cleansing of the popular memory' managed to defame it. The people were so traumatized they no longer accepted 'the right to their own past as it actually took place'. The ideological abuse of history became a daily, almost ritual event.[32]

In *Balkan Express* Drakulic encourages an opposite tendency, a desire to understand ethnicity as a cross-pollinated and hybridized form rather than an immutable, timeless category which operates within a prescribed cultural territory through which others cannot trespass. Drakulic shares the concerns of Werner Sollors in *The Invention of Ethnicity* that nationalism is not a repository of originality and authenticity or a legacy of European romanticism. For Drakulic, ethnicity is not an external, stable entity, but is constantly changing and evolving in constant interaction with external stimuli. Drakulic shares the modern and postmodern concept of 'invention', therefore, to describe ethnicity not as an object but a historical process, a set of 'widely shared, though intensely debated, collective fictions that are continually reinvented'.[33] *Balkan Express* is a collection of such fictions – biographical and autobiographical narratives about life in a civil war zone and about the loss of identity which tragically results from a politics which denies the need for restructuring. In a country where the ideal of cultural essentialism has come of age with a vengeance, an actress is seen to lose her homeland, a mother her daughter, a woman an apartment, a street its name, a country its history – all in the name of authenticity. If, as Milan Kundera says, the 'struggle of man against power is the struggle of memory against forgetting',[34] then Drakulic resists the totalizing narratives of the new Croatian nationalist state and turns her back on the revisionist strategies which militant Croats like Franjo Tudjman are using to interrupt the movement of history. Underlying her critique is the belief that styles of authoritarianism tend to lead an independent existence beyond ideology and that the search for legitimacy in history is subject to a continuous process of rebirth.

Drakulic inhabits a border region. She distances herself from the xenophobic politics of Tudjman's new nationalism where history has become a 'frighteningly uniform' tribal doctrine rigorously encoded in a 'new bolshevism' or quasi-fascism. She also resists the temptation to purify herself in the company of those who annihilate the past and tamper with its language, its street names, its educational curriculum, merely to settle an 'account' with Communism. For Drakulic, Croatia is a mongrel place with a miscegenated past, a region riddled with friction and contradiction which her personal history reflects. We see her life as an intriguing muddle, a jumble of cross-cultural encounters, multiple collaborations and multi-ethnic debates. Drakulic is a hybrid, a woman of mixed belief and syncretic heritage who has lived and travelled gladly, and gratefully, on the border of different cultures and diverse political systems. Her history is an act of growing up with different ideologies and racial memories: capitalist and Communist, Serb and Croat, Western and Eastern European. In *Balkan Express* Drakulic acknowledges the disparateness of Croatian life and confronts the dilemma of the individual as nationalist whose right to utilize the past is frequently suspended by the 'correcting hand' of the state in its search for purity. In her conflict with the 'new historical justice' Drakulic resists the partisan approach to memory, the attempt to wipe clean the collaboration between Nazis and Ustashes during the 'quisling' period of the 1940s and the targetting of those who cling to the memory of an unreconstructed past.[35]

As nationalist supporter and nationalist critic, Slavenka Drakulic straddles the psychic fault lines of history, welcoming the arrival of the new Croatia but not at the expense – as Tudjman insists – of a Muslim,

Communist, Yugoslavian heritage, each element of which is an essential part in the personality of the country in which she grew up. For Drakulic, the multiple histories of the Croatian people invalidate the essentialist rhetoric of the state: hence the need for a politics of openness rather than one which subsumes individualism and restricts the role of memory and the imagination. Although 'the war', she says, 'has become the pivotal point in our lives and it determines everything else', she chooses to resist the politicization of memory.[36] Instead, her work embodies the elemental tensions that are the shaping patterns of her nation's culture.

In a formative period of national and ethnic awareness, Drakulic explores the tensions that exist between rival histories as well as the sins and omissions that are common to both. Like Yael Tamir in *Liberal Nationalism,* she avoids the exclusivities and pieties of fundamentalism and provides an ethical grounding for nationalism in liberal principles and multi-ethnic aspirations (shared language, shared social practices, shared history). Like Tamir, Drakulic sees our last hope as lying in intersecting circles of autonomy for different national groups within territorially defined states. For Drakulic, as for the American poet Carolyn Forché, memory and identity are based on the need to celebrate a kinship rooted in difference.

Notes

1. Augustine (1949), p. 32.
2. Baritz (1985), p. 30.
3. Ibid.
4. Rasmussen and Downey (1991).
5. State of the Union Address, United States Information Service, 29 January 1992, pp. 1–2.
6. Hobsbawm (1993), p. 64.
7. Elon (1993).
8. Ibid., p. 4.
9. Ibid.
10. Ibid., p. 5.
11. Ibid.
12. Bradbury (1990).
13. Ibid.
14. Gott (1994).

15. Traynor (1994).
16. Hobsbawm (1993), p. 63.
17. Ibid.
18. Eco (1995), p. 27.
19. Womack (1994), p. 12.
20. Hearst (1994), p. 20.
21. Woollacott (1994), p. 22; Meek (1994), p. 22.
22. Aronowitz (1992), p. 13.
23. Block (1995b), p. 12; Block (1995a), p. 8.
24. Hobsbawm (1993), p. 63.
25. Slotkin (1986), p. 86.
26. Drakulic (1993a), p. 13.
27. Ibid., p. 75.
28. Glenny (1992), p. ll.
29. Le Goff (1988), p. 334.
30. Glenny (1992), p. 12.
31. Drakulic (1993b), pp. 21–2.
32. Ibid., p. 22.
33. Sollors (1989), pp. xi–xv.
34. Quoted in Schlesinger (1992), p. 52.
35. Drakulic (1993a), pp. 124, 2.
36. Ibid., p. 75.

Bibliography

Aronowitz, Stanley (1992), *Politics of Identity: Class, Culture, Social Movements*, London: Routledge.

Augustine, Aurelius (1949), *The City of God, vol. 1 of the Works of Aurelius Augustine, Bishop of Hippo*, ed. and trans. Marcus Dods, Edinburgh: T. & T. Clarke.

Baritz, Loren (1985), *Backfire: A History of How American Culture Led Us into Vietnam and Made Us Fight the Way We Did*, New York: Morrow.

Block, Robert (1995a), 'The madness of General Mladic', *New York Review*, 5 October, pp. 7–9.

Block, Robert (1995b), 'Serbs idolise Bosnia's bloodstained warlord', *Independent on Sunday*, 30 June, p. 12.

Bradbury, Malcolm (1990), 'Frontiers of Imagination', *Guardian*, 15 February, p. 21.

Drakulic, Slavenka (1993a), *Balkan Express: Fragments From the Other Side of War*, London: Hutchinson.

Drakulic, Slavenka (1993b), 'Nazis among us', *New York Review*, 27 May, pp. 21–2.

Eco, Umberto (1995), 'Pointing a finger at the fascists', *Guardian*, 19 August, p. 27.

Elon, Amos (1993), 'The politics of memory', *New York Review*, 7 October, p. 3.

Glenny, Misha (1992), *The Fall of Yugoslavia: The Third Balkan War*, Harmondsworth: Penguin

Gott, Richard (1994), 'End of the party', *Guardian*, 3 November, pp. 2–3.

Hearst, David (1994), 'Small war is a big gamble', *Guardian*, 1 December, p. 20.

Hobsbawm, Eric (1993), 'The new threat to history', *New York Review*, 16 December, p. 64.

Le Goff, Jacques (1988), *Medieval Civilization, 400–1500*, Oxford: Basil Blackwell.

Meek, James (1994), 'Sad pantomime of Boris the Bad', *Guardian*, 14 December, p. 22.

Rasmussen, Karen and Downey, Sharon D. (1991), 'Dialectical disorientation in Vietnam war films: subversion of the mythology of war', *Quarterly Journal of Speech*, vol. 77, no. 2, p. 178.

Schlesinger, Jr., Arthur M. (1992), *The Disuniting of America: Reflections on a Multicultural Society*, London: Norton.

Slotkin, Richard (1986), 'Myth and the production of history', in Sacvan Bercovitch and Myra Jehlen (eds), *Ideology and Classic American Literature*, Cambridge: Cambridge University Press, pp. 70–90.

Sollors, Werner (1989), 'Introduction: the invention of ethnicity', in Werner Sollors (ed.), *The Invention of Ethnicity*, New York: Oxford University Press.

State of the Union Address, United States Information Service, 29 January 1992, pp. 1–2.

Traynor, Ian (1994), 'The bookie who backed a winner', *Guardian*, 3 November, p. 3.

Womack, Helen (1994), 'Why has Yeltsin sent the tanks in now?', *Independent on Sunday*, 18 December, p. 12.

Woollacott, Martin (1994), 'The risks the big powers take through fear and fantasy', *Guardian*, 14 December, p. 22.

Index

Index

Index

republican movement, 61–4, 68
  see also Great War, Second World
    War
Israel, 257
It Started With Eve, 167

Japan
  Anne Frank Diary, 10–11, 13
  Hong Kong, 45, 48, 49
  see also Second World War
Janner, Greville, 34
Jenninger, Philipp, 248
Jewish Chronicle, 7, 15
Jews
  Anne Frank Diary, 11,16
  Britain, 9
  Holocaust, 6, 9, 256
  Hungarian, 37
  nationalism, 6
  war crimes trials, 6
  see also, Holocaust, Palestine
Johnson, Lyndon, 178

Kennedy, John, F., 178
Kessler, David, 7
Klein, Michael, 186
Kohl, Helmut, 245
Kops, Bernard, 9

Lacombe Lucien, 156
Lady Hamilton, 167
Lamp Still Burns, The, 167
Lefebvre, Henri, 164
Levin, Meyer (Anne Frank Diary), 5, 7,
  11–13
Liberalism, 224–34 *passim*
Love Story, 169
Lynn, Vera, 113

Machery, Pierre, 210
Man in Grey, The, 170
masculinity, 112–13, 171, 230
mass media, vii, 191
Mass Observation, 170, 196
Mayer, J. P., 168–9
memory
  mass, 164–5, 170, 172–3
  national identity, vii, 177, 191–3, 255,
    259

occlusion of, 29–32
popular, 163–4, 168
private, vii, 99, 125, 157, 179
public, vii, 99–101, 125, 136–9, 157,
  177–8
social discourse, 46, 52–4, 163, 165
trauma, 51–2, 258
see also myth, Second World War
militarism, 191, 192
Millions Like Us, 167
Mills, Sir John, 172
Ministry of Information, 165, 173
Mitterand, François, 246
Morgan, Kenneth, 27
Mrs Miniver, 169
museums, 90–1
  Imperial War Museum, 91–4, 99, 105
  Winston Churchill Museum, 92–4, 97
myth, xvii, 255, 259–63
  Blitz, 89–90, 192
  American frontier, 177–8, 186–7, 256
  popular culture, 27–8
  public, 178–9, 257
  tradition, 191–2, 263
  see also memory

National Federation of North African Ex-
  Servicemen, 76–83
Neue Wache, 250
New World Order, 258–9
Noisseville memorial, 144–5
Nolte, E., 247
Nora, Pierre, xvii, 125, 126, 128, 154
novels, x, 33
  Algerian war, 76
  Gulf War, 215–17
  Second World War, 32
Nuremberg
  see Internal Military Tribunal

oral history, viii, 59

Palestine, 32, 256–7
Perfect Strangers, 166
Platoon, 80
Poliakov, Leon, 7
popular culture, x, 89–90, 163, 210, 215,
  217
  see also myth

Index